CHAMBER MUSIC

Also by Will Ashon

*Strange Labyrinth: Outlaws, Poets, Mystics, Murderers
and a Coward in London's Great Forest*

CHAMBER MUSIC

WU-TANG AND AMERICA (IN 36 PIECES)

Will Ashon

FABER & FABER

First published in the USA in 2019
by Faber & Faber Ltd,
Bloomsbury House,
74–77 Great Russell Street,
London WC1B 3DA

First published in the UK in 2019
by Granta Publications,
12 Addison Avenue, London W11 4QR

Printed and bound by CPI Group (UK) Ltd,
Croydon, CR0 4YY

A CIP catalogue record for this book is available from the
British Library

ISBN 978-0-571-35000-1

FSC
www.fsc.org
MIX
Paper from
responsible sources
FSC® C020471

1 2 3 4 5 6 7 8 9 10

For Rodney

What if history was not a reasonable citizen,
but a madman full of paranoid guile and
these boys his agents, his big surprise!
His own revenge?

RALPH ELLISON, INVISIBLE MAN

The only thing I rely on is truth,
so therefore I rely on nothing.

THE RZA

CONTENTS

1ST CHAMBER
THE PICTURE

It starts with the picture, back in the time when the
picture comes first. Before we've slipped out the white
paper inner, before we've pulled out the black disc
inside—three fingers on the label, the meat of the thumb
resting along its edge. Before we've lifted the lid of the
turntable, placed the record over the spindle, before
we've set the whole thing running. Before the needle
comes down, before that bump and crackle as it rides
the run-in grooves. Before the music. A creation myth.
The very first time.

A big room, hard to make out, curtains and a gilt mirror
at the back, half of a reflective, misshapen globe, a sun
sinking (or rising?) through clouds and smog. The floor
wooden, or brown lino etched with double lines to make
it look wooden, the pinstripe on the suit of a god. A ring

of votive candles, seven or eight in shot, each set on a
thin stick stuck into a blob of gold, the flames running
horizontal—quite a distance—in such a way as to suggest
an open door, or fan, or a complete lack of walls, as if
the shot were taken on a platform high up in the sky,
levitating above a city. But not a gust, nothing variable,
utterly under control. Each flame uniform, of a set,
so that the candles seem to be pointing at something
or someone just beyond the frame.

There are six figures. It's possible, if we squint, to
see a seventh, distorted by the light from the sun at the
back. But what we can interpret as a head and shoulders
blocking the light is in fact a cutaway and what we've
seen as a circle—that rising sun—is a huge, stylised W,
their emblem. So, six figures in a line, one behind the
other, leaning out to left and right to see and be seen.
Legs bent, shoulders hunched, arms out in front of
them. Gun fingers toward the back, thumbs cocked.
The hand of the second figure distorted, so that the
thumb seems to grow over the top of its index finger.
The front-most figure making signs, right hand pointing
downward, left hand the kind of shape you form to
throw shadows of a duck or alligator on to a wall.
Fingernails very white, over-exposed, long and thin and
graceful. Maybe we know how to interpret these hand
signals, maybe not. It doesn't matter. It's not important.

All the men (do we presume they're all men?) are
wearing black hoodies with the cords on the hoods
pulled tight round their faces. On the front two we can
see the patch sewn on their chest. It reads WU-TANG
in the middle of that same stylised, kung fu-backdrop
'W', and underneath, looping round the bottom of the
circle, PROTECT YA NECK and, after a gap, something
else which could be KID or K1⁊ or K⫯⁊. The stitching at

the top looks like a waveform on music software but this is probably accidental and, anyway, we don't recognise it as such. At a glance, we might think the second figure is wearing crazy, crepe-soled cowboy boots, but when we look closer, we see it's probably Clarks or Timberland and the guy has his jeans rolled up to his knee.

The music starts. This should make things easier but we're not sure it does. A man is talking about sword styles in the clipped tones of a 1930s Hollywood announcer. A beat kicks in—a compact lump of recycled funk, as solid as a boxing technician on the defensive—and someone hollers, over and over again, to *BRING THE MOTHERFUCKIN' RUCKUS*. The beat stops, a clown car seems to fall apart in the background, and the first of a series of voices rips into his verse. A finger snap turned up so loud, mixed so hard, it sounds like someone chipping marble from a sculpture, slices of another beat stabbed in here and there, slathered in reverb as if recorded in the middle of an ancient stone hall, so that the size of the room they're occupying magically grows and shrinks. A strange, gossamer melody is twined between these elements, the kind of tune aliens might use to communicate in a black and white TV special. A slowed-down piano sample, so ponderous and covered in hoar frost it sounds like the drums are cracking it to pieces. And over it all, the voices, one after another, indomitable, unstoppable, at this point utterly unfamiliar.

But we're still staring at the picture, letting the music soundtrack the image. It doesn't matter how they're standing or what they're wearing. The thing that sets our heart beating or our mind working or our subconscious bubbling is this: the figures have no faces. Or rather, they have white material pulled down over their features, so that a hint of their shape—their bone structure, the size of their noses—can be made out while making them anonymous, empty, in some way inhuman; a cross between bank robbers, shop dummies and extras from a horror movie. The light is coming through so brightly, right to left, that the front figure's lips and nose are spread out in silhouette across the inside of the mask, a scan. The face of the figure furthest left appears in absence, a flattened, Turin Shroud effect. The others display varying gradations of blankness, the one at the back dyed blood red, more a shield than a visage.

The power of the image lies in this negative fact: that its subjects are unidentified and, more important, unidentifiable. The six men are masked and meaning multiplies out from this. A picture like this traditionally functions as a clue to help understand the music contained. This one does and it doesn't. The group (we presume it's the group—or at least some part of it) are deliberately disguised, deliberately hidden, deliberately *obscure*.[1] This must be the conclusion we're supposed to draw—that what's contained inside is of hidden significance, an encrypted message, a mystery. That it is, in the word's most literal meaning, occult. We are invited to speculate, to search for clues, to unpick and re-stitch, but at the same time remember that— whatever we do, however long we take, regardless of the hours spent listening to the music inside—those six figures will remain masked. Treat it as an invitation to embrace enigma, to be eaten up by it. Lose face, lose skin, lose self in it.

This is not a document. This is a rite.

---

1   Late Middle English: from Old French *obscur*, from Latin *obscurus* 'dark', from an Indo-European root meaning 'cover'.

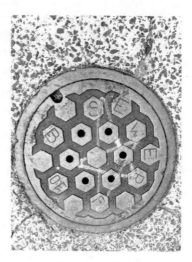

2ND CHAMBER
DON'T CRY

In 1942, a young tenor saxophonist from Texas stepped
up to take a solo on a number called 'Flying Home',
his first studio recording with the Lionel Hampton
Orchestra. In *The Devil's Horn*, Michael Segell recalls that
sax player, Illinois Jacquet, telling him that the night
before the session, 'me and God had a prayer meeting.
I just asked him to let me be original'. God did his best.
It's a moment that has gone down in the history of jazz.
To the sinuous, almost polite take that Jacquet has on
the tenor blueprint of Coleman Hawkins, the 19-year-
old brings a few moments of gruff overblowing and,
towards the end, vamps on a single note, repeating
it in two batches of twelve, building the tension and
swinging the beat hard.

The record—and in particular Jacquet's solo—was
an instant sensation and the young man was asked

to close each of Hampton's shows with it, expected to bring down the house night after night. The effect on his playing was marked. Two years later, for the very first of the Jazz at the Philharmonic concerts, on 2 July 1944, Jacquet played a tune called simply 'Blues—Part 2'. Most of Hawkins has gone from his playing now. He offers an utterly contemporary, bluesy, gruff, honking, wild solo and, at around the minute-thirty mark, he makes the saxophone scream. Really scream. It sounds like a fox copulating with a razor, or a hyper-intelligent if understandably neurotic goose on Christmas morning. African American music had never been short of emotion—it had moaned, it had wailed, it had sobbed, it had laughed. But it hadn't screamed. Illinois Jacquet had opened that box, he'd let the scream out. 'After that,' Jacquet confided in Segell's book, 'saxophonists went berserk.'

Jacquet ushered in the era of the honkers. A whole subset of the newly emergent rhythm & blues genre[2] was devoted to instrumental music on which the saxophonist (most often a tenor player) would scream and squawk, often on one note, at as much length as possible. Artists like Arnett Cobb, Big Jim Wynn, Hal Singer, Dick Davis, Joe Houston, Lynn Hope and Earl Bostic (the last on alto) all had hits with records of this sort. Most famous of all, Big Jay McNeely used to play lying on his back, dressed in the brightest zoot suit imaginable, with a full light show, apparently an early influence on Jimi Hendrix. His 'Blow, Blow, Blow' sums up the genre—fast, frantic and opening with repeated

2   Rhythm and blues was arguably both a new sound and a convenient way for the labels to market what they'd previously called 'race records'. The chosen euphemism around the time of the release of *Enter the Wu-Tang* would have been (still is?) 'urban'. It's up to the reader to decide whether this is any sort of progress.

high screams, as if a particularly exhibitionist woman is reaching her climax in a neighbouring hotel room, the drum beat a bedstead thumping the wall.

In the worthy opinion of men of judgement this was not, however you looked at it, music. Arnold Shaw, who had worked as a songwriter before becoming a publicist for a series of labels after the war, put it like this in his book, *Honkers and Shouters*: 'The musician was not playing music. In the monotonous honking and catlike screeching, he was mocking the audience and destroying the music.' Or, as Dean and Nancy Tudor saw it, 'frustration, hostility and alienation were vented through crude emotional responses, such as honking or squealing contests with saxophones'. The poet and activist LeRoi Jones, who would later change his name to Amiri Baraka, offers the subtlest response in his classic, *Blues People*, narrowing and sharpening the implication: 'The point, it seemed, was to spend oneself with as much attention as possible, and also to make the instruments sound as unmusical, or *non-Western*, as possible.' Esteemed jazz critic, Leonard Feather, damned this tide of noise. 'By resorting to such tactics as the use of freak high notes, the relentless honking on a single note for an entire chorus, and the use of low notes with deliberately vulgar tonal effects,' he said, these saxophonists 'have been able to achieve great popular success.' And there, in that *great popular success*, is the simple thing that all of them ignored. At its best, it sounded great. It was thrilling, exhilarating, new, raw and exciting. It was city music. It was the sound of traffic-jammed car horns in the street, of altercations, of people collapsing in fits of laughter, of drugs, of sex.

*

The same screaming, though, was not apparent among the vocalists. Known as *shouters*, the singers in R&B combos certainly had to holler to be heard above the clamour of their band and, as a result, it was a great time for big men and women with capacious lungs. Whoever made suits for the likes of Amos Milburn or Wynonie Harris must've gone through a lot of cloth. But this was good-time music and though they wanted to be loud, these singers didn't seem keen to lose it in the same way as their accompanists (not, at least, when they were recorded). They aspired to a certain level of urban slickness. They didn't want to speak in tongues. And perhaps the clue's there back at the start when Illinois held his prayer meeting. The screamers were for God. Because this is the other place that the scream was heard in African American music as the forties moved into the fifties: gospel.

Or, more accurately, hard gospel. The template for the gospel vocal group had stayed more or less static since the Fisk Jubilee Singers embarked upon their first tour in 1871, only eight years after the Emancipation Proclamation ended slavery. Smooth, close-harmony music where the blending of the voices was what was important, it was a sound whose elegance and restraint was supposed to convince White audiences of the sophistication of the people singing. But in the late forties, a new wave of groups, moving out of the South to cities like Chicago, began to make music which relied upon 'sheer vocal power'. Foremost among these were the Five Blind Boys of Mississippi, who featured the monstrous talents of Archie Brownlee on lead vocals. Bobby Womack (who briefly played guitar for the group when he was only thirteen) would later recall that 'Archie could demolish huge halls with the bluest version of the Lord's Prayer ever recorded. He would interrupt his songs with a falsetto shriek that conjured up images of witchcraft or bedlam. He started that scream that all the big soul singers that followed used. Plenty of them screamed, but Archie was the first, and maybe the best, too.'

Nothing much appears to be known about Brownlee, other than that he was blind, that he died in 1960 (possibly of pneumonia, possibly of a perforated ulcer, more fancifully, having sung himself to death) and that he had an extraordinary set of pipes. In some accounts, even the blindness is in doubt. Both Womack and Robert Darden (in *People Get Ready!*) report that Brownlee could get around quite admirably despite his lack of sight and Darden quotes a witness to his live performance: 'I seen him... jump *all the way* off that balcony, down on the floor—*blind!* I don't see how in the world he could do that.' Womack also reports his penchant for whisky, placing his myth very much within the blues tradition of sainthood. His voice is remarkable. The Blind Boys' first hit, *Our Father* (one of the earliest gospel records to hit the mainstream R&B charts) finds him singing the Lord's Prayer over the backing of a simple drum hit on the one and three and his fellow singers' repeated intonation of the title to a blues progression. But Brownlee tears it up, and his scream at 1:31 is the moment the record really catches light, ripped out of the back of his throat and the back of the bar, a trick he repeats twice again in the last chorus of the record, powerful and wild, possibly anguished, most of all *alien*.

Not everyone in the world of gospel approved of Brownlee's style, but the influence of that eardrum-shattering noise cuts right through everything that follows. Sam Cooke—who himself started out singing in gospel groups—claimed that Brownlee was the only singer who could consistently bring him to tears. And he must also have influenced the two greatest screamers of American music, both of whom were playing and singing gospel in 1952, when 'Our Father' was released. One of these was Little Richard. The other was James Brown.

'He'd scream and scream and scream', writes Nik Cohn of Little Richard in his study of the birth of pop, *Awopbopaloobop Alopbamboom*. 'He had a freak voice, tireless, hysterical, completely indestructible, and he never in his life sang at anything lower than an enraged bull-like roar... He sang with desperate belief, real religious fervour.' The religious fervour was never faked. Though he was homosexual and started out performing as a drag act, Richard Penniman grew up poor and Black and very much in the church. In fact, he went to them all, from Pentecostal to Baptist to Methodist to Foundation Templar. At one point, he even retired from the music business to concentrate on being a Seventh Day Adventist. As a child, he liked the Holiness Church best, both for the holy water in which they washed their feet and for the opportunity 'to imitate them talking in tongues, though we didn't know what we were saying.' This babbling may have influenced his vocal style, which was already well developed when his family entered church singing contests as the Penniman Singers: 'The sisters didn't like me screaming... and threw their hats and purses at us', he recalled in his memoir, *The Life and Times of Little Richard*. 'They called me War Hawk because of my hollerin' and screamin' and they stopped me singing in church.'

When 'Tutti Frutti' became a hit, Penniman was whisked off to LA to record new material, even though he had a series of dates booked. James Brown was managed by the same man in Macon, Georgia, and was persuaded to step in—not instead of Little Richard but *as* Little Richard. On the few occasions the crowd realised Brown was an impostor, he worked harder, jumped higher, screamed louder than the real thing in order to win them over. Back to Cohn again, this time writing about Brown: 'he lets out a series of screams, mad anguished shrieks that last ten seconds each. Probably they're the loudest sounds you've ever heard any human being make and, physically, you can't not be moved by them. That's the way he works on you. That's the way he hurts you and beats you up.' RJ Smith, Brown's best biographer, knows exactly where the Godfather of Soul's shattering scream comes from, both its roots and how it builds on or transforms those roots. 'The scream was a transfer from the black church', he writes of Brown's legendary show, recorded in 1962 at the Apollo Theatre in Harlem, only seven years after he'd been faking it as Little Richard. 'For the previous hundred years, where else in public could a black man yell like he could at church? Where else would he not have been whipped, or institutionalized, or shoved to the margins for making the sounds that Brown is luxuriating in making right now at the Apollo? It is a scream activated by the church but not of it, a scream that is an agent of change.'

In March 1970 James Brown fired his band. Again. There's nothing so remarkable in that. By now, another eight years on from that show at the Apollo, Brown was one of the biggest names in music and he ruled his groups with a fierce, autocratic, often rather arbitrary discipline. This was, though, a particularly fine band, featuring as it did, Maceo Parker, Fred Wesley and Pee

Wee Ellis, plus Clyde Stubblefield on drums. They had recorded a host of classic tunes, not least 'Ain't It Funky Now', 'Funky Drummer' and 'Say It Loud', in the process becoming stars in their own right. Unfortunately for them, these players had written down a list of grievances and given it to Mr Brown before a show. Having said he'd think about their complaints, Brown put in a call to his trusty lieutenant, Bobby Byrd. He told him to go to Cincinnati, find the bunch of teenagers who hung round the King record label, playing on the odd session for free, put these kids on the Learjet and fly them out to the next date. Once they arrived, he sacked the previous players and told these arrivistes to get on stage. He had a new group now.

This band, known until this point as the Pacesetters, included the brothers Collins among their number, Catfish and Bootsy, and they would go a long way towards revolutionising funk, first with Brown, then with George Clinton and Parliament-Funkadelic. In the single year that they worked with Brown, the band—which he christened the JBs—recorded 'Sex Machine', 'Super Bad', 'Soul Power' and 'Get Up, Get Into It, Get Involved', which would be enough for any ordinary mortal's entire career. They toured Nigeria and Europe as well as the USA, expanding Brown's mind as the world expanded theirs. And, in moving the focus of the groove from the drums to the bass, they changed the music, permanently.

The problem Brown had was that his band didn't take him too seriously. Not yet in their twenties, they just wanted to play. They weren't worried about fines or being ticked off—they didn't have families at home relying on their wages. Bootsy gobbled LSD like there was no tomorrow. Once he collapsed on stage, wrestling with his bass, which he believed had turned into a python in his hands. When Brown tried to discipline him after the show he laughed, utterly unbothered. Part of the way the Godfather tried to keep his group motivated, then, was with constant sessions—rehearsals, recordings, whatever. He even told them he was going to produce an album by the JBs, make them famous. In the end King only released a single from the sessions, though the full record surfaced forty-five years later.

That single, 'The Grunt', starts with a saxophone squeal. Not any old squeal. Some kind of glissando which works its way like an arpeggiated razor cutting through the cloth of two octaves, up, up and then, when you think something will surely give, still upper. It starts incredibly high-pitched, forced and overblown, and ends even higher, even more forced, even more over-blown. The effect is amplified by the mix, which places this scream front and centre, very loud compared with everything around it, so that when the horns come in they sound like they're in the room next door. What follows is a tight piece of instrumental funk, Bobby Byrd's piano syncopating in the right channel against Phelps Collins' rhythm guitar in the left, Bootsy Collins becoming increasingly manic on bass as the tune progresses (Brown claimed that 'when I met him he was playing a lot of bass—the ifs, the ands, and the buts. I got him to see the importance of the *one* in funk'). The reason for the extra volume on Robert 'Chopper' McCullough's saxophone quickly becomes apparent—he's the soloist on the piece. After that initial screech he sits back a bit, lets the groove establish itself, vamping and riffing until—*SQUOOWEEEEEE!!!*—he leads the band into the bridge with a nod to that first upwardly mobile cry. Besides that, he maintains control and plays a neat solo, only really letting go when Bootsy does, the two instruments tracking or chasing each other through those last bars, that tumbling finale brought to the abrupt, disciplined end you'd expect from a group of musicians working under the strict, volatile control of Mr Brown.

What is it about that squeal? What gives it the power it so obviously possesses? Ben Sidran has written about the importance of the *cry* to the roots of African American music: 'The "cry" was the trademark of the rural individual, derived from the Arwhollies, or field-hollers, and the vocalizations of the spirituals. It signaled that the individual was feeling in such-and-such a way, that he was alive and present, and that he was black.' Moreover, the saxophone—introduced into the USA as a cheap, novelty instrument—has been used in jazz since the thirties as an extension and heightening of the human voice. 'The introduction of the saxophone as a solo voice,' Sidran says, 'made the quality of vocalization more readily available to black instrumentalists, as that horn sounds like the human voice throughout its registers.'

As lead soloist on an instrumental tune, McCullough tries to replace his boss, Mr Brown. He doesn't reach this target, except in those screams, which—through the use of saxophonic technology— time-stretch, amplify, distort and warp Brown's own trademark sound. The moment represents a coming together, a synthesis, of those two screaming traditions—hard gospel and honking—a sonic wedding in the Church of Funk, the kind of collision that rips a hole in the space-time continuum. But at that moment? Nobody noticed. One more step was necessary.

Only two years after 'The Grunt' was released,
hip hop began to make its first foetal movements in
the cultural womb of New York City when a Jamaican
émigré, Clive Campbell, imported the sound-system
culture he remembered from his early childhood and
began playing parties in the Bronx. The chief innovation
of Campbell, better known as DJ Kool Herc, came when
he began buying doubles of records so that, using two
turntables and a mixer, he could cut back and forth
between the most rhythmically intense and exciting
sections of those records—known as *the breaks*—to
keep the crowd dancing, a looping process he called
the merry-go-round. Herc had invented or discovered a
manual form of sampling, although in many ways it was
an extension of Brown's use of his band, in particular
his habit of utilising two drummers and cutting back
and forth between them. The further developments of
hip hop as a musical form all flowed from this initial
innovation.

It did, however, take technology (or, more
accurately, the misuse of technology) another fifteen
years to catch up. It was only in the mid-to-late eighties
that the machinery needed to really play around with
the sampling and sequencing of music became both
cheap enough and manageable enough to move out
of super studios and the set-ups of ageing rock stars
and into the hands of the people with the imagination
and flexibility to do something interesting with it.
The result was a bunch of musicians who, contrary to
popular belief, rather than *stealing*, collaged and melded
sounds from any number of sources to make something
new. For a few short years—before older musicians
caught on to the pillaging of their back catalogue and
lawyers discovered a lucrative new way to pass their

time—sampling was the most creative way you could make music, bar none.

There is another way to think of a *break*, which is as the particular section of any piece of music which carries the most data—in most cases, rhythmic. This, obviously, involves a slightly different way of conceptualising data than as a series of bytes. The file size for this book, for instance, would be the same whether it contained ideas, thoughts, jokes, descriptions, metaphors and similes or simply the same word written again and again for as many pages. But in the same way that written language is more than just a series of letters, music is more than just a series of notes. And the break is where music explodes, where rhythm in particular starts multiplying and complicating and copulating—where there is almost *too much information* for the body and mind to deal with. Such data-peaks are manageable when isolated and finite, but the DJ liberates them and loops them, extending them indefinitely. Dancing, on this reading, becomes an involuntary response to this sudden data overload, this tsunami of information, which causes not so much a slaying in the spirit as a bumping and grinding in the spirit, an unchosen twitching and twisting to the beat, as if Saint Vitus and not the Devil had all the best tunes. The crate digger becomes a kind of data-miner, the producer a data-arranger. What hip hop does with sampling is liberate these seams of data, mould them and then fit them together into one long, never-ending, golden chain. The tsunami never ceases, the wave keeps on coming—and is a wave even a wave any more if it never ends, or has the sea just got fifty fathoms deeper?

*

It's fitting that a new generation of musicians, keen to redefine and redeploy soul, to make it new through the creative use of technology—to, in effect, give soul back its soul—should come across Chopper McCullough doing exactly the same thing seventeen years earlier and hear in it a way to make that tradition live again. Because, once you've established the break as a short section of another record packed with the most intense data then it's no longer just about rhythm and McCullough's bringing together of the two 'scream' traditions of African American music is a rich seam indeed.

The Bomb Squad—the production crew behind the band Public Enemy—may not have been the very first people to use Chopper's opening notes on 'The Grunt', but, if not, they used them best. They took the first bar, the first four notes of that rising howl, and looped it right through their 1987 single, 'Rebel Without a Pause'. 'That weird screechy sound,' Chuck D remembers, 'was sampled to have a clean sound, and it just didn't feel right, so we... redid it with... a two-bit sampling rate, which made it really gritty sounding, almost unpresentable, and then we looped that at a point where it was kind of imperfect.' The positioning is key. Hank Shocklee, a key member of the Bomb Squad, recalls 'that sample had to be taken off of the two. But then placed on the one.' Remember Brown teaching Bootsy 'the importance of the *one*'? In this case, the Bomb Squad switch the one and the two and in doing so, they break the sample open and release what it contains, unleash its intensity.

Repeated over and over again, the sound goes straight up your spine like electricity, part muezzin call, part free jazz howl, part street noise. It's also bizarrely catchy—a *hook* for fuck's sake!—so that you find yourself

19

humming its strange, rising whistle, its weird upward swirl, the most unlikely of earworms. And the link to free jazz isn't as crazy as it sounds. McCullough was a jazz player first and foremost and, plying his trade in the late sixties and early seventies, was aware of developments in that field. Indeed, it's McCullough who takes the solos on Brown's 'Super Bad', recorded a month after 'The Grunt'. As he goes in hard on an abstract, roiling, babbling solo (sadly too low in the mix), James Brown eggs him on: 'C'mon! C'mon Robert! C'mon brother! Blow, Robert! Blow me some 'Trane, brother!' The solo is issued in by Brown's own shriek, impossibly high, a piercing reminder of the remarkable strength of his voice. As for Coltrane, along with Brown he represents an apotheosis of the scream in African American music, as celebrated by Don L. Lee (who later changed his name to Haki Madhubuti) in his poem 'Don't Cry, Scream':

> i didn't cry,
> i just–
>> Scream-eeeeeeeeeeeeeee e-ed   sing loud
>> SCREAM-EEEEEEEEEEE EEEEEEE-ED   & high with
>> we-eeeeeeeeeeee eeeeeeeeee ee   feeling
>> WE-EEEEEEeeeeeeeee EEEEEEEE   letting
>> WE-EEEEEEEEEEEEEEEEEEEEEEEE   yr/voice
>> WHERE YOU DONE GONE, BROTHER?   break

The sound, the sample, became something of a hip hop craze from this point onward, much like the honking craze of the 1950s. The data was unleashed. Appropriately, considering it was an ode to Long Island, where both they and Public Enemy came from, J.V.C. F.O.R.C.E. recycled the sample (probably direct from

'Rebel…') on 'Strong Island'. Ultramagnetic MCs used it the following year for 'Ease Back' and Curt Cazal took a stab of it for MC Shan's 'Juice Crew Law'. In the UK, according to Coldcut's Matt Black, it became known as 'the kettle noise', proving that only a nation of tea-drinkers could hold Public Enemy back. It was used in Britain by Bomb da Bass, by Coldcut themselves and by Norman Cook, who seemed to slip it into every remix he worked on between late 1987 and 1989, including his 'Funky Drummer Remix' of 'She's The One' by none other than… James Brown. The start of the nineties saw no diminishment in the sample's popularity. In Philly, Jazzy Jeff & The Fresh Prince referenced it in one of their early suburban-teen takes on the music, 'Who Stole My Car?' (1990). The first breakout group of Southern rap, Texas's Geto Boys, used it on the album track 'Trophy' (1991), and a year later California's The Pharcyde deployed it to pay explicit tribute to Public Enemy on 'Officer'. Back in New York, Showbiz & A.G. also utilised the sample—pitched up right near the roof—on their 'Soul Clap', an early example of jazz fetishisation (and none the worse for it). And in this way, the sample continued to collect more data, a history as well as a pre-history, a whole hierarchy of uses and abuses, of second- and third-hand reconditionings which spoke to the music and where the music came from, adding and expanding upon this rapidly growing universe.

So when Robert Diggs aka the RZA used the same sample for the Wu-Tang Clan's first single, the self-released 'Protect Ya Neck', he must have known how much weight that snippet of sound carried in it, how much information adhered to it. Which is why he chooses to reinvent it, turning a scream into something else altogether, some kind of cold, magic-lamp sliver of beauty. Although it's instantly recognisable it's also transformed. He thins the sample until it sounds like a note bowed on a single string, then takes the first interval and loops it round so that there's no start and no finish to the phrase. This loop runs through the verses like a spider picking its way through a web. There's something almost *stop-motion* about how it works, a Švankmajerish quality, that same scuttling, surface sheen. Although it references the anger of Public Enemy and the recent scream history of African American music, it offers a kind of calm centre to this essentially chorusless introduction to the voices of the band. It floats—both ghost melody and thereminic tech-fragment.

It's been traditional to think of hip hop as noise, as malevolence, and it's true that the Wu-Tang are full of anger and violence and bravado (as well as humour). It's easy to remember the words LeRoi Jones used, back before he became Amiri Baraka, of a Lynn Hope gig. 'There was no compromise, no dreary sophistication,' he wrote of Hope's playing, 'only the elegance of something that is too ugly to be described.' What you hear most of all as you focus in on Chopper's reconstituted, re-shaped scream on 'Protect Ya Neck' is *balance*—a kind of poise, the pieces of this musical puzzle orbiting each other, fitted together in ways both simple and complex, so perfectly that the fact you can see every join becomes exactly what makes it work. The joins *are* the music, with what's between them just a way to emphasise them, to show them off. And you're left wondering, questioning—what is ugly and what is beautiful, anyway? What is elegant and what is crude? Are these opposites at all, or do they emerge only when they are held in this delicate—this powerful—equilibrium?

3RD CHAMBER
RULES OF ENGAGEMENT

Robert Diggs begat Rakim Allah begat Prince Rakeem
begat the RZA.
Gary Grice begat Allah Justice begat The Genius begat
the GZA.
Russell Jones begat Ason Unique begat Ol' Dirty Bastard
begat Big Baby Jesus begat Osiris.
Clifford Smith begat Shakwon begat Method Man.
Corey Woods begat Shallah Raekwon begat Raekwon the
Chef.
Lamont Hawkins begat Universal God Allah begat
U-God.
Jason Hunter begat Rebel INS begat Inspectah Deck.
Elgin Turner begat Jamel Arief begat Masta Killa.
Dennis Coles begat Ghostface Killah. And it is said that
none could be iller.[3]

---

3   Something which we will aim to prove later.

*

This book tells the story of the first album made by the Wu-Tang Clan, entitled *Enter the Wu-Tang (36 Chambers)* and released at the tail end of 1993. It sounds straightforward put like that, but there are lots of ways to tell a story, as the Wu-Tang Clan are all too well aware. This isn't, for instance, one of those volumes which talks you through each recording session, who was there, what they were wearing, who popped out for a smoke and so on (though some of that information sneaks in, anyway). Instead, it's an attempt to reflect the shape and ethos both of the album it focuses on and of hip hop more generally—the genre, or more accurately, the *culture* to which that album belongs. The period from 1993 to 1994 was a key moment in the development of hip hop, a kind of high renaissance, twenty years on from its birth in the slums of the South Bronx. *Enter the Wu-Tang* came out right in the middle of this golden age, on the same day as A Tribe Called Quest's *Midnight Marauders*, two weeks before Snoop Dogg's *Doggystyle*, and nestled in between classic releases from Souls of Mischief, Freestyle Fellowship, KRS-One and Black Moon on one side and Nas, Notorious B.I.G., Jeru The Damaja and Outkast on the other.[4]

It will be part of the aim of this book to show the unique genius of hip hop's operation, the way it re-boots many of the traditions of African American music and culture in completely new ways, moving away from the

---

4   This list barely scrapes the surface. We could add The Roots, Brand Nubian, Leaders of the New School, Scarface, De La Soul, Del the Funky Homosapien, Onyx, Digable Planets, Tha Alkaholiks, 2Pac, Lords of the Underground, Organized Konfusion, Pete Rock & C.L. Smooth, Common Sense (later known simply as Common), The Beatnuts, Gang Starr, The Coup, the crew behind Project Blowed and many more, all of whom released classic albums in this two-year period.

linearity of the Western music tradition and embracing quotation not merely as a tool or technique but as the very ethos of creativity, of originality. Of course, every lover of hip hop has their own favourite record or group, but it's this book's assertion that the genius of hip hop reaches some kind of wild, ramshackle apogee on *Enter the Wu-Tang*, and that to come close to understanding that record is also to understand something about America—a place which, like the music it has birthed, creates beauty and boldness, humour and warmth, all out of underlying horror. In order to reflect its subject matter, *Chamber Music* itself will take a largely non-linear, sample-heavy, magpie approach as its template.

Picture our nine protagonists as particles moving at the speed of light away from some cataclysmic beginning. As they travel, they drift further apart, their velocity drops, some of them collide with other particles. They are heading outward and as they do so, they leave a universe in their wake. Now imagine we take a snapshot just nanoseconds after that beginning and we call that snapshot, *Enter the Wu-Tang (36 Chambers)*. What if, using this image, we could move through time, plotting the particles' trajectory back to where they came from and forward to the present and beyond? Imagine 36 experiments based on aspects of data from that snapshot. Some of these experiments interrelate, some don't. Some teach us new things about the particles, others less so. Some are baffling, frankly. You quickly come to realise this isn't really science, but then people aren't really particles.

Instead of opening a book, you've opened the box of a jigsaw puzzle. You tip the pieces out onto a tabletop covered in green baize and there you start sorting them.

Painstakingly, you piece the image together, agonising over this piece or that, trying to get it to fit. Eventually you realise it's the cover to the album *Enter the Wu-Tang (36 Chambers)*, only the pieces which should show the group's masked faces turn out to be missing.

You live in a city built of scrap metal and recycled rubbish, the whole put together with such ingenuity it shines in the night with a strange, unearthly lustre. To travel between neighbourhoods, you step through a door which can deposit you in any of the other thirty-five districts. You have a choice—devote your life to figuring out the exact pattern in which the teleport system moves you round the metropolis, or just go with it and live the best you can.

You're listening to an album with 36 separate tracks. The tracks seem disparate and all over the place at the start—and in fact are disparate and all over the place at the start—but somehow they gradually cohere together in your mind into one magnificent, beautiful suite of music. You're not sure if it's the album which has done this or you.

You're playing a game with complex rules and the only one you've been taught is that they won't be explained to you.

Listen. A man is breathing—in, out, in, out, in, out. You don't know if the man is scared or angry or excited, or some mixture of those, or none of them. You're not even certain it's a man. As you listen, though, you try to match his breathing to your own. At first you find the rhythm, then you try to couple your lungs to it, so that you inhale and exhale exactly the same volume of air at just the same speed. You experiment, trying to hold your throat as tightly or loosely as he does, all so that you make precisely the same sound. Is it possible that, if you can do this, if you can synch your respiration completely to his, you can figure out his thoughts, his feelings, whether he's running towards something, or away from it?

4TH CHAMBER
HERE AND THERE

It's a basic requirement of any cultural product that
it has an origin myth, a story which can be told (and
embellished) over and over again and used to explain
something about that item's essence. The story of how
Enter the Wu-Tang (36 Chambers) came into existence is a
case in point, a complex series of interlocking narratives
all designed to suggest that the rise to prominence of the
group behind that album was somehow fated. One of
its key tropes is that the Wu-Tang Clan consisted of two
warring factions who united and put their differences
behind them in order to conquer the rest of New York
and then the world. Those factions were geographically
based, tied to two of the biggest housing projects on
Staten Island—New York City's fifth, least fashionable,
and most suburban borough. The rivalry was fuelled in
part by the proximity of the Stapleton Houses and Park

Hill Apartments: you can walk from one to the other in less than ten minutes. Both built in the early sixties, the initial history of these two developments is very different, almost as if architecture or geography is trying to reflect the group's storied schism.

The Stapleton Houses were always designed to be public housing for the poor. Apart from the red-framed enclosure of the stairwells, the six eight-storey blocks probably look much the same now as they did back in 1962. Consisting of almost 700 separate apartments, they are big, squat red-brick structures, external walkways leading to the front doors, the walls haunted by the ghosts of graffiti. The residents are protected from falling—or throwing themselves off—by high, diamond-lattice wire fences that give the place a slightly unfortunate penal atmosphere. It's the single biggest public housing estate on the whole of Staten Island, though its badlands reputation has been somewhat eclipsed by Park Hill, on the land above it.

Park Hill Apartments went up around the same time as the Stapleton Houses, but were privately built and privately let. You could argue that they were among the final fruits of the policies of Robert Moses, the city planner who had dominated New York City's architectural existence for the preceding thirty years. The building of the Verrazano-Narrows Bridge from 1959 onwards was to be his last major project, a massive edifice, the towers of which reach around seventy storeys above the water below. Moses called the bridge 'a triumph of simplicity, and of restraint over exuberance', while President Lyndon B. Johnson described it as 'a structure of breath-taking beauty and super engineering'. It was also the first physical linkage of Staten Island to another city borough (Brooklyn), and an influx of New Yorkers looking for cheaper housing was predicted. That's exactly what happened, only their reasons for coming were perhaps more complicated than originally envisaged.

On 16 July 1964, only a couple of weeks after the Civil Rights Act was signed into law and four months before the Verrazano-Narrows Bridge was opened, off-duty police officer Thomas Gilligan shot and killed fifteen-year-old James Powell on the Upper East Side of Manhattan. Two days later, protesters marched to a Harlem police station to mark the boy's death and were met with batons. When local residents started to throw bottles and dustbin lids down onto the police, they began firing into the sky—two thousand rounds on that first night alone. The riots that ensued lasted for four nights and spread to Bedford-Stuyvesant, an area of Brooklyn with a predominantly Black population. It's a key moment in understanding the changes which were to affect America for the next thirty years and more, but one of its immediate consequences was to cause Irish and Italian Brooklynites to consider leaving the borough to move somewhere newly accessible but seemingly safer. '"White flight," of course,' suggest Daniel Kramer and Richard Flanagan, 'is one of the primary causes of the population boom after the opening of the Verrazano Bridge in 1964.' When they arrived, these incomers soon realised that houses in the borough were cheap to buy and they abandoned the new blocks in favour of all the attractions of suburbia: 'larger homes, green lawns, a garage' (and, of course, White neighbours). To this day, Staten Island is the only one of the five boroughs of New York City where homeowners outnumber renters. By the end of the decade, Park Hill had largely been handed over to federally-subsidised 'Section 8' low income housing, where it remains to this day.

The Park Hill blocks are flatter on the sides than the Stapleton Houses, six storeys of red brick with their bases painted a deep burgundy. From the outside they're about as characterless as social housing can get, a succession of identical lumps, gigantic capital C's presenting their backs to the road. Although officially smaller than the Stapleton Houses, this is partly because the twelve blocks are split into differently named estates: Park Hill, Fox Hills, Concord Court (where GZA once lived), St George Plaza and so on. It adds up to something like 1600 units in total and you get a sense of the scale of the development when you see them rearing up behind the carpark of the local Home Depot on Targee Street.

Perhaps because of the notion that it was somehow already in decline, a place deserted by anyone who could afford to get out, the Park Hill area seems to have been hit particularly hard by the crack epidemic of the late 1980s, first becoming known as Crack Hill and then Killer Hill, thanks to a series of drugs-related shootings (we will return to crack later). GZA gives a shout out to the area on 'Wu-Tang: 7th Chamber' when he says his 'style jumped off in Killa Hill-a'. It's Inspectah Deck, however, who sums up what living in these areas is meant to do to you. 'I'm mad vexed,' he says, referring less to an emotion than a state of being. 'It's what the projects made me.'

The rates both for murder and for drug offences have dropped precipitously in these estates since the early nineties, although this isn't obviously to do with any great improvements in the housing stock. Locals say that there were always worse projects on the North Shore of the Island anyway, and it's just the Wu-Tang's fame which has resulted in the notoriety of these particular enclaves. You only have to listen to Ghostface's 'All That I Got Is You' from his debut album *Ironman*, though, to understand something about the levels of poverty these boys experienced growing up and hence the attraction of any activity which held out the possibility of lifting a family out of destitution. The opening line recalls a time when his mother's three-bed in Stapleton was home to fifteen people. He goes on to recall having to sleep four in a bed, picking cockroaches out of the cereal box, being sent to a neighbour with a note from his mom begging for food and so on. Although the poet Kevin Young has pointed to the nostalgia in the Wu's recollections of childhood, what he calls 'struggle as a form of sustenance', this doesn't detract from the bare facts of poverty presented. In such circumstances, you might ask yourself, who wouldn't want to sell drugs? Of course the old irony is that you're selling drugs to your own poor neighbours or fighting for the right to sell drugs with your own poor neighbours, feeling a sense of resentment and rivalry not with your real enemies, but with kids the same age from the building just a little way down the road.

Number 134 Morningstar Road—the house where RZA is said to have convened the meeting at which he persuaded his disparate band of rap assassins to bow to his authority for a period of five years—is no longer standing. Instead the site now makes up half of a garage and auto-repair shop, somewhere on the edge of nowhere. Thinking back to bluesman Robert Johnson and his fabled deal with the Devil, there's a certain irony to that street name. After all, 'morning

star' translates as 'lucifer' in Latin and a (probably
misunderstood) reference in Isaiah linked that name to
the Devil: 'How art thou fallen from heaven, O Lucifer,
son of the morning!' What you notice in travelling to
Morningstar Road is how far it is from both Stapleton
and Park Hill. It's right across the other side of the
Island, either a trek through the luxury uplands of the
interior or a long schlep around the shoreline. The area
crouches underneath the struts of the Bayonne Bridge,
one of three major car routes into New Jersey, giving
it a slightly harried feel, as if you're a rabbit sensing
the shadow of a hawk on your back. Coming here, so
far from everywhere else RZA had previously lived,
seems deliberate. It's as if he had first decided to remove
himself from the theatre of war and then—having
formulated his master plan—summoned the other
members of the group away from it, too, in order to
parley for peace.

Of course, except as a foundation myth, this
take on events is flawed. When you break down the
numbers, the Wu was never really a coalition of two
warring armies. Only Ghostface Killah comes from the
Stapleton Houses. Method Man, U-God, Inspectah Deck
and Raekwon all came from Park Hill. RZA and GZA
both moved around, flitting between areas and never
completely belonging to one side or the other, the former
living in and around Stapleton, the latter Park Hill.
Ol' Dirty Bastard was from Brooklyn. Indeed, it could
be argued that the three cousins in the group (RZA, GZA
and Ol' Dirty) were all from Brooklyn originally and
that it was their distance from the traditional rivalries
of Staten Island that made the group possible. You could
also argue, though, that this distance (and their blood
ties) made for another faction within the Clan, one

which the residents of Stapleton and Park Hill might come to resent with much more fervour than they had ever resented each other. As is often the case with stories, this one obscures as much as it illuminates— as stories are supposed to.

5TH CHAMBER
CREATIVE REORGANISATION

Here's a different narrative, one operating on a
broader level. It seems likely that any culture born
out of slavery will be re-referential, in that its mode
of communication will always be, at root, to *say* one
thing and *mean* another. There is no room for an
honest exchange of views with a master—even (or
particularly?) a master who thinks that there is. Your
own culture, religion and language are all forbidden, the
master's ignorance of them weaponising them, turning
them into a conspiracy. Everything which makes you
human has to be nested within the alien structures
of the aggressor culture. As this disjunction of saying
and meaning develops, it becomes a shadow system in
which all forms of communication—language, music,
movement—are re-wired while still maintaining the
appearance of the dominant culture which is in fact

being subverted. This is, of course, work requiring huge ingenuity and imagination. However, during this transference the original meanings of the enslaved culture will inevitably be warped and changed, too, so that something new is created in the gap between what is forced upon its constituents and what they remember. Both cultures are transformed—in some sense, transcended—in this act of creative necessity.

Amiri Baraka, in his classic work on African American music and culture, *Blues People*, suggests Christianity as the point of cultural ingress for captured Africans brought to America. These slaves weren't allowed to practise their own religion—central to their understanding of every aspect of the lives they had been ripped from—so adopted the only version of spirituality on offer. Having done so, though, they discovered that—in the early days, anyway—it was the sole area of their existence where they were left to themselves, 'the only times when the Negro felt he could express himself as freely and emotionally as possible'. Under cover of piousness, the deities of diverse African religions were smuggled into the Christian pantheon of saints, as outlined by Robert Farris Thompson, who shows how Yoruba-Americans, for instance, 'outwardly abiding by the religious proprieties of the Catholics who surrounded them, covertly practiced a system of thought that was a creative reorganization of their own traditional religion'. The particular way the African-becoming-American was allowed to express him or herself in church was through music, the spirituals being hymns rebuilt and repurposed to express the secret longings of a people ripped out of their world and deposited in a brutal hell. Later, secular forms of this music began to be marketed and sold by entrepreneurs

(America's core religious practice?), and these re-wired expressions of loss spread, multiplied, expanded, forming new shapes as they went, eating up any raw material they came across. Until, eventually, we arrived at a point where almost all of us—possibly even high court judges—know that 'wicked' can carry a very different meaning from the same word in the King James Bible.

Hip hop has often been treated as a collapse or retreat from the 'high' African American culture of modern jazz, a kind of bastard offspring lacking the musicality, sophistication, complexity, even the spirituality or morality of its besuited forebear. It's understandable on one level, the lack of traditional instruments and hence the absence of a recognisable corpus of technique leading to the conclusion that no technique is required at all. On top of this is the issue of the language sometimes used, of swearing and misogyny and violence, a sense that this is not a music which presents the best of Black American life. It's inarguable that it's a long way from *A Love Supreme* to *Supreme Clientele*. But if you think of the music of the African slave diaspora as a music of re-reference then it's possible to suggest that hip hop is, in fact, its highest, most realised form, a late renaissance rather than a descent into decadence: the most re-referential music ever made. This begins with the DJ 'cutting breaks' across two turntables and finds its own ultimate expression with the sampler (Grandmaster Flash described himself, after all, as a 'human sampler'). Sampling recontextualises sound. It is re-reference made concrete, brought front and centre where it's unmissable. To collage sound and, in doing so, to alter the meaning of every constituent element, is a form of ecstasy, stepping outside of oneself in order to more fully inhabit oneself. It represents a system in which this re-wiring, this recontextualisation, is the central form of self-expression. In which, in effect, Self is built from Other—and hence collapses the distinction between Self and Other—over and over again. For ever.

No one exemplifies the particular dynamics of this renaissance better than Method Man, and the only technologies he employs are his mouth and his mind. 'Method Man' the song is one of only two solo tracks on *Enter the Wu-Tang* and Meth uses it for a master class in re-reference. For a start, the nursery-rhyme spelling out of 'Method' on the chorus itself—sounding as if it naturally follows the cadences of the piano sample beneath it—is in fact a quotation from the Hall & Oates hit, 'Method of Modern Love'. The hook which follows on the bridge ('I got fat bags of skunk...' etc.) seems so natural and immediately recognisable that when you hear it you imagine it as a chant on a hundred other hip hop records. In fact, it's a version of 'Come Together' by the Beatles. 'Even if I didn't know the words to the song,' Method Man explains, 'I had my own version of the words'—his memory acting as a filter, warping and changing the original so that the result is familiar and unfamiliar all at once. And where does the lure of nostalgia lie if not in this tension of something familiar and forever lost?

This 'sample', though, is even more refracted than we might at first imagine, because what Meth is referencing isn't the Beatles at all, but Michael Jackson's cover of that Beatles song, itself a kind of re-referencing. This is a trick the artist pulls twice on 'Method Man': the first line of his first verse is apparently a straight steal of the chorus from the Rolling Stones' 'Get Off Of My Cloud', but when asked about it, Method Man once again points to a Black artist's cover or re-appropriation, in this case Bootsy Collins' use of the line in the Rubber Band's 'Disciples of Funk' from 1990. In view of Keith Richards' recent comments when asked about cultural and musical appropriation ('I'm black as the ace of fucking spades, man. Ask any of the brothers'), the double repurposing of this line seems even more apposite (though so, too, does a smack in the chops).

This is just the start, though. The Man describes his method like this: 'I was sampling it in my fucking head and saying it like it would be sampled'—in effect, using the sampled backdrop of the beat and music as the basis for a sample solo stitched together in his mouth. In the same song, Meth works in references to George Clinton's 'Atomic Dog' and Captain Sky's 'Super Sporm' (which had led to boasts about super *sperm* ever since Sugarhill Gang's 'Rapper's Delight'—and presumably before, as that manufactured concatenation of bouncers and pizza parlour managers were renowned for stealing most of their boasts). Then there are nods to both Busta Rhymes' group, Leaders of the New School, and Humpty Hump, the alter ego of Shock G from Oakland act Digital Underground. But he also re-purposes children's nursery rhymes (a little bit of pat-a-cake), children's stories (the Big Bad Wolf) and children's books (Dr Seuss and Sam-I-Am), as well as at least three TV catchphrases running the gamut from Tweety Pie and his puddy-tat friend to the Bill Cosby cartoon Fat Albert and the bluesman Calhoun Tubbs from *In Living Color.* Throw in a bit of Dick Van Dyke in *Mary Poppins*, and at least one re-worked advertising jingle and you have a fudgy melange of pop-culture references which should trigger little hits of recognition in the brains of a whole range of listeners.

Something else should be pointed out. Method Man is known as Meth, and meth is Wu-slang for cannabis. Much of the song 'Method Man'—particularly the Beatles-warping bridge we started with—is a paean to smoking weed. We can think of being stoned as something like watching an internal firework show of our own brain cells. One by one, ideas fly up into the mind's sky to detonate beautifully (the death of that single cell), a moment of excitement almost instantly forgotten as we focus in on the next. In the way that 'Method Man' succeeds in actually mimicking this feeling through its compacted re-referencing of pop culture—this succession of tiny dopamine hits—it's arguable that this is not only a highly sophisticated work of the African-diasporic renaissance but one of the finest musical evocations ever recorded of the sensation of being baked. That it manages to be both at once is not to disparage it or the form but to suggest quite the contrary—that a music this complex and flexible, a music of re-reference, can be both at once. And also everything in between.

6TH CHAMBER
PARENT TRAP

The parents of Clifford Smith didn't live together but he
spent time with both growing up, staying out in Long
Island with his father and on Staten Island when he
was with his mother. The father of Robert Diggs left his
family when Bobby was three, holding him in one arm
as he smashed the furniture up with the other. Elgin
Turner lived with a great-aunt and great-uncle in South
Carolina from the age of four until he was thirteen. Both
Jason Hunter and Dennis Coles were six when their
fathers went. Hunter's, a trumpeter and artist, died,
while Coles's just walked out. The parents of Russell
Jones split up when he was sixteen. His dad said Russell
never got over it. Gary Grice's father seems to have been
around at least into his teen years, probably longer—the
evidence is sketchy. Lamont Hawkins said he only had
a mother. This is not yet scientifically possible. Corey

Woods said that 'none of us had fathers', which isn't strictly true, either.

There are only three mentions of fathers on *Enter the Wu-Tang*, and two of them come from Raekwon the Chef. On 'Can It Be All So Simple' he says that his father was a *fiend* (a drug addict) from the age of sixteen, and on 'C.R.E.A.M.' he remembers his mother leaving the man and moving to Staten Island. The only other reference comes courtesy of Method Man, who, during a skit recorded from an early radio interview, explains that Ol' Dirty Bastard is so named because he has 'no father to his style'.

But the mothers who were left behind and who often had to raise their sons alone receive much the same treatment. As well as referring to his own mum on 'C.R.E.A.M.', Raekwon recalls pointing a gun at someone else's on 'Can It Be All So Simple'. Inspectah Deck also refers to his mother on 'C.R.E.A.M.' and in particular to seeking her advice, though it's unclear exactly how useful that advice turns out to be. Beyond that there is RZA's fictionalised first-person story rhyme on 'Tearz', in which he 'recalls' how his mother sent his brother out to buy bread, an excursion which ended when the boy was shot dead. Even here, the mother—presumably grieving—is absent after the initial errand is set.

We are invited, over and over again, to view the collapse of the traditional family unit in the inner cities of the developed world as a tragedy, as a blight, as something that ruins lives. The analysis of why it's happening, whether it's cause or effect, may differ depending on where you sit on the political spectrum, but nobody is claiming it as anything other than bad. And yes, of course there's deep sadness here, issues with abandonment, emotional repercussions and poverty.

For the young artist, though, as for the young crook, being cut loose from your parents—from their attempts at instilling discipline, from their fear, their shame, their sense of exactly who you are—might also feel a lot like liberation.

In the case of Wu-Tang, this liberation offered a group of young men the opportunity to form their own brotherhood, a fraternity shaped both by the realities of the New York drugs trade and by the imaginative universe of Hong Kong cinema, as well as by the esoteric religious philosophy they adhered to. The structure they created shared many of the strengths of other fraternities as well as the weaknesses (most obviously, the lack of women). There is a tendency, though, to view any grouping of young African American males as threatening rather than as self-protective, as destructive rather than creative. A society which always treats the actions of particular members of that society as a problem is, in fact, the problem—much more so than a lack of parental role models.

7TH CHAMBER
IMPURE THOUGHTS

Family runs horizontally as well as vertically. As we've already seen, Robert Diggs (RZA), Russell Jones (Ol' Dirty Bastard) and Gary Grice (GZA) are first cousins. They share a grandfather, Fred Cuffee, and Fred, it has been claimed, was a sachem (chief) of the Shinnecock Indian Nation. The Cuffees are, indeed, one of the four major families or clans of the Shinnecock Nation. Absalom Cuffee was among only the second set of trustees elected by the tribe, in 1793, and by 1983 he had been followed in this role by Aaron, Noah, Vincent, Wicks, Elias, Paul, Wickham, Nathan, Andrew, Emerson, Eugene, Deforest and Cortland. Paul Cuffee was a famous preacher, whose grave at Canoe Place is still marked. Wickham Cuffee was held to look so much like George Washington that he was (somewhat bizarrely) held up as yet another example of those exceptions, 'pure blood' Indians, when he died in 1915.

The Shinnecock Indian Nation, based on the eastern tip of Long Island, isn't the most storied or legendary of Native American tribes. Small to begin with, it shared with its neighbours the singular misfortune of being located on the east coast of America, where the devils from across the sea arrived in their ships. First contact with Europeans, it should be all too apparent, never works out well for those thus contacted. The Shinnecock's continuing survival is, in and of itself, a remarkable achievement. Located on land whose ownership was disputed between the Dutch and the British, the Shinnecock found themselves coming under pressure not only from these parties, but from a variety of larger, more powerful tribes trying to muscle in on the manufacture and supply of 'wampum' beads after the colonising powers declared them currency in New England in 1637 (the tribes, who quickly became reliant on the manufacture of these beads, were dealt another blow when the Europeans started using metal drill bits to mass-produce them).

In 1640, the Shinnecock agreed a deal with the British which relinquished a large proportion of their land in exchange for protection, only grudgingly and occasionally given. By 1657, the authorities had managed to saddle the tribe with a debt of £400 for the actions of one man in burning down some English houses. In the years immediately after the agreement, plague (probably smallpox) swept through the Indian communities of Long Island, reducing their size by around two thirds. By 1703, a new deal was agreed, incorporating yet more land, though including a thousand-year lease back to the tribe of the Shinnecock Hills—a lease which was swiftly abrogated in 1859 when the railway was due to be built through that land, massively increasing its value. The result of all these *agreements*, plagues, tricks, false signatures and intimidations was that the Shinnecock were left with a reserve of just 800 acres, on which it was impossible to maintain their traditional lifestyle. 'When an Indian was dispossessed of his land, he lost all hope of finding any niche,' Francis Jennings, director of the Center for the History of the American Indian, points out, 'except that of a servant or slave.'

Once the Shinnecock had signed away whatever rights they were felt to have in the land around them, the full force of American society was concerned mainly with their destruction. Or, to put a marginally kinder spin on it, with their dissolution. The reason for this was simple, and best understood in legal terms. If there was no longer any tribe, then there was no longer any party to previous agreements and hence no party to either challenge or enforce those agreements. The Montaukett, the neighbours of the Shinnecock—and, due to the English, at one time the dominant force on the Island—were made the exemplars of this practice. In 1909, they sued various parties (including the rail company) over land taken from them since the 1703 agreement, which they were also party to. The defence's case rested on the assertion that the Montaukett were not a tribe at all, but 'a diffuse community of thoroughly assimilated individuals who were seeking a lucrative monetary settlement'. The way the defence went about 'proving' their case was by playing on 'prevailing racial and class prejudices', in particular emphasising the tribe's intermarrying with African Americans. The judge eventually ruled that the Montaukett had indeed 'disintegrated and been absorbed into the mass of citizens'.

Much the same rhetoric has bedevilled the Shinnecock. The historian John A. Strong, until recently a professor emeritus of history at Long Island University and a dogged chronicler of the Algonquin Indians of Long Island, has catalogued references to the 'last of the "pure blooded" Shinnecocks' running from 1867 to 1936 and relating to at least thirteen different 'last' individuals. He also explained to the *New York Times* exactly what was held to underpin this obsession with purity, recalling when he moved to the area after the Second World War. 'When I first came here, the talk, particularly in the bars and so forth, was that they are simply posing as Indians, that they were really blacks, although the terms used were much more derogatory.' Despite this ongoing claim—that they are just 'Blacks' playing at being 'Indians' for what they can get out of it—the Shinnecock Indian Nation has continued to fight for justice and self-determination, resulting, at last, in formal federal recognition in 2010 and, with it, the right to build a casino on their land, as well as to pursue the return of land (or compensation for that land) from the people who took it from them. Members of the Shinnecock Nation can be proudly counted among the protesters against the Dakota Pipeline at Standing Rock. Their annual powwow is 'one of the largest Native American gatherings on the East Coast'.

For some, though, they will remain 'Blacks' 'posing as Indians', and this isn't a coincidence. Patrick Wolfe has outlined how America 'required the dispossession of Indigenous people just as foundationally as it did the enslavement of Africans'. In fact, the two were part of the same dynamic, the capture of more land requiring more slaves to work that land. And within this system of appropriation, there was a dual purpose to anti-miscegenation laws suggesting that 'one drop' of Black blood made a child Black. 'In addition to rendering the exclusion of Black people complete,' he says, 'the one-drop rule was integral to the statistical elimination of Indians, in that where Indians shared parentage with Black people it... provid[ed] for the immediate transmission of non-Indian status.'

Let's look at a particular example, that of Fred Cuffee, a probable ancestor of RZA, GZA and ODB. Records show that Fred was admitted to the Carlisle Indian Industrial School on 4 September 1892 and expelled from the school on 8 September of the same year. Started in Carlisle, Pennsylvania, in 1879 by Captain Richard Henry Pratt, the institution was a federally funded boarding school for Indians, with Pratt's over-riding aim being to 'Kill the Indian, save the man'. The method for achieving this purpose, later expanded across a whole network of educational establishments, was brutal. 'Cut off from their families and culture, the children were punished for speaking their Native languages, banned from conducting traditional or cultural practices, shorn of traditional clothing and identity... taught that their cultures and traditions were evil and sinful, and that they should be ashamed of being Native American', write Donald Wharton and Brett Lee Shelton. 'Far from home, they were frequently neglected or abused physically, sexually, and psychologically.' Unsurprisingly, the effect attained wasn't always what Pratt was hoping for. A child of the Lakota people, Plenty Horses was taken from the Rosebud reservation in South Dakota to attend Carlisle from 1883 to 1888. In 1891, he shot and killed Lieutenant Edward W. Casey during negotiations following the massacre at Wounded Knee. At his trial, he stated that when he returned to his tribe from Carlisle, 'I was an outcast among them. I was no longer an Indian. I was not a white man. I was lonely. I shot the lieutenant so I might make a place for myself among my people. I am now one of them.' Among Native Americans, the name of the Carlisle Indian School sits alongside those of massacres at Sand Creek, Camp Grant, Wounded Knee and so on.

Fred Cuffee, however, escaped after only four days, or rather was rejected, and sent the three hundred or so miles back home. The reason given on his student file card is as simple as it's bleak: 'Too much negro'.[5] This presents us with something of a contradiction. Fred Cuffee was saved from being 'de-Indianized' by dint of being too Black. The racial category meant to damn him was in large part responsible for preserving his identity and, we can presume, his sense of self. If we extrapolate from this incident we are left with a new, broader question. Were the Shinnecock as a whole delivered from complete destruction in part because of *their lack of purity*? When it comes up against a totalising system of categorisation does the very resistance of hybrid culture to easy classification operate as a broader cultural resistance? And isn't hip hop a hybrid culture, too—moreover, a culture of hybridity?

5   The Carlisle Indian School Digital Resource Center is a remarkable act of online remembering, offering a searchable database of resources relating to the school, including full scans of student files, which is where Fred was found.

8TH CHAMBER
THROWING AWAY THE KEY

Escape isn't always so simple. Seven of the nine
members of the Wu-Tang Clan have been in jail and
this shouldn't surprise us. Not because they're rappers,
or drug dealers, or drug users, or owners or possessors
of illegal firearms—though each member of the group
could have ticked more than one and often all of these
categories at some point in the first twenty-five years
of their lives—but simply because they're all African
American and grew up in the 1980s. It's an excuse
and it's not an excuse, an explanation or part of an
explanation. It's America and its story since the 1960s.

As the historian Michael Flamm has pointed out,
16 July 1964—the day James Powell was killed by Officer
Thomas Gilligan on the Upper East Side of Manhattan—
was also the day on which Barry Goldwater received

the Republican presidential nomination.[6] 'Security from domestic violence… is the most elementary and fundamental purpose of any government,' he said in his acceptance speech. 'History shows us—demonstrates that nothing—nothing prepares the way for tyranny more than the failure of public officials to keep the streets from bullies and marauders.' Although Goldwater would go on to lose the presidential race to Lyndon B. Johnson, 'his embrace of law and order shaped the political debate for the coming decades'. Johnson, who claimed that every night of rioting that summer was costing him 90,000 votes, re-branded his War on Poverty as 'a war against crime and a war against disorder', but it was the Republicans who made the issue their own (at least until Bill Clinton reclaimed it). The issue was not crime, not really. Instead, it was an electoral strategy revolving around 'the use of crime as a proxy language for race'. While it's easy to blame politicians for this nefarious practice, it's always worth bearing in mind that the tactic only works if the electorate contains a lot of racists.

It's salutary to remember, though, particularly at this time, that 'the New Right's "authoritarian-populist" project' goes back even further than the Nixon Whitehouse (Nixon gets a mention from Ghostface Killah on the first verse of the first track on *Enter*, the rapper revelling in his villainous role and threatening, like the former president, to 'damage your whole era').

---

6   Gary Grice, the oldest member of the Clan, was born just over two years later, on 22 August 1966. Method Man, the youngest member, was born on 2 March 1971. So, although they all entered this world in the decade following the enactment of the Civil Rights Act, seven of the Clan were born during the Nixon presidency. If history does indeed repeat itself, we could expect another burst of brilliant musical creativity in the USA to hit some time in the early 2040s.

However, it's Ronald Reagan, first elected as governor of California off the back of his heavy-handed response to the Watts Rebellion in Los Angeles, who concerns us most here. The Wu-Tang Clan were aged 11 to 16 on 2 October 1982 when Reagan used one of his weekly radio broadcasts to the nation to declare war. 'The mood toward drugs is changing in this country,' Reagan told his listeners, 'and the momentum is with us. We're making no excuses for drugs—hard, soft, or otherwise. Drugs are bad, and we're going after them... We've taken down the surrender flag and run up the battle flag. And we're going to win the war on drugs.'

Reagan's unique contribution to this particular debate is that he seems to have taken his own rhetoric seriously, putting in place many of the changes which made American penal policy, in the words of Michelle Alexander in her remarkable book, *The New Jim Crow*, 'a system of social control unparalleled in world history'. Although the process went right back to the 1960s, it was the 1980s which saw the most pronounced expansion of the criminal justice system. 'Between 1965 and 1993, crime control expenditures jumped from $4.6 billion to $100 billion... and the rate of incarceration in the United States is now the highest in the industrialized world'— higher than in Russia, China or Iran. In particular, Alexander shows, 'no other country in the world imprisons so many of its racial or ethnic minorities... The current system of control permanently locks a huge percentage of the African American community out of the mainstream society and economy. The system operates through our criminal justice system, but it functions more like a caste system than a system of crime control.'

Of course, this is all much more widely

acknowledged now than it was a few years ago—is almost a commonplace, in fact—which is not the same as saying that anything's been done about it. First there was Alexander's book, then Ava DuVernay's Oscar-winning documentary, *The 13th*, which took these observations into the mainstream. All the same, let's quickly outline the processes by which 'more than half of the young black men in many large American cities' came under the control of the criminal justice system or suffered the difficulties and indignities which result from having a criminal record.

Presidents have a problem when it comes to law and order, something they tend to keep quiet about on the campaign trail. In that 'street crime' tends to happen on a street and hence in a state, it doesn't fall under federal control. The Reagan administration, though, wasn't going to allow itself to be stymied by a small matter like jurisdiction. The main thrust of the war on drugs was finding ways to influence policy towards drug crime at a state as well as a federal level.

The first plank was federal funding. In addition to huge increases in direct anti-drug funding for the Federal Bureau of Investigation (FBI), the Drugs Enforcement Agency (DEA) and the Department of Defense, money was poured into federal training schemes like the DEA's Operation Pipeline, launched in 1984 to help in the training of state police. By 2000, over 25,000 officers had been directly trained by the DEA under the auspices of Operation Pipeline, and many more were then trained by these officers. Basically, Pipeline encourages police officers to stop people on any pretext and then use their authority to pressure them into submitting to a search. Research shows that very few people are aware of their right to refuse to be searched, and even those that are can be bullied into it. As such, Operation Pipeline led to a tripling in the number of drug arrests between 1980 and 2005, even though it's estimated that 95% of Pipeline searches yield no drugs. Put these two statistics together and you get some sense of the scale of the trawl being undertaken.

In addition to the training offered by Operation Pipeline, federal grants also encouraged local law enforcement to concentrate resources on the war on drugs. From 1988, the Byrne Program was used to encourage the formation of narcotics task forces at state level. In fact, Alexander says, 'it is questionable whether any specialized drug enforcement activity would exist in some states without the Byrne program'. The Pentagon also armed these task forces, pouring weaponry and body armour into the inner cities. The quantity of funding received *was linked to the number of arrests made*. This encouraged the kind of trawling that Pipeline promoted, because the more drugs arrests a department made, the more money it would receive.

Just as important in convincing the public that all this was necessary was a media campaign, spearheaded by Robert Stutman of the DEA, which happened to coincide with the appearance of crack. We will return to the issue of crack in the next chamber, but it's worth saying here that the panic around it was not limited to the media but also infected both the legislature and the legal system. The Fourth Amendment should protect American citizens from 'unreasonable searches and seizures' (i.e. general stop and search policies like Pipeline), but the Supreme Court became so supine as Reagan's appointees moved it to the right and the newspapers trumpeted the *drug scourge* that by 1991, one of its own members, Justice Stevens, could conclude that 'this Court has become a loyal foot soldier in the Executive's fight against crime'.

Meanwhile, as early as 1984, Congress amended the law to allow police and other bodies to keep a huge proportion of any cash and assets seized during drugs investigations. As this could be done even on suspicion of illegal drugs-related activities, Alexander points out that 'this drug forfeiture regime proved highly lucrative for law enforcement', augmenting the stream of federal funding and further incentivising mass search and arrest tactics. In addition, the Anti-Drug Abuse Acts of 1986 and 1988 were 'extraordinarily punitive', in particular in the introduction of minimum mandatory sentencing and 'civil penalties', where housing and federal benefits could be denied to anyone convicted of a drug offence. The 1988 Act went as far as introducing a minimum sentence of five years for a first-time offender caught in possession of crack. This had the effect of passing unrivalled power to public prosecutors, who could now 'load up' defendants 'with charges that carry extremely harsh sentences in order to force them to plead guilty to lesser offenses'. The plea bargain system, combined with harsh mandatory sentences, forced people to plead guilty whether they were or weren't—the costs and risks of going to court to plead your innocence became too high. This, in brief, is how a country with five per cent of the world's population could end up with twenty-five per cent of the world's prison population.

But that's not all. 'In the drug war, the enemy is racially defined.' As Alexander shows, 'although the majority of illegal drug users and dealers nationwide are white, three fourths of all people imprisoned are black or Latino'. In that the buying and selling of drugs is a consensual act, no one reports it. The police are sent out to try to uncover it. In doing so, they are granted a huge amount of discretion over who they stop and search. And they tend to stop and search people from ethnic minorities living in inner cities. This then becomes self-reinforcing. Police statistics seem to show that most drugs arrests come from ethnic minorities living in inner cities and so they target ethnic minorities in these areas even more, in the belief that these are the most likely to yield results. Unless they publicly acknowledge that they are searching someone solely because of their race, the courts defend a police officer's right to stop and search whoever he or she likes. Throw in a media-driven panic about the *crack epidemic* in predominantly Black inner-city neighbourhoods and higher mandatory sentences for possession of and dealing crack—and in particular, the way prosecutors used the threat of these sentences both to push convictions through outside the court system via plea bargains and to gain tip-offs from informants—and you begin to gain some clarity as to how the whole set-up is rigged.

As for prison, there are perhaps certain economic advantages to having a large incarcerated population. As RZA has noted, 'slavery just meant that 3 to 5 million Americans were providing free labor for the entire country. After the civil war, they were freed but they filled the jails with blacks, and now they working again... Where's the profit going? They're building highways, running industries, and you come to find these institutions are privately owned business. It's [the] same thing all over again.'

Prison, though, is not the end of the ordeal. Once you have a criminal record you are stuck in what Alexander describes as 'a closed circuit of perpetual marginality'. It's hard to gain access to social housing or benefits. You're often left with debts from your time in jail or on parole, where so many services have been privatised and you are expected to pay for them. You have to declare your record to any potential employer but are in breach of parole if you don't have a job. The National Association for the Advancement of Colored People (NAACP) states that 'a criminal record can reduce the likelihood of a callback or job offer by nearly 50 percent. The negative impact of a criminal record is twice as large for African American applicants.' Often you are banned from jury service and, even in states which don't restrict your right to vote, getting yourself back on the electoral register is complicated and deliberately abstruse.

The situation is summed up best by the poet, novelist, playwright and essayist, Ishmael Reed. 'Whites have their government,' he says, 'with its three branches and innumerable services. The police are my government. They can regulate my comings and goings with all the leeway accorded modern-day patrollers, which they are. They can request an I.D. check with or without cause. They can invade my home without a warrant and the criminal justice system will tolerate this invasion with a wink and a nod. They can arrest me without cause, judge me, and in some cases carry out the sentence. Sometimes they decide that the penalty is death.'

Unsurprisingly, the police and the criminal justice system were very much a focus of anger for rappers by the end of the 1980s. N.W.A's 'Fuck tha Police' (1988) and KRS-One's 'Sound of Da Police' (1993) are probably the two best-known examples of this phenomenon.

But LL Cool J included 'Illegal Search' on his 1990 album, *Mama Said Knock You Out*, and Public Enemy flipped the script by talking about the unresponsiveness of the emergency services to calls made from predominantly Black neighbourhoods on '911 Is A Joke' (also 1990). LA crew The Pharcyde rapped about the fear of getting pulled over when you'd lost your licence on 'Officer' (1992), while Brand Nubian's 'Claimin' I'm A Criminal' (1994) sets out the dynamics and politics involved as clearly as you could hope. And there are many, many more. The Wu-Tang Clan, though, stay more or less silent.

The only place where this issue is fully addressed is during Inspectah Deck's verse on 'C.R.E.A.M.' Even here, though he mentions unscrupulous policemen and how 'the court played me short', there's no doubt from the rest of the rhyme that his trip to jail aged fifteen was because he was caught selling crack, not because he was some innocent indiscriminately swept up by the system. If anything, the message of the verse concerns the wisdom contained in the teachings of the Nation of Gods and Earths[7] and the importance of self-education. It's about transcending hopelessness and nihilism through self-actualisation, not through a critique of America.

Beyond this, *Enter the Wu-Tang* largely inhabits a universe free of authority—except for the group's own and the tenets of their belief system. There are very few references to imprisonment or constraint of any sort on the record. On the opener, 'Bring Da Ruckus', Ghostface suggests that the uncompromising will either end up in prison or shot, while Raekwon talks about being as

---

7   Also known as the Five Percenters, this breakaway sect of the Nation of Islam has counted all the members of the Wu-Tang Clan among its number at some point and played a definitive role in their intellectual development. We will be returning to them in much more detail in the 11th Chamber.

careful to watch his back as he would be in jail. Method Man turns theft into a kind of conquest on 'Shame on a Nigga' when he suggests no one can capture his 'stature'. On 'Wu-Tang: 7th Chamber', Deck says he's just busted out of prison, having been 'charged by the system for murdering the rhythm'. Ghostface returns with the last reference (beyond Deck's verse on 'C.R.E.A.M.') when he commands the listener to 'Open the cage' before getting out of there as fast as 'a runaway slave'.

The Wu-Tang Clan, it might be presumed from this brief overview, are interested in escape, and there's some truth in this. But their escapism is of a very particular sort. First, as already suggested, they largely choose to ignore authority. This can't be an accident. Their disregard is, in effect, a refusal to acknowledge the authority of authority. The only grounds on which they would submit to that authority is the grounds of superior force—and an authority which can only maintain its authority through superior force is no authority at all. This might not sound too different to the anarchism of Emma Goldman, who maintained that 'the State is not a social organisation; it is an organisation born of despotism and maintained by force, and imposed by force on the masses'. Having passed through the American penal system, Inspectah Deck emerges knowing that 'living in the world [is] no different from a cell'. But the Wu-Tang aren't anarchists in any recognisable form. They see the prison outside of prison but they're still escapers first and foremost. The question then becomes—how do you escape from a prison which encompasses the entirety of your existence?

9TH CHAMBER
CRACK IN THE SYSTEM

In his history of the relationship between hip hop and capitalism, *The Big Payback*, Dan Charnas spells out how the mania of crack gripped the pre-Wu and their entourage in the years before the group got together. This wasn't necessarily the mania you'd expect, the mania of substance abuse. Instead, some of these young men found themselves caught up in the mania of substance *supply*. Oliver 'Power' Grant—who would go on to be one of four executive producers on *Enter The Wu-Tang*, along with RZA, his brother and Ghostface Killah—grew up in the Park Hill projects. When a crew of older kids moved in on the neighbourhood, stopped him selling weed and started shifting crack, he approached them and asked to buy in. Very rapidly, he was making good money and bringing in friends to work for him. Charnas argues that it's 'a measure of how addictive the drug was to both its buyers and sellers. One taste of crack made you a fiend. One taste of crack money made you a dealer.'

Both RZA's older brother, Divine,[8] and Power's close friend Raekwon worked for Grant during this time (there are persistent rumours, always denied by Raekwon, that his moniker, 'The Chef', referred to his talents at 'cooking' crack). Inspectah Deck was jailed when he was only fifteen for something connected to dealing. U-God ran his own operation out of Park Hill at around the same time and Method Man worked for him. Later, at a point of particular desperation, RZA and Ghostface Killah, finding the New York scene already a little too crowded, headed out to Steubenville in Ohio—where RZA, GZA and ODB had visited family as children—to set up in the drugs game. They were joined there by Ol' Dirty Bastard. 'We made money and were able to feed ourselves,' RZA recalls, 'but it was the most negative point in my life. I never wanted to be a drug dealer—I thought I was killing my own people—but for my own survival I entered that world. I betrayed myself.' When he talks about those times, RZA sounds very much like a recovering addict. Only Masta Killa and the GZA have sidestepped stories of hustling and dealing in the past, though even the latter included a track on his debut album (as The Genius) called 'Life of a Drug Dealer'.

Everyone wants to get high—which is another way of saying that everyone wants to escape from something. Alcohol, tobacco, heroin and connected opioids, marijuana, speed, crystal meth, angel dust, caffeine,

8 Or Mitchell, as he was probably still known then. The power of self-naming in hip hop is a strange sort of magic, working retrospectively to delete the user's previous identity, regardless of whether they wish it.

LSD, MDMA, magic mushrooms, cocaine, solvents, poppers, laughing gas, spinning round until you fall over. There are lots of ways to do it. 'The drive to achieve intoxicated states is a universal and abiding one.' How we choose to get high—or even if we do choose—is, of course, another matter.

How about some of this? 'I inhaled. Smoke invaded my mouth and lungs. The rush hit me almost instantaneously, euphoria detonating in my brain and spreading quickly to every part of my body' Or this? 'He feels the high at first as a flutter, then a roar. A surge of new energy pounds through every inch of him, and there is a moment of perfect oblivion where he is aware of nothing and everything... It storms through him—sexual, euphoric—like a magnificent hurricane raging at the speed of light. It is the warmest, most tender caress he has ever felt.' How about this? 'You feel this great wave of massive, totally unhandleable energy rolling through you, until you feel you can't actually contain it, and it's about to burst through your finger-ends, and you know you won't ever do this again. Then you let out your breath and you feel *so* beautiful... you feel like a king.' Or even this, from a slightly less literary source? The hit is like a 'whole body orgasm'. Want some? Who wouldn't want some? You'd be crazy not to give it a go.

There is, of course, a problem. The high being referred to is that delivered by crack cocaine. It lasts about fifteen minutes tops and all four users are referring to their first ever use. The god of diminishing returns seems to have chosen it as his very own narcotic. Bill Clegg, the former literary agent turned crack addict turned memoirist and novelist, is responsible for our second testimony. The passage finishes, '...and then, as it recedes, the coldest hand. He misses the feeling even before it's left him and not only does he want more, he needs it.'

The active substance in coca leaves was first isolated at some point in the 1850s. The drug went through a half-century or so as a panacea for everything from catarrh to piles to addiction to other drugs before it became apparent that it could also be quite addictive itself. The move towards its prohibition, though, was driven, as these things tend to be, by a panic. Craig Reinarman points out that cocaine was 'first criminalized when the addict population began to shift from predominantly white, middle-class, middle-aged women to young, working-class males, African-Americans in particular'. This shift was reflected in the rhetoric of Dr Hamilton Wright, appointed the US Opium Commissioner by President Theodore Roosevelt in 1908. 'There is no doubt,' Wright claimed, 'that this drug, perhaps more than any other, is used by those concerned in the white slave traffic to corrupt young girls, and that when the habit of using the drug has been established, it is but a short time before such girls fall to the ranks of prostitution.' In case the subtext wasn't quite clear enough, Wright also claimed that 'cocaine is often the direct incentive to the crime of rape by the Negroes of the South'. Unsurprisingly considering the rhetoric, the substance was banned, drinks like Coca-Cola and Vin Mariani were forced to remove the ingredient or stop producing and this hugely popular 'health' product was cast into the wilderness.

It wasn't until the 1970s that cocaine staged something of a revival, this time because of 'its aura of elite unaffordability', an odd reinvention for what was previously an over-the-counter cure as common as aspirin. In this new iteration, coke became a drug of the rich and beige, glamorous not because of the effects it produced but because of its high cost alone, as if its dealers had learned a trick from those furniture stores who shift unwanted sofas by increasing their ticket price. The appeal of the drug, Stuart Walton argues in *Out of It*, his overview of the human desire to get blasted, became exactly that 'the sensations offered by snorting [it] are more modestly tame than any'. As such, 'it is a perfect capitalist construct', he says, 'delivering tormentingly brief satisfaction that requires further lavish expense to sustain'.

The user response to this problem of tameness was dealt with, though, when freebase was invented, either as an attempt by a chemist to return powdered cocaine to something like the coca paste—known as *basé*—that Latin American peasants traditionally smoke, or as a by-product of dealers checking the purity of their goods. With the chemistry of freebasing already a dangerous and difficult process for the amateur alchemist, the resultant effect of the drug was also transformed into a sharp, extremely intense hit—and one that wore off even more quickly. To extend Walton's metaphor, it was late capitalism to powder cocaine's industrial revolution. At some point, someone made the technical leap which created 'rock'—lumps of freebase cocaine that could be dried out, broken into small hits and sold.

This innovation is often attributed to 'Freeway' Ricky Ross, a Los Angeles drug dealer and former tennis prodigy who began to flood the city (and eventually the country) with crack in the early to mid-eighties. Reading Ross's recent autobiography, there's nothing about any *eureka* moment where he either discovered how to make crack or moved from selling one to selling the other. 'Powder cocaine appeared as a bright, shining star of opportunity', he says, and then later, on the same page, 'We cooked like a hundred kilos every night. We didn't call it crack. We called it Ready Rock.'

As Reinarman has pointed out (this time with Harry Levine), 'crack was a marketing innovation. It was a way of packaging a relatively expensive and upscale commodity (powder cocaine) in small, inexpensive units.' The joy of that powerful hit, you see, is that it means you can sell in quantities small enough that the price comes down to twenty or ten or even five dollars, all using amounts of powder that your average snorter wouldn't notice had even entered his/her nose, much less get any kind of a high from. Indeed, Ricky's real innovation seems to have been a highly aggressive attitude towards price, a sense that 'the key to a good product is making it affordable to everyone, not just the privileged few'. This 'misuse' of a high-end drug (massively cutting his margin and selling in bulk exactly in opposition to the product's traditional marketing) was both Ross's moment of genius and the action which so outraged powder cocaine's normal user-base, many of whom were, of course, part of the country's ruling elite.

Ross was aided in his price-cutting tactics by having access to a supply of cocaine which was cheaper than almost anyone else was offering at the time. It's well known now, but for a number of years Ricky's main supplier was a Nicaraguan called Danilo Blandón. While Ross was used to paying $40,000–45,000 per kilo, Blandón ended up offering him a price that was well under $20,000. This was partly because of the quantities Ross was buying, of course, but was perhaps also a reflection of the lack of overheads Blandón had in dealing with law enforcement. Blandón himself had a background in marketing but, more importantly, he was well connected to the high command of the CIA-assembled FDN (Fuerza Democrática Nicaragüense) 'Contras', committed to the overthrow of the left-wing Sandinistas back in their home country.

Not everyone in the American government felt that the US administration should be funding the overthrow of foreign governments and hence financial support for the Contras was subject to a series of funding crises—for most of 1981 and between October 1984 and October 1986 in particular. Some of the shortfall was made up by funds from escapades like Colonel Oliver North's arms sales to Iran. Some was made up with drugs money. Short of the CIA releasing all documentation—or the Russians giving the documentation to Wikileaks—we will never know how much of the money Blandón raised by selling cocaine made it to the FDN, but he certainly led a charmed life. 'All the way through the first half of the 1980s, the prime wholesaler of cocaine to Los Angeles was not once raided or inconvenienced in any way by any authorities.' Blandón wasn't only selling cocaine to Ricky, either. In his autobiography, Ross recalls gifts of a boxed Uzi submachine gun and a .22 pistol with silencer. Other sources mention 'miniature video cameras, recording equipment, police scanners and Colt AR-15 assault rifles... Blandón even tried to sell [Ross's] partner a grenade launcher.'

When Blandón was arrested in October 1986 (perhaps not coincidentally, only ten days after the lifting of the Boland Amendment, which had prevented US state funding of the Contras), it turned out that his warehouses were all miraculously empty. It was only in 1991 that he was finally caught and charged, and sentenced the following year to a mere four years in prison. By 1993 he had become an informant for the DEA and Department of Justice and was freed after serving just twenty-eight months in jail. And in 1995, he fronted a sting operation to catch Rick Ross—a bizarre example of someone higher up the drugs food chain getting time off his sentence for entrapping not the person who supplied him, but the person he supplied.

Unsurprisingly, when this information became public knowledge, there was a sense that the CIA had perhaps deliberately encouraged the selling of crack in the inner cities in order to damage or destroy the Black community. It seems much more likely that the CIA simply didn't care. The effects are all that can be measured, not the intention, and on these the judgement seems clear. As Ross himself puts it, 'none of us knew the side effects that could and would occur amid the crack epidemic that would sweep over black neighborhoods across the land'. In 2014, the *Village Voice* ran a feature looking back at the rise of crack in New York in particular. 'Crack literally changed the entire face of the city,' a former DEA agent, Robert Stutman, was quoted as saying. 'I know of no other drug that caused the social change that crack caused. You can't name another drug that came close.'

This narrative has a fatal flaw, though, and the former DEA agent is it. Stutman made a guest appearance in the previous chamber. 'In October 1985,' Michelle Alexander points out, 'the DEA sent Robert Stutman to serve as director of its New York City office and charged him with the responsibility of shoring up public support for the administration's new drug war.' As we've already seen, 'crack was a godsend to the Right', and Stutman was one of the people most vigorously pushing this agenda. And, let's be fair here, he did a fantastic job. NBC devoted fifteen hours to features about crack in the seven months leading up to the 1986 congressional elections. *Newsweek* called it the biggest story since Vietnam and Watergate and its editor-in-chief was moved to comment that 'an epidemic is abroad in America as pervasive and dangerous in its way as the plagues of medieval times'. It was *Time* magazine's Issue of the Year. ABC News described it as 'a plague... eating away at the fabric of America'. The *Washington Post* ran 1,565 'drug crisis' stories (that's over 28,000 column inches) in the three years from October 1986 to October 1989. All of these stories were predicated on the simple notion that 'crack is the most addictive substance known to man'.

It's not. To think so is to fall into the trap of something known as 'pharmacological determinism'— to believe that the chemical make-up of a substance is not just the key determinant of how humans interact with it, but the *only* one. There is no pharmacological difference at all between crack and powder cocaine, and yet Congress voted through sentences one hundred times harsher for the possession of crack than for that of powder cocaine, based on the 'faulty testimony that crack was fifty times as addictive as powder cocaine. Congress then doubled this ratio as a so-called "violence penalty".' Perhaps the key factor behind this agenda was exactly Ross's Walmartisation of a product previously reserved for a privileged few. Poor people were being punished for expecting to have access to something which the elite felt should only belong to them. The actions of Congress certainly weren't backed by any scientific data. 'There is no evidence,' John Morgan and Lynn Zimmer state, 'that smoking crack cocaine is markedly more addictive than sniffing cocaine powder.' Ironically, considering that something similar is currently happening in our attitudes towards sugar, they go on to draw the following analogy: 'Like food consumption, drug consumption must be understood primarily as a social-psychological phenomenon.'

This is not a new idea. It's just an idea that's largely been ignored. Clarence Lusane set it all out in his 1991 book, *Pipe Dream Blues*. 'The drug problem,' he says, 'is, at its roots, a crisis of economic inequality, social disintegration, misplaced political priorities, and pervasive hopelessness.' That is, it's a very neat way of packaging up a very messy, very tragic story. As if the situation for Black and Hispanic people was not difficult enough in the America of the early 1980s, the collapse of the country's industrial base disproportionately affected them. Unemployment shot up just as Reagan's policies were beginning to bite. In addition, the war on drugs, by massively increasing penalties across the board, incentivised the selling of whichever product had the best margin, so that marijuana dealing, for example, became less attractive and crack more so. Furthermore, the onslaught of increased criminalisation of drugs removed fathers and mothers from the community, and destabilised a drugs market already being shaken by the economics of crack production. This breakdown of traditional controls in the home and in the drugs market sparked a massive upsurge in violence—not caused by the *drug*, but by selling the drug.

This was a crisis of capitalism—in particular, unregulated black market capitalism—not of pharmacology. 'Black people's need for money and consequent desire for psychological escape,' Lusane goes on to say, 'exacerbated by the alienating and iniquitable environment of poor communities, go a long way in explaining the drugs crisis.' While Rick Ross's memoir is obviously partial in what he chooses to remember and emphasise, the reader is struck most by just how much of his time is taken up with sorting out new vendors rather than new buyers. The book takes on some of the fevered atmosphere of tulip mania. Everybody wants in on the crack game—for the simple reason that it's the only way for anyone to make serious money: 'Just about all of the mothers in the apartment complex a couple days before the first of the month asked me about investing their welfare checks. It looked like an organized plan, because so many of them voiced interest.' Everyone wants to be a seller. Being a seller, after all, offers the possibility of a more concrete or permanent form of escape. Finding buyers seems to take care of itself.

The buyers, in fact, are often the same people as the vendors. 'The primary means for supporting... crack consumption was crack selling.' Ross's success is largely predicated on the fact that he's one of the very few who never partakes. The real driver here is a supply-side addiction, not a demand-driven one, or rests exactly in the disappearance of the gap between the two, the collapse of the distinction—fundamental to the classical model of economics—between supply and demand. It's an escape mania driven by fantasies of wealth more than the momentary release of the hit.

The propaganda of the war on drugs colludes in this fantasy. Drug scares promote the drugs they're supposed to warn us against. Rather than reinforcing conservative notions of self-responsibility, the notion of *instant addiction* excuses the user from any responsibility. The mania runs right through and across society, so that everyone but the addict is absolved of blame for their actions. Representative David McCurdy described the drafting of the 1986 Anti-Drug Abuse Act as 'out of control' before going on to say that 'of course I'm for it'. Walton argues that 'drug-taking disrupts the operations of the post-industrial economy', but the crack scare/ boom of the 1980s functions more as a heightening or intensification, almost a pastiche of the operations of the mainstream post-industrial economy, where all sides are trapped into a kind of magical thinking and go for hit after hit after hit.

Only on one side, though, is this magical thinking built on a complete lack of opportunity, on poverty and hopelessness. 'If all you have in life is bad choices, crack may not be the most unpleasant of them.' And selling crack may not be the most distasteful of them, either. If you think of the sampler as the technology that hip hop was waiting for in order to express itself, then crack was the technology US society as a whole was waiting for in order to express itself. And it expressed itself in a racist penal policy combined with a pyramid scheme which would eventually kill you or put you in jail.

Craig Reinarman has written extensively about the successive drug scares which swept twentieth-century America and has tried to get a handle on what it is about American society that makes it so susceptible to them. He focuses first on the temperance culture brought to the USA by Protestantism and the way it combined with industrial capitalism. 'Self-control,' he argues, 'was both central to religious world views and a characterological necessity for economic survival and success in the capitalist market.' However, as is the way with capitalism, a contradiction snuck in. American society became stuck on a mass consumption model of expansion which relied on 'the constant cultivation of new "needs", the production of new desires', he says. 'Drug scares continue to occur in American society in part because people must constantly manage the contradiction between a Temperance culture that insists on self-control and a mass consumption culture that renders self-control continuously problematic.' As we've seen, the crack panic was a generalised loss of control (of addicts, of suppliers and of those fearful of the first two), an unleashing of this tension in an orgy of drug abuse and abuse of drug abuser.

This same dynamic tension between self-control and mass consumption, between holding it down and getting out of it—as well as the manipulation and exploration of that tension—runs right through the Wu-Tang Clan's work. Although RZA was ashamed of his time selling crack, he learnt about the operation of American capitalism from it—intimately, uncomfortably. What he learnt, in particular, was how it *actually* functions rather than how it's supposed to work in the textbooks and the wet dreams of neoliberals—as a result of compulsions and panics and manias, in a world where your consumer is exactly the same man as your dealer.

10TH CHAMBER
DEALING

At some point in 1992, Robert Diggs aka the RZA
persuaded the other members of what would become
the Wu-Tang Clan to sign a deal with his company,
Wu-Tang Productions, and devote five years of their
lives to his master plan. He was aiming to do two things
which had never been done before: first, to 'unite
eight talented, unique, individual MCs as one'; and
second, to negotiate recording deals for the collective
and, crucially, also for each individual. With this
in mind, the group recorded two tracks—'After the
Laughter' (later re-named 'Tearz'), featuring the RZA
and Ghostface Killah, and 'Protect Ya Neck', featuring
Inspectah Deck, Raekwon, Method Man, U-God, Ol'
Dirty Bastard, RZA, Ghostface Killah and GZA. The cost
of the latter recording session, at Firehouse Studios in
Brooklyn, was covered by each MC paying $100 to appear

on the track, or maybe $50, or was possibly paid by RZA and Ghostface, or wasn't paid at all. According to legend, the group then pressed up 10,000 12-inch singles and began selling them out of the boot of RZA's cousin's car. They recorded 'Protect Ya Neck' in October 1992, had their first proper radio play in December and claimed that they had sold out of singles by March 1993, although a good few of them went into mail-outs for DJs and journalists (and there doesn't tend to be much of a paper trail for records sold out of the back of a car).

Steve Rifkind, the young boss of new label Loud (at the time a part of RCA, itself in turn part of Sony), was interested in the Wu-Tang Clan. The story goes that one day he was sitting in his office listening to the single at high volume (in some versions actually at his meeting with the members of the group) when the door burst open, and a kid he had never seen before leapt into the room, hollered, *'THAT'S THAT SHIIIIT!!!'* and departed. This spectre or harbinger convinced Rifkind to bet the house on Wu-Tang. He claimed never to have seen the kid again, adding to the narrative's supernatural overtones, the sense that everyone connected with the story likes to foster of a series of events that were pre-ordained and unstoppable.

Unable to compete financially with some of the other offers that were coming in, Rifkind gave RZA and his business associates what they wanted: the removal of the standard record company clause which would prevent any individual member of the group from signing a solo deal with another label. An advance was agreed of just $60,000, and before the contract was even fully negotiated, Def Jam had signed Method Man as a solo artist for $180,000 and Elektra had snapped up Ol' Dirty Bastard for a similar sum. Eventually, after more than a bit of fuss from the higher brass at RCA, Rifkind signed Raekwon and Inspectah Deck on solo deals, while GZA went to Geffen, Ghostface Killah to Sony and the side project RZA was working on, Gravediggaz, went to Gee Street/Island. 'Every label except one,' recalls Dan Charnas, 'now had some stake in the Wu-Tang Clan's success.'[9]

It's worth taking a moment to think about exactly what had been achieved here. First, the Wu-Tang broke the standard industry deal where a large advance buys complete control over the output of all signatories to that deal—where signing a deal for an advance means in effect that all recordings produced by any of the individuals covered by the deal are owned by the record company. 'You bargain for less money up front, more freedom in the longer run and higher earnings total,' RZA explained. 'The contract we signed with Loud in 1993 changed the way hip-hop artists negotiate, the way deals are structured; it changed the whole rap game.' In effect, RZA repackaged a series of products into a more marketable whole.[10] Having created a frenzy around this supergroup, he sold it cheap in order that,

9   To explain, when Charnas refers to 'every label', he means the major labels that dominate the music industry, not the individual imprints under their control. In 1993, the majors were Sony/RCA (which owned Loud and had a 50% stake in Def Jam), Warner (Elektra), MCA (Geffen), PolyGram (Island/Gee Street) and EMI. Every conglomerate except EMI had a financial interest in a member of the group. Two years after the release of *Enter*, MCA and PolyGram merged to form Universal Music Group and in 2012, the latter bought EMI, meaning that there are currently only three majors left. The current deals these labels have with Spotify for access to their catalogues mean that this number should stay stable–at least, until Spotify decides it can manage without them.

10   Both RZA (as Prince Rakeem) and GZA (as Genius) had already been signed and dropped by reputable hip hop labels Tommy Boy and Cold Chillin'. RZA, Ol' Dirty Bastard and GZA called themselves All In Together Now; RZA, Method Man, U-God, Raekwon and Inspectah Deck were known round Park Hill as D.M.D.

like Ready Rock, he could snap off chunks and re-sell them all over again (that is, the individual MCs from the Clan). The consumers of these offcuts (the major labels) then had to sell on the product they'd bought to the general public, in a manner similar to street dealers further down a cocaine supply chain. And rather than operating in competition with one another, they all had an interest in making it work, in convincing the world and themselves that this was the best high going. If the debut album flopped, a lot of investments would look shaky. No one could afford for this to happen. Hence the business was gripped by a kind of collective mania in which the Wu-Tang's success was all that mattered and everyone told everyone else that it would, in U-God's words, *rock and shock the nation*. 'I wanted my artists under many umbrellas because I wanted the industry to work for me,' explained RZA. 'That was my original strategy—to have artists placed in different locations and get those different labels to work together for my brand.'

RZA has claimed that only $36,000 of Loud's advance was spent on recording *Enter*. By this time Firehouse had moved to Manhattan and it was here that the album was recorded and mixed, apparently with very few changes from the demo versions recorded in RZA's apartment in Staten Island. During recording, Loud re-released 'Protect Ya Neck', this time backed with 'Method Man', a tune that Def Jam was now as keen to promote as the label selling it. *Enter the Wu-Tang (36 Chambers)* was released on 9 November 1993. Much of its reception on the east coast of America was further

---

(Dig 'Em Down); and RZA and Ghostface had originally been the only members of the Wu-Tang Clan.

enhanced by a sense that, after the recent domination of product from Los Angeles (Dr. Dre's *The Chronic* had come out at the very end of 1992 and Snoop Dogg's solo debut, *Doggystyle*, would follow two weeks after *Enter*), this was a return to the gritty, grimy hardcore style which was New York's own. This was a record completely without compromise, with no R&B choruses (occasionally with no choruses at all), nothing but hard beats and hard rhymes. *Enter* sold 30,000 records in its first week of release, was certified gold (500,000 record sales in the USA) by April 1994 and platinum (one million record sales in the USA) by May 1995.

It's worth noting that *Doggystyle* debuted at No. 1 on the Billboard Top 200 (*Enter* peaked at 41), sold over 800,000 records on its week of release, went quadruple platinum in the States, platinum in the UK and Canada and gold in France, selling in excess of eleven million records in the process. There are people who will tell you that the most important part of the whole Wu story is the deal which RZA and his associates cut with Loud. But these people would probably also tell you that the sales history of *Doggystyle* makes it as significant, as important a work of art as *Enter*. Those people, it should hardly need stating, are wrong.

11TH CHAMBER
YOUNG GODS

Any artistic or cultural movement has moments where,
rather than developing in a logical fashion, step by step,
it leaps. Someone makes a conceptual move which opens
up a door and, quick as you like, everyone else pours
through. You're in a different room, you're—maybe, in
those rarest moments of all—*outside*. Hip hop has had a
few of these moments (more than most), but a key one
came in 1987, when William Griffin Jr., better known
as Rakim, recorded 'I Ain't No Joke'. He had already
hinted at what he could do on the first record he and his
DJ/producer, Eric B, had recorded and released, 'Eric
B Is President', but it was on this, their second single,
that his innovations found their first full and complete
expression. Up until this point, MCing (as rapping is
referred to within hip hop culture) stuck largely to its
roots in the hosting of parties. The rhyme schemes and

rhythms used were simple and largely unchanging.
But on 'I Ain't No Joke', Rakim packs rhyme on top of
rhyme on top of half-rhyme in every line, alters lengths
and rhythms at will, stretching and compressing ideas
and punchlines as he sees fit. The result is not chaos,
however, but a highly thought-out, ultra-compacted,
condensed flow of language which keeps coming
and coming, the end of each discrete section already
containing the seeds of the next. He delivers it all calmly
and methodically, his bragging backed up and proved
by the words and the way in which he's doing it, utterly
without fear, so that you're carried along as if bobbing
on the surface of a great river, barely able to make out
the banks in the distance. You are listening, possibly for
the first time in your life, to the words—to the voice—of
a god. The next step is to understand that voice—where it
came from and what makes it divine.

W. Fard Muhammad started the Lost-Found Nation
of Islam in Detroit around 1930. Originally arriving in
the area selling what he claimed were Middle Eastern
silks, Fard drew upon the teachings of Noble Drew Ali's
Moorish Science Temple, Ahmadiyya Islam and a very
original reading of the Bible to teach his followers (and,
in particular, Elijah Muhammad, who would come
to succeed him as leader and chief theologian of the
organisation) the key tenets of his new belief system
before he himself vanished forever in 1934.

Fard claimed that the original people of the Earth
were the tribe of Shabazz, Black people who lived a
civilised and enlightened life in the area around what
is now Mecca and the Nile valley. Six thousand six
hundred years ago, an evil scientist called Mr Yakub
(Jacob in the Bible) starting gathering followers in

Mecca. He and 59,999 of these followers were eventually exiled to the Greek island of Patmos for causing trouble. Here, Yakub began a breeding programme by killing the darkest infants of his followers. After 600 years he had bred blonde-haired, blue-eyed white devils, and he returned to Mecca with these devils to cause trouble. He and his army of hairy savages were escorted out of Mecca at gunpoint and taken to Europe (in particular, to the Caucasus mountains). The rest, as they say, is history.

The Lost-Found Nation of Islam is so called because its members are descendants of the lost tribe of Shabazz, who have now found themselves again. The prophets (Moses, Jesus and Muhammad) all tried to civilise or tame the white devils in some way but this was always a failure—they cannot be reformed, only grafted back to original man (a process which would take another 600 years) or destroyed. The prophesied destruction of the race of white devils is near at hand. God is not a 'Mystery God' but a human being. Anything else is, in the words of Elijah Muhammad, Christian 'spooky mindedness'— while Christianity itself is viewed as a perversion of Jesus's teachings, used by the (White) Devil(s) 'to make slaves out of all he can so that he can rob them and live in luxury'. Fard, Elijah Muhammad stated, is Allah, and he, Elijah, is his prophet.

When we talk about religious fundamentalists we imagine them, always, as conservatives, as reactionaries, as those people who justify their outmoded beliefs with reference back to the Law of ancient books. But is it possible to be a liberatory fundamentalist? Between around 1960 and 1963, Harlem's Temple no. 7 of the Nation of Islam—at that time under the ministry of

Malcolm X—was attended by one Clarence Smith, or, as he was now known, Clarence 13X. By the end of that period, Clarence 13X had noted and tried to resolve what he saw as certain contradictions in the theology of the Nation of Islam (as the Lost-Found Nation had come to be known under Elijah Muhammad's leadership). These contradictions would lead to him leaving the movement, not in a rejection of that theology but as a refinement— or, as he felt, a realisation—of its philosophy.

Clarence 13X was exercised by the role assigned to W. Fard Muhammad by Elijah Muhammad. It ate at him. How could Fard be Allah? Clarence asked. Members of the Nation of Islam were not supposed to believe in a 'Mystery God' but Fard had vanished nearly thirty years ago and must be dead. Even if he were not dead, he acted in all particulars like a 'spirit', occasionally whispering in Elijah's ear when no one else was listening. Furthermore, the answer to Question 1 of the 'Student Enrollment' lesson of the NOI's *Supreme Wisdom* (the very first text a new member was given) states: 'The original man is the Asiatic Black man; the Maker; the Owner; the Cream of the planet Earth—God of the Universe.' How then could Fard—by Elijah's own account the son of a white woman and hence a 'grafted' man—be Allah? After all, didn't the answer to the first question of Lesson #2 state that 'the Holy Koran or Bible is made by the original people, who is Allah, the supreme being, or (Black man) of Asia'? Allah must be a living Black man, hence Fard could not be Allah. As the man who had uncovered this contradiction, Clarence decided it was he who must be Allah. Clarence 13X declared himself God and excused himself from the Nation. In a jujitsu move often used by religious sects, he turned the Nation of Islam's teachings against itself.

The organisation preached that eighty-five per cent of the world's population were enslaved, that ten per cent used a Mystery God to enslave them and profit from them, and that five per cent were the Poor Righteous Teachers who knew the truth and tried to emancipate the eighty-five. As the hierarchy of the Nation of Islam were teaching the existence of a Mystery God (Fard) while becoming rich themselves, Clarence saw himself and those who would come to follow him as the five per cent within that belief system. Hence his own followers would come to be nicknamed the Five Percenters.

There is a countering argument that Clarence—or Allah, as he now called himself—was thrown out of the Nation for, among other things, drinking, gambling with dice and turning up to Temple wearing shorts. But there's no contradiction here at all, when you think about it. If you are a god then of course none of the rules of a mere religion apply to you. You choose to behave as you see fit. From 1964, Allah began teaching his interpretation of the lessons of the *Supreme Wisdom* together with new lessons of his own to young Black men on the street corners of Harlem, which he re-named Mecca (Brooklyn was Medina). And by 1966 at the very latest, he had followed his original insight to its logical conclusion. If you took the answer to Question 1 of 'Student Enrollment' seriously—literally—then *every* Black man was God of the Universe. This insight, which in effect calls an end to religion, an end to following other people's rules, was eventually formalised as point number 7 of 'What We Teach', the nine fundamental tenets of the Nation of Gods and Earths: 'We teach that the Blackman is God and his proper name is Allah.'

What does it mean to declare yourself a god? And then, what does it mean to declare yourself a god devoid

of supernatural powers, of 'spooky mindedness'?
It's a question which deserves to be taken seriously.
The temptation is to view the sentiment as a healthy
corrective, an expression of Black pride, a kind of
aspiration rather than a reality. But we're not dealing in
metaphor here. Fundamentalism is extremely resistant
to metaphor (and perhaps poetry should be, too).

The Nation of Gods and Earths began to grow first
among the young street kids of New York City, of course,
so it's worth mentioning precisely this youthfulness as
an idea of what it must be like to feel oneself a deity, as
in Virginia Woolf's description of her sister, Vanessa:
'she was tawny and jubilant and lusty as a young God'.
It seems uncontroversial to claim both that every child
should consider him or herself immortal and also that
it's how we move from this position into acceptance
of our own mortality that, eventually, characterises
adulthood. Although, once again, this leaves us steering
dangerously close to that ill wind, metaphor.

Perhaps a better question (at least a simpler
question) is to ask what being a god does to art. The
first two lessons Allah gave to his followers, to go before
the texts the Five Percenters inherited from the Nation
of Islam, were called the *Supreme Mathematics* and
the *Supreme Alphabet*. The former gives meanings to
individual digits, while the latter offers up the words
hidden behind every letter of the alphabet, in order to
turn the whole of the *Supreme Wisdom* into backronyms.
The idea is to dig for the deeper meanings, to draw
connections, to use this method to *drop science*. But the
method itself is viral, uncontainable. If each letter of a
text is said to represent a word (for instance, D is *Divine*),
the text thus created must itself be liable to breaking
down into still more meanings (that Divine 'D' could

itself become Divine Eye Victory Islam Now Equality,
for instance). Language becomes an infinitely regressive
meaning machine. And on top of the lesson of the
Supreme Alphabet, more personal alphabet-meanings
begin to make themselves felt. In honour of the fact that
Allah is a human being, Five Percenters break the word
down as *Arm Leg Leg Arm Head*. *Islam* itself is expanded
from its constituent parts into *I-Supreme, Lord And
Master*. Everything is a code for something else. Meaning
expands laterally, infinitely, from every linear sentence.

We started with Rakim. It's possible his style
(and hence his status as one of the most influential
hip hop lyricists of all time) bears no relation to his
membership of the Nation of Gods and Earths. But the
way that he constantly unpacks language, uncovering
hidden rhymes and assonances, playing with meaning,
rhythm and sound—and, as importantly, the way that
these *games* (or exercises?) never really cease, the way
in which one uncovering only leads to the next—all that
hints back to a training with the *Supreme Alphabet*.
And perhaps that's what a god is—someone who sees
connections where no one else can. It's tempting here
to draw on the literature of schizophrenia, and there is
an obvious link to be made: 'Like cubist chemists, they
break things down and rearrange the elements.' But at
the same time, it seems as important (perhaps more so)
to resist an explanation by madness as it does to resist
an explanation by metaphor. Both are a kind of cop-out,
a refusal to take something seriously on its own terms,
an attempt to reduce it to a mode we understand and
hence rob it of its power.

But what choice to do we have? The last lesson,
passed down most clearly of all in the work of the
Wu-Tang Clan, is that being a god makes no sense, can

make no sense—but still it is so. From 1987 until 1995 (which, perhaps uncoincidentally, is also the period that many people consider to be the Golden Age of hip hop) the influence of the gods was at its height. Groups like Poor Righteous Teachers and Brand Nubian preached the gospel of this non-religion and, indeed, the first side of Brand Nubian's debut album, *One for All*, is probably the funkiest, most remarkable exposition of an untheology since reggae was at its height in the late seventies. References to the Five Percent can be found in the work of Busta Rhymes, Nas, Erykah Badu, Gang Starr. The very language of hip hop owes a debt. Using 'Peace' as greeting and farewell is claimed as a tradition started by Allah himself, who took issue with the phrase *As-salaam-alaikum* because it wasn't in his own language. The almost universal use of 'G' (as in *Wassup, G?*) didn't originally refer to *Gangsta* but to *God*. The phrase *Word is bond* originates with the Nation of Islam but was animated by the Five Percenters' acronymic obsessions to become an essential trope in an artform built on language, where words are absolutely all you have.

But in 1993, the Wu-Tang largely forego proselytising and instead focus on the true work of gods—building a world, surviving through the pure act of creation. Why, after all, would a god care whether you believed in him? This may be hard to comprehend if you find the repeated, shouted statements '*WU-TANG CLAN AIN'T NUTT'N TO FUCK WIT*' and '*BRING THE MOTHERFUCKIN' RUCKUS*' threatening rather than exhilarating, but throughout the record, the Wu are defiantly 'jubilant and lusty', to follow Woolf's definition of godliness. They explode and implode language, unpacking boxes with all the mania of

85

three three-headed Rakims, punchlines overlapping and doubling back on themselves, a stream of nihilist invention delivered in nine voices. And they take the implications of the Nation of Islam mythology as seriously as anyone has ever done. There is no 'mystery' heaven and hell. Hell is Satan's realm and Satan is the White devil. Hell is America.

Their response to this reality, on 'Wu-Tang Clan Ain't Nuthing Ta F' Wit', is surprisingly chipper, jokes and threats kept in divine equilibrium. In the words of Inspectah Deck, they resolve, individually, to 'bake the cake, then take the cake / and eat it, too, with my crew'. Over a beat held together by a stepped bassline, a finger snap that lands so far off anywhere it should that it creates funk despite itself, and what sounds like a cartoon Valkyrian choir riding through the clouds, singing over their shields, the vocalists (in this case, RZA, Deck and Method Man) attack with verses which take the tradition of MC bragging and use it as nothing more than a scaffold—a kind of gallows—on which to hang weaponised language; a barricade from behind which to spit fire. As the RZA points out right at the end of this particular burst of controlled aggression and outlandish humour, the Wu-Tang's language is 'choppin' heads, boy./ It ain't safe no more!'

If you want to know how the Wu-Tang sound without ever hearing the Wu-Tang, you need to go down to the underworld and look for clues there: 'With scorching flames and boulders tossed in thunder, / The abyss's Fiery River. A massive gate / With Adamantine pillars faced the stream, / So strong no force of men or gods in war / May ever avail to crack and bring it down. / And high in air an iron tower stands.' These aren't gods on some idyllic hilltop listening to the harp, these are gods fighting their way through a landscape utterly inimical to their survival, plunged into the depths with no golden bough. Which is why, despite the litanies of violence, the gun-brags, the apparent *nastiness* of much of what they say, the effect is actually rather clean and pure, spiritual, strangely liberating. They evoke a world in which self-belief in its most literal sense—belief in oneself as God—is the *only possible* weapon of survival. It isn't optional. It isn't esoteric. It is not metaphor or madness. As Allah said on the streets of Mecca, New York, 'You know you are Allah, never deny yourself of being Allah.'

12TH CHAMBER
A PROBLEM IN MATHEMATICS

Imagine that there are 36 x 36 x 36 people living in the
USA, but instead of thinking of them as people think
of them as beetles. The beetles are all different shades
of brown, from very pale to very dark, but everyone
refers to these insects as either Black or White (some
of the White beetles are darker than some of the Black
beetles but everyone seems very certain which are
which, except when they're not). Beyond this there is no
discernible difference between them. They are separated
into different habitats. There are 36 Black beetles in the
habitat which represents New York City, plus a load of
White beetles. Imagine that a year passes every hour and
that the year of Ol' Dirty Bastard's birth, 1968, is midnight
on a Monday morning. GZA is born at 10 p.m. on Sunday
night, RZA at 1 a.m. that Monday morning, and most of
the rest of the Clan are born between 2 and 3 a.m.

In the ten hours from 4 a.m. to 2 p.m. on that Monday, the number of unemployed Black beetles increases by 140%. The overall unemployment rate among Black beetles hits almost 20%. That's one in five of the Black beetles. In certain areas of the habitat it's even worse. During some part of the hour between 2 p.m. and 3 p.m., over 30% of the Black beetle labour force is jobless. Between 2 a.m. and midday, the number of Black beetles living in the poorest areas of the habitat increases by 230%. While unemployment among White beetles is also at its highest rate since 1 a.m. on Sunday morning, the rate of unemployment among Black beetles is double that among White beetles. Among Black beetles aged between 16 and 24 hours, the situation is even more severe. Back at midnight, 19% of young Black beetles were out of work. By 8 p.m. on the evening of that Monday the number is up to 44%. For teenaged Black beetles, the rate hits almost 50% around 2 p.m. This is almost 28% higher than for White beetles in the same age bracket. Midday is one of those times when the beetles elect a new president. Very few of the Black beetles vote for the winner on this occasion, a White beetle who used to appear in second-rate beetle movies. In the first hour of his presidency, the real median income of Black beetle families falls by 5.2%.

Think of housing as the underside of a mulchy, decaying log. At 5 p.m. on Monday, 40% of the Black beetles—almost 15 of our 36 Black beetles—don't have affordable logs to live under. This means that they spend at least 70% of their income on decaying logs to huddle beneath, before paying for food or clothing or anything else a beetle might need to survive and thrive. Between midday and 10 p.m., funding for subsidised logs is reduced by 90%. Between 2 a.m. and 5 p.m., the number of Black beetle children living in mother-only households goes up from 30% to 50%. Ninety per cent of Black beetle children living in a single parent household with a mother Black beetle below the age of 30 hours are living in poverty. As late as 6 p.m. on Tuesday (only a few hours before *now*), 34%—one third!—of all Black beetle children are still living in poverty, as opposed to 10% of White beetle children.

On the afternoon of that Monday, high school dropout rates go up as high as 50%. By 10 p.m. at night, between half and three quarters of Black beetles who dropped out of high school have no legal employment. Even among Black beetles who finish high school, their chance of entering college within one hour of graduating is less than half that of a similarly qualified White beetle. As of midday on that first day, only one in five Black beetles aged 18–24 hours are enrolled in college.

At 8 a.m. on Tuesday, a survey of the beetle police finds that over 51% of Black beetle officers feel that their fellow officers treat White beetles better than Black beetles and other minority insects. An even larger 57% believe that these officers are more likely to use physical force against Black beetles or other minority insects. A study of FBI statistics running from midday on Monday to 8 p.m. on Tuesday shows that male teenage Black beetles are 21 times more likely to be killed by the police than male White beetles in the same age group. Of those killed while 'fleeing or resisting arrest', 67% are Black beetles. The average age of the Black beetles killed is 30 hours. The number of beetles in prison in the New York habitat increased in twenty hours by 550%.

*

Calculate how many of the 36 Black beetles survive until 1 a.m. on Tuesday. Calculate how they survive. Calculate what they think of White beetles. Calculate what they think of police officers. Show all working.

13TH CHAMBER
CROSSING THE BORDER

It takes twenty-five minutes to ride one of the Staten Island ferries from St George terminal across the Upper New York Bay to Whitehall terminal in Manhattan. The boats go every half hour, day and night, every fifteen minutes during rush hour. Back when *Enter* came out, a round-trip ticket would set you back 50 cents but today it's free.[11] Sitting on one of these boats—down on the lower decks where the locals gather, leaving the views to camera-happy tourists—everything suddenly becomes clear. You're making passage across an ocean.

You can smell it as soon as you get anywhere near to the water. Upper New York Bay is the place where the

---

11   A week before the album was released, Rudy Giuliani won the New York City mayoral elections, relying on Staten Island votes. Part of the price the rest of the city paid for these votes was the removal of ferry fares.

icy fingers of the Atlantic, funnelling down through the East River and up through the Narrows, meet each other and the Hudson in a churning, roiling mass of cross currents. Salt—you feel it in your nostrils and you know, somehow, that it means a significant journey, an epic. You don't cross any stretch of water by boat without the journey carrying extra consequence, but the sea is water as deity, not merely a minor break or interruption in landmass, but a thing unto itself, a whole different category. The sea is powerful and capricious, changing shape, shifting, liaising with the moon. It makes the sky larger as well, scale altered by its flatness, so that mere humans are spots, insects trapped on the meniscus between one and the other. Or, as Inspectah Deck puts it, melding together references to both 'America the Beautiful' and Robert Crawford's U.S. Air Force song and hence removing any landfall from the equation, 'Across the clear blue yonder / Sea to shining sea!'

Even before the horrors of the Middle Passage, Africans of many nations and peoples had an intimate relationship with water, physical and spiritual. Those dragged into slavery from inland regions may have been culturally, religiously and linguistically diverse but they were united most strongly by their engagement with the Niger-Senegal-Gambia river complex. 'For the Bambara in Senegambia,' W. Jeffrey Bolster points out in *Black Jacks*, 'an androgynous water spirit called Faro maintained an individual's soul or vital life force after death... Ibo peoples from near the Bight of Benin had similar associations with the transmigration of souls in water... For historic Kongo peoples a watery barrier called the Kalunga line divided the living from the spirit world... To Africans water was clearly a potent metaphor for life beyond this world.' This tradition is both continued and transmogrified in the 'marine maroon colony' of Drexciya, the utopia imagined by the Detroit techno duo of James Stinson and Gerald Donald, where slaves thrown overboard during the Middle Passage learn to breathe water and build a new civilisation beneath the waves. It can be seen, too, in the notion that death will somehow 'undo the transformative Middle Passage', so that the singer Bessie Jones could state that 'the sea brought us, the sea shall take us back'. More prosaically, for many, many years, jobs at sea offered African Americans both (relative) freedom and the ability to make a living. Black seamen were common in whaling crews, as evidenced by *Moby Dick*. When the pirate Blackbeard (Edward Teach) was finally killed in 1718, five of his eighteen-man crew were people of colour. And while Northern, abolitionist army regiments were still segregated during the Civil War, it has been estimated that 20–25% of sailors in the integrated navy were Black.

African water traditions collided and melded with European ones, both in terms of seamanship and in the way those sailors conceptualised the ocean. To the beliefs they brought from their homelands were added stories of Moses parting the waters, of Noah and his ark, of Jonah in the belly of a whale. The ancient Greeks provided Poseidon and Proteus the shapeshifter and the story of Odysseus, his boat tossed hither and thither on his return from the sacking of Troy, washed up on this island or that, challenged on each one, scrabbling for survival. RZA mentions having read a version of this book as a child, but it's the stories of the Hong Kong film industry (another city separated by a huge bay, crossed by ferry, another place where cormorants bob and duck between boats) which he chose to repurpose.

All the same, think of those isles. The ferry picks its way past Liberty Island, where a siren welcomes travellers towards her with a promise which Ellis Island shows she can't necessarily keep. The irony of this icon of immigration can't be lost on people whose ancestors were shipped here in chains—and perhaps Method Man and U-God pondered this as they worked at Liberty's feet. To the other side is Governor's Island, traditionally a symbol of state power, from the British onwards, now transformed into a fairground, much like American politics. Further away up the East River, out of sight, lies Rikers Island, a cyclops-cave prison, where members of the Wu-Tang (Ghostface Killah leaps to mind) have spent time against their wishes. And full steam ahead lies Manhattan—Mammon!—the site not just of high finance but of some of the most expensive land in the world, humans pushed upward in a dizzying profusion of towers, helicopters flying in low overhead like a corporate re-enactment of *Apocalypse Now*. There are pleasure boats out here, jet skis coming down the East River in a line, the sailboats of the wealthy, but what lies behind you is *work*. A barge carries three huge trucks. Ranks of cranes lie ready to disgorge goods from vast container ships, their arms mimicking the angle of the raised limb of Liberty. Two great grey hulks moored up in New Jersey look like warships, though they're just unliveried, the colour of undercoat. A landscape of lunar silos huddles near to Bayonne. The Verazzano Bridge, at your back, makes the Williamsburg and Brooklyn bridges look like toys.

Staten Island lies *outside*. Its status as part of New York is contingent, unlikely—and certainly other New Yorkers seem to have very little time or interest in the fifth borough, the only one among them to vote Republican, the land itself hunched tight up against New Jersey as if for protection beneath a bigger brother's muscled arm. If the feeling isn't exactly mutual, there's some kind of wounded pride involved in coming from the outskirts, from feeling excluded. 'It's an area that's not noticed,' says the photographer Christine Osinski, who has lived on the North Shore since the early 1980s. 'The people are not noticed. It had an edge to it. It's not happy. It's a tough edge. The people and the houses and the landscape—I think that's where the edge comes from.'

Once you see Ellis Island you understand New York as a border, a kind of Kalunga line. Staten Island comes *before* the border. Any journey into Manhattan involves crossing that line—literal, social, metaphorical—and in doing so, it becomes an invasion, at the very least an incursion. You've travelled past the gate, avoided the sentinel, you've dragged your boats up on shore, ready to wreak havoc in the counting houses of this, the new Rome. Stuck on a small piece of rock which can never provide everything its population needs, comfortable with water, inured to the devastation it can wreak, island people are marauders. So watch them maraud.

14TH CHAMBER
COLLECTIVE INSULATION

The first thing you learn listening to the 1992 Wu-Tang
Clan demo tape is that it's hard recording rap in your
apartment.[12] The vocals all sound literally *enclosed*,
constrained, as if the MCs are afraid to raise their voices
to full volume for fear of disturbing the neighbours.
Or alternatively, going into the red on the recording
(which they still manage to do). It makes the group
sound physically caged, blocked in, more than a little
inhibited. After hearing this, some of the sheer verve
and attack you find on the finished album presents as

12   In case you're imagining the author tracking down this demo on original
cassette and paying hundreds of dollars to get hold of a copy, it only seems fair
to point out that the whole thing is available via YouTube. The age of the true
crate-digger (even the true aficionado) is over. Personally, I always found the whole
authenticity-through-superior-knowledge schtick a little wearying, but perhaps
it was a price worth paying to be able to feel commitment.

relief, as the liberation of hitting a big, well-appointed, sound-proofed room where you can shout and holler to your heart's content, where you can make all the noise you want and nobody—not your mother, not the people living above you, not the police—can stop you.

The next thing that strikes you is that it isn't much of a clan. Of the sixteen verses across the eight tracks on the demo, eleven are delivered by RZA himself, or at least Prince Rakeem, as he's still calling himself. Ol' Dirty Bastard—under his previous alias, Ason Unique—delivers two (a whole verse on 'The Wu Is Comin' Thru' and two half-verses of trading bars with RZA on 'Cuttin' Headz', the final version of which would end up on his debut solo album, *Return to the 36 Chambers: The Dirty Version*), and Ghostface Killah, Raekwon and Inspectah Deck get a verse each. 'Bring Da Ruckus' is present and correct, only stripped down to just two verses, Deck and Raekwon running through their stuff, with Rae offering a completely different lyric to the one he serves up in the final version. As well as the verses, most of the choruses are delivered by Prince Rakeem, too. So yes, the Clan part of the equation is more a theory at this point than a reality. (Though at the same time, the absences do cement RZA's central role in putting the whole thing together. Less than two years before their debut album came out, the Clan as anything more than a name was just a glimmering in his mind.)

Only two tracks from the final album are here in demo form. 'Tearz' (here called 'After the Laughter') is pretty much as it appears on the final record, except for minor differences in delivery and the odd word change. 'Bring Da Ruckus', on the other hand, is barely recognisable. The drum break used is the same—Melvin Bliss's 'Synthetic Substitution'—only it's mixed

differently (or not mixed?) so that the snare has less
snap. It's also missing the second beat used on the final
record, taken from a drum breaks record, that provides
the cavernous snare hit which erupts every so often,
adding an extra dimension to the loop, making it feel
like a landscape to be navigated. The other samples are
completely different—much fuller and more musical—
and along with the flatness of the looped beat, they
make the whole thing drag a little. It certainly doesn't
sound like an album-opener. Ethan Ryman, who
engineered the final version of the song while working
at Firehouse Studios, recalls that the original version
'had this blues sample that RCA couldn't clear, so we
re-recorded the sample and some of the other tracks'.
It's this space, though, together with the detailed
manipulation of the remaining elements, that gives the
tune its unique ambience. It's what makes it a Wu-Tang
production as opposed to any old East Coast hardcore
tune (Naughty By Nature used the same beat a year or
two before for 'O.P.P.'—a track that Ghostface references
on 'After the Laughter'). It's somehow fitting that what
was almost an accident—having to remove a sample that
couldn't be cleared—could be so definitive in terms of
the sound of the music, as if RZA stumbled onto his style
partly as a reaction to the end of the golden free-for-all
era of sampling.

RZA isn't a man to waste good music. A tweak of the beat
on the opener, 'Enter the Wu-Tang', would be used on
the Gravediggaz album he was already working on as he
recorded the Wu-Tang album and which was released
a year after it, in 1994. As we've already noted, 'Cuttin'
Headz' would end up re-recorded and released on ODB's
album (in early 1995). One of the standout treats of the

demo, it should be said, is Dirty/Ason's rhyming on this track, where he sounds nimble, quick and well-balanced—less distinctive maybe, but more clearly a very skilled MC—before his role and purpose as jester (or wild man)[13] has been established. But it's interesting to look at the four tracks which never made it beyond demo form to see what their future absence tells us.

'Wu-Tang Master' comes first, and the truth is it's just not good enough. The samples are all overly familiar, despite a clever bit of break-chopping on the drum track to make a fill. Prince Rakeem rhymes pretty well on it, but you could argue that he hasn't really found himself. The delivery lacks any of the staccato attack which makes him so compelling. 'The Wu Is Comin' Thru' is more interesting. It's built round one of RZA's favourite sample sources, the jazz pianist Thelonious Monk (and you can't help wondering if his name was what first led RZA—aka the Abbot—to check him out), but the lyrics from him and ODB really don't have that much to recommend them. It's not that they're bad, exactly, but they're not distinctive. They lack the deep back-myth roots which make the finished album so intriguing.

'It's All About Me' is an oddity. In the lyrics, Rakeem references De La Soul's 'Me, Myself & I' and the tune has a jaunty, off-kilter catchiness that will have no place in the finished Wu universe. In many ways, the reference to De La is not so surprising. Rakeem met Prince Paul (who produced the first three De La Soul albums, including the ground-breaking debut, *3 Feet*

<hr />

13 Or clown? Or chaotician? Everybody thinks they understand ODB, but while his importance to the group is clear, his role is harder to pin down than you might imagine. We will, of course, devote our full attention to him, but not until the 31st chamber.

High and Rising) in the late eighties and would work with him on the Gravediggaz record. Indeed, if you're looking for a producer to compare RZA to, particularly the RZA of *Enter the Wu-Tang*, you could do a lot worse than the beatmaker and DJ from Amityville who began his career with Stetsasonic, who was largely responsible for bringing in the *sampledelic* era in hip hop, and who shares a similarly developed sense of space with his Staten Island collaborator. Both this tune and 'Wu Is Comin' Thru' show an artist putting together some of the building blocks of a style without having figured out how to assemble them into something completely personal and new.

'Problemz' is a slow blues, another tune built around a familiar sample, this time from British funk group Cymande (although its most famous uses came later).[14] It's the pick of the rejections, with a kind of downbeat, depressed, dread-drenched atmosphere, but it doesn't completely convince as a blank-eyed suicide note and it lacks the bravado, the sheer *fuck you* panache of classic Wu. And that's perhaps because, like the previous track, 'it's all about me' rather than the 'We' of the Wu collective. And really that's the piece of the jigsaw which most clearly hasn't yet fallen into place—the collective, the brotherhood of martial artists standing back to back against the world, wielding their liquid swords in defence of one another. Although the demo tape shows the basis of the Wu vision residing with an individual, it also shows that this individual on his own would be incapable of delivering it.

Part of what makes the Wu-Tang unique is that they

---

14   In particular, on 1996's 'The Score' by The Fugees, which featured the one and only Diamond D.

roll so deep they become a world of their own—and that means they don't have to care what anyone else thinks. In their attempts to present themselves in the way they think they should appear, rappers can sound as mannered, as finicky as the most pyrotechnic soul diva. By the time of *Enter*, the Wu-Tang Clan have perfected the art of not giving a fuck. They holler and shout and relish every minute of it. They don't care what you make of it, whether you get it, what you understand by it—and it's this lack of neediness that's so attractive. Perhaps what we hear is not a response to the insulation of the recording studio but a response to the insulation of the gang.

The use of that word might seem controversial, suggesting some criminal intent or focus, but in this context nothing is meant to be implied beyond the notion of a tightknit bunch of friends caught up in a common project or, perhaps more accurately, a common projection—Tom Sawyer rather than Michael Corleone. If it's the possibility of being allowed to join this gang which animates the listener's fantasies, then it's the reality of already belonging, of being protected by your fellow members, of being answerable only to these fellow members, which animates the voices of the group. They shout and holler and we dream about being able to, mumbling to ourselves as we listen, protected by our own insulations—reverie and headphones.

15TH CHAMBER
SECRETS AND LIES

Another aspect discussed by the Detectives was that of a
shooting and car jacking that occurred on Staten Island by
an associate of WTC.   attempted to rob
*   during a drug deal for angel dust.   shot*
*   twice and stole his car during this drug deal*
gone bad.   survived his wounds and he and
*   identified the shooter as   is also a*
suspect in an unsolved homicide which was supposedly
ordered by the WTC. Intelligence indicates that
*   area. The Detectives have reliable*
information as to the exact whereabouts of

Examining FBI reports released under Freedom of
Information legislation is a little like reading the
work of a particularly abstruse contemporary poet.

You might know deep down that what you're looking at is important but you can't, for the life of you, work out why. As you trundle through page after page of badly reproduced pdfs, your eyes become heavier and heavier and nausea settles upon you with all the horrible finality of an arrest. You begin to wonder if the website you're on—helpfully provided by the FBI itself—is deliberately designed to make your body react this way, to limit your forays there to minutes rather than weeks or months. There is an art to redaction and that art is to render the document as meaningless as possible. This is entirely appropriate. The story of the Federal Bureau of Investigation is, after all, the story of secrets—those gaps left on a page of text, the holes in the narrative. Secrets taken from other people, secrets held, secrets used to achieve particular results. And, as J. Edgar Hoover put it, 'there's something addicting about a secret'.

The Federal Bureau of Investigation began life as the Bureau of Investigation in 1908, and wasn't renamed the FBI until 1935. It was an organisation waiting to discover its true purpose, its crusade, and it found it when the USA entered the First World War. In reaction to both the Bolshevik revolution and fears 'that blacks would be particularly receptive to the blandishments of German enemies', Theodore Kornweibel suggests, 'modern political surveillance had its birth.' And it found its embodiment in the young J. Edgar Hoover. Although he didn't become head of the bureau until 1924, as an assistant to the Attorney General he helped set the post-war priorities for the organisation. 'Black radicalism,' he would later state, 'was one of the major preoccupations and targets of the federal investigatory network during the Red Scare.'

To put it bluntly, 'Hoover was a racist.' *Black radicalism* in its many forms would remain a major preoccupation of the man and his Bureau over the fifty or so years he was in charge. This was evident both in the priorities he set for investigation and in the type of organisation he ran. 'Edgar kept the Bureau in a state of apartheid as long as he possibly could', claims his biographer, Anthony Summers. Even before he had taken over, Hoover launched his first all-out vendetta against a popular Black leader when he determined that Marcus Garvey was 'the foremost radical amongst his race'. It took four years, but eventually he saw Garvey convicted for mail fraud after he included in some literature for his Black Star Line a picture of a ship he hadn't yet finished buying. This was enough to imprison him and then have him exiled from the country.

This pattern was to repeat itself over and over again. Once Garvey was dealt with, the Bureau turned its attentions to the singer Paul Robeson, who was spied on for over thirty years. Twenty years after the death of Garvey in his London exile, Martin Luther King was to feel the full weight of the Bureau bearing down upon him with the purpose of 'neutralizing [him] as an effective Negro leader'. To this end, Hoover began 'a massive surveillance operation', bugging almost every room the civil rights leader stayed in, spreading rumours about his sexual appetites and proclivities, even sending a doctored tape to his wife with a note suggesting that King should commit suicide. In between, agents briefed the press against King at every turn, and Hoover himself used an interview with a group of women journalists to brand King 'the most notorious liar in the country'. When King was assassinated, it was announced that Hoover was personally running the investigation, but there seems to have been little urgency in his approach. Rumours have swirled ever since of some kind of FBI involvement in the killing, but perhaps it didn't need to be directly connected. As Andrew Young, a former colleague of King's, put it, the FBI 'created the climate in which Martin's assassination was acceptable'.

If the treatment of King was demonstrably appalling, the COINTELPRO (Counter Intelligence Program) tactics used covertly by the FBI against the Black Panther Party were so effective that to this day the latter's image is tarnished by 'the very lies and racist caricatures which the Bureau promoted', so that even broadly sympathetic observers tend to overlook 'the fact that the FBI and police harassed, vandalized, beat, framed and murdered Panthers for years before finally provoking the party's retaliation'. The FBI's campaign could be said to have reached its height with the killing of Fred Hampton and Mark Clark by Chicago police on 3 December 1969. Although the Bureau wasn't directly involved in the raid in which the two men were shot, it was FBI agents who sketched out a map of the floorplan of the apartment they were staying in, including the exact location of Hampton's bed. A former FBI man recalled that a colleague from the Chicago Bureau told him, 'we set up the police to go in there and kill the whole lot'. At four in the morning, fourteen cops burst in, carrying between them a mind-boggling 'twenty-seven guns, including five shotguns and a submachine gun'. Hampton, drugged with secobarbital (whether he had taken it by choice has never been established), was shot in his bed. Mark Clark is credited with firing the one retaliatory shot to the police's ninety-eight. It went into the floor, as a bullet penetrated his heart at the very moment the front door was broken open.

The Chicago incident was not an accident. Hoover had exhorted his agents to convince all and sundry that 'to be a black revolutionary is to be a dead revolutionary'. Those they couldn't kill were imprisoned. As just one example, Elmer 'Geronimo' Pratt, a war veteran and high-ranking member of the Los Angeles Panthers, spent twenty-seven years in prison, eight of them in solitary confinement, based on the testimony of an FBI informant whose status as such was not revealed to the jury.

This being America, where the issue of race sits like poison in the collective psychic well, Anthony Summers suggests that Hoover's reaction to African Americans wasn't merely a result of a Southern white upbringing, but rather was a response to a generally held belief that he himself had 'black roots'. As Gore Vidal (possibly not the most reliable of sources, though undoubtedly one of the more entertaining) recalls, 'there were two things that were taken for granted in my youth—that he was a faggot and that he was black. Washington was and is a very racist town, and I can tell you that in those days the black blood part was very much the worst... To be thought a black person was an unbelievable slur if you were in white society. That's what many people flatly believed about Hoover, and he must have been so upset by it.' Summers goes on to suggest that there was more weight to the rumour that Hoover was a homosexual. He also claims that this information was used over a number of years by Meyer Lansky and other elements in organised crime to deflect the FBI's attention on to other, less well-equipped targets. Black radicals, for instance...

You might think, then, that the FBI would've

sorted itself out after Hoover's death in 1972, that this was a personal rather than an institutional crusade. Certainly attempts were made to build a 'new FBI' after his passing, and to investigate some of the worst excesses of the past. It should be noted, though, that by 1990, almost twenty years later, the number of serving Black agents had only risen from seventy at Hoover's death to five hundred—still representing less than five per cent of the Bureau's 10,360 agents, a stunningly low number. Moreover, former agent Tyrone Powers points to a succession of racist incidents during his training and while working, including fellow trainees disguising themselves as Klan members, superior officers explaining to him that racism wasn't as important as how someone looked after his family, agents referring to a Black woman as a 'bitch', and on and on. He also points to the case of Donald Rochon, a Black Special Agent who joined the FBI in 1981 and was subjected to such sustained racial harassment that his final legal settlement was the highest ever paid out to an individual FBI employee as the result of a discrimination case. As reported by the *New York Times*, Rochon suggested that 'the bureau agreed to settle the case because it feared a trial would expose how white F.B.I. agents had made death threats against his family and how bureau supervisors, confronted with evidence of brutal racial harassment, had tried to cover it up'.

As for COINTELPRO, Hoover officially abandoned the program before he died. But what was abandoned was the name and the centrally directed nature of its actions. 'It did not,' Brian Glick points out, 'cease its covert political activity against U.S. dissidents. The documents show that the Bureau evaluated the COINTELPROs as "successful over the years."

It disbanded them only "to afford additional security to our sensitive techniques and operations." Continued reliance on those same techniques and operations was officially authorized, only now on a case-by-case basis, "with tight procedures to insure absolute security."'

Today, you can investigate online the long, sorry history of FBI enquiries into all manner of groups and individuals. They put it on their site, for everyone with access to the internet to see. You could call it a counter-narrative if it wasn't for who put that narrative together (and for everything they've taken out). In there you can find over 3,000 pages devoted to the study of Noble Drew Ali's Moorish Science Temple of America, whose members are, agents conclude again and again, 'religious fanatics and apparently somewhat mentally unbalanced'. You can search through the files of W.D. Fard (aka Fard Muhammad, who starts off described as Caucasian and ends up as Negro, more due to the passing of time than to any new information) and the Nation of Islam. In 1955, researchers characterise it in a special monograph as 'a fanatic Negro organization purporting to be motivated by the religious principles of Islam, but actually dedicated to the propagation of hatred against the white race'. In wartime reports on both organisations, a variety of informants are more than a little horrified by how sympathetic these parallel religious groups are to the Japanese. There's also a quite massive series of files on Malcolm X and a huge amount about Muhammad Ali. The latter, having only been recently released, conform to the new redactive standards—where black-lined white boxes are placed over text, presumably using a computer, rather than the classic thick black pen splurges. There are a few pages on the 'Five Percenters', but no one seems too bothered about them. They're characterised as 'a loosely knit group of Negro youth gangs in the Harlem section of New York City', the contempt for this particular offshoot unconcealed. The New York office even goes as far as to state that it 'does not feel that the Bureau should become involved with every ordinary Harlem rowdy and street fighter who shouts invectives'.

And then we come to the Wu-Tang Clan. The files relate specifically to Russell Tyrone Jones aka Ol' Dirty Bastard after a Freedom of Information request in 2012. They concern the group not as a political or religious threat to the state but as a criminal enterprise. What do we learn from them? That police files are repetitive, the same stories cropping up again and again, as if their earlier existence in those pages gives them credence on its own. That most of them are banal: for some reason, a newspaper report about Sean 'Puffy' Combs being caught with a gun is interleaved in the file, along with an advert for microwave ovens. That redaction breaks any sense of a narrative chain, that they are released out of sequence, so that rather than being able to build any kind of judgement of the facts involved in the case, all you're left with is statements like the one from August 1999 that 'the WTC is heavily involved in the sale of drugs, illegal guns, weapons possession murder [*sic*], car jackings, and other types of violent crimes'.

The fact that this is the FBI, the fact that no corroborating evidence is presented, the fact that it's actually impossible to follow the sequence of events they try to tie together, none of this means that any of the previous quote isn't true. And this leaves us in a difficult, uncomfortable position, stuck somewhere between (or behind) truth and falsehood, certainly a long way off any verification. In that Hoover's position was built and maintained by the secrets he accumulated, you might think that anything that opens these secrets out to scrutiny is an unalloyed good. But did the legacy of Russell Jones or the lives of the surviving members of the Wu-Tang benefit from these files being made public?

Rich Jones certainly thinks so. He's the self-proclaimed 'radical freedom of information activist' and hip hop fan who filed the Freedom of Information Act request which resulted in Russell Jones's files being released. Most of his requests relate to 'computer security and surveillance', but he has also done 'a few dead celebrities and hip hop icons'. As if to prove the point, he sends over a hilarious photo of Insane Clown Posse in full face paint at an American Civil Liberties Union press conference that came about because of the revelation that the FBI had carried out an investigation of their fans, the Juggalos, on the grounds that they were a 'loosely-organized hybrid gang'.

Rich is pretty pleased with the revelations contained in the files. 'As a FOIA requester, you really can't ask for a more interesting celebrity file,' he explains via email. 'It's super, super fascinating! ODB saving a little girl's life! ODB being the first person ever charged with a body-armour crime! ODB in a *previously-unknown shoot-out with the NYPD!* The whole clan being investigated on a fucking RICO! [see below] Plus if I remember correctly it had to do with gun running out of some bumblefuck place in Ohio or Florida.' He admits that not everyone sees it quite that way, though. 'I've actually been accused of being a snitch because of this,' he says, 'but I don't really see it that way and those accusations don't bother me.'

He does see the tension, of course. He's happy to admit that 'the FBI is quite responsive to celebrity requests compared to other kinds of requests', although he doesn't analyse why that might be. He's also keen to emphasise that 'the discerning reader will obviously note that this file is only from the perspective of law enforcement, a perspective from which everybody is demonized'. And yet at the same time, he can't help getting caught up in the excitement of the whole thing, both personally ('when was the last time a nerdy white hacker got his name in *The Source*?') and through his view of it as a hip hop fan interested in the notion of 'kayfabe', a wrestling term for presenting obviously faked events as real—literally 'be fake' muddled up. 'I think a big part of the response is that so much of the rap industry is built around this idea of "kayfabe"— is the shit that they rap about actually real, or are they just acting tough to sell more records to suburban white kids? This is what everybody really wants to know, and I think it actually does matter... when it comes out in the documents that not only are the Wu Tang legit gangsters, but are in fact even *more* gangster than their lyrics imply, so much so that the FBI was using RICO powers normally reserved for the actual mafia to investigate them, that's pretty major.'

Except that's not what RICO powers are usually reserved for. Passed in 1970 as part of Nixon's 'Crime Bill' (and hence an early and essential component of the New Right's law and order agenda), the Racketeer Influenced and Corrupt Organizations Act was originally envisaged as an anti-Mafia bill but has been applied in the interim in all kinds of cases, involving both anti-obscenity protesters and pornographers, the tobacco industry and unions, bankers and doctors—even the police.

Indeed, the broadness of RICO's drafting has led some libertarian elements to compare the Bill to Britain's eighteenth-century Black Act as an overarching and extremely punitive piece of criminal legislation used in situations far beyond its original conception: 'Federal prosecutors have discovered that RICO is a powerful weapon that can be wielded against most business owners, should the feds choose to target them.' The *Los Angeles Times*, meanwhile, described the legislation as 'an open invitation to prosecutorial abuse'.

Furthermore, what comes out in the Russell Jones FBI documents is *not* that the FBI used RICO legislation against the Wu-Tang Clan, but that they failed to find enough evidence to do so. And this despite harnessing RICO and its power to 'overturn the protections inherent in due-process guarantees of the U.S. Constitution'. In fact, the more you think about it, the more you're left with the sense that the FBI themselves were trying to look behind the curtain and see whether their own reading of what 'rap' was all about was *actually true* or another example of kayfabe. It's almost as if law enforcement's own ideas about hip hop and authenticity have operated in a narrow feedback loop. This is signalled perhaps most clearly by the *Godfather*-style claim—completely unverified and, in fact, unverifiable—that 'once individuals have proved themselves as good and loyal members or associates of the WTC… they are offered record contracts to record Rap type music'.

Indeed, there's a further irony here in that the Wu-Tang Clan are not 'gangsta rappers' anyway. While it could be traced back to the lyrics of New York rapper Schoolly D, 'gangsta rap' as a genre—and in particular its spin-off, G-funk—was predominantly a West Coast phenomenon, set in commercial motion by NWA's 'Gangsta Gangsta' and then jumped upon, expanded, packaged and weakened by the acts that followed and, in particular, by the labels profiting from this new style. Arguably, Raekwon's solo album, *Only Built 4 Cuban Linx*, is one of the classics of the 'gangster' genre, but in fact the whole thing is so stylised, so clearly influenced by totems of popular culture like *Scarface*, that you would have to be pretty unsophisticated in your reading of narrative to interpret it as *true* rather than a fictional construct.

As for *Enter...* it's not even a *crime* album, let alone an organised crime album. Which isn't to say that there aren't multiple references throughout to guns, to drugs, to beat-downs, to murder and so on. It's just to say that most of such references have to be understood within a very particular context. As Rich Jones concludes our email exchange, 'It's not the whole story, it's just an interesting part of it.' Which is another way of saying it's not the story at all.

16TH CHAMBER
WALKIN'

RZA escaped from Staten Island, not by leaving the
environs of the island but by in some way transcending
them. He walked his way out. Up in Steubenville
dealing crack, he had got into a dispute with a rival
gang over a girl who Ghostface was seeing. Shots were
fired, someone was hit, and despite Diggs's assertion
that he was acting in self-defence, he was charged with
attempted murder, for which the prosecutor wanted to
see him jailed for eight years. After a jury found him not
guilty, he returned to Staten Island, determined to
make the most of this second chance. He moved his
girlfriend and newborn baby away from the area he'd
grown up in to a place on the other side of the Island,
where they slept on a boxing mat on the floor in a
two-bed apartment shared with two of his brothers,
his sister and Ghostface. Then, day after day, he would

set out and walk his way all over the island. He was following in the (literal and nonliteral) footsteps of his favourite monk, the Bodhidharma (known in China as Da Mo, Damo or, in RZA's formulation, Da'Mo), whom he had seen a film about, *Master of Zen*. Later, he would recall being particularly moved because the Chinese, noting the colour of Da'Mo's skin, had called him 'the brown monk'. 'I walked every day for hours. I mean, *walked*, like Da'Mo walked all the way from India to China. I'd walk from the Park Hill projects to the Staten Island ferry dock, from New Brighton to the Stapleton projects, walking through May, June, July.'

— — —

Outside the Wholly Fellowship Ministry some kind of mini-zephyr picks up tiny pieces of leaf—dried and browned and ground down over two or three seasons—and the sunlight catches them as they twirl up into the air, painting the dust gold.

— — —

First up, this walking was an end in itself, a way to get free. RZA likens it to a meditation, but there's an element of storying in that, of justification after the fact (though it isn't wrong). Just as good a starting point is Frédéric Gros' notion that walking takes you out of yourself. 'By walking, you escape from the very idea of identity, the temptation to be someone, to have a name and a history.' Sometimes we need to get out of ourselves, to find an acceptable, non-lethal way to oblivion or something close to it. After all, 'the logic of identity is, always and everywhere, entangled in the logic of hierarchy'. Later, you find that coming out of yourself is the first step in finding perspective on yourself—and everything around you.

— — —

Frank's Pizza is doing brisk business before noon. Built into a corner unit so that it's a rounded-off triangle, it's frequented by just about every demographic in the area. A super' from one of the nearby buildings grabs a slice with a friend. Members of some kind of family unit— an older couple with two adult young men of different ethnicities to them and to each other—pass round pots of sauce (they eat like a family, anyway: methodically and in silence). A girl, maybe late teens and overweight, orders two slices of thick crust. Two adolescent boys in basketball gear count out change. They keep on coming.

— — —

Picture him walking, almost marching, talking to himself, a monologue rapped out to the beat of his feet. His hair growing out and wild-looking, that thin face and high, prominent cheekbones. The roll in his gait and accompanying swing of his arms. He looks nuts, frankly, so that people step out of his way, and laugh when he's gone past. But he doesn't notice. He's caught up in something else, fantasising as much as plotting, figuring it all out. Something about walking, the pace of that movement, seems to free your mind after a while to a torrent of fantasy, a reimagining of self. It's as if the process of placing one foot in front of the other occupies just enough of your cautious, sensible self—the one who checks everything, who advises against any particular course of action, the one who always finds a problem, a gap which can't be jumped—and leaves the rest of your mind free to go where it wants.

— — —

On the sidewalk opposite, another walker, this one
patrolling the same twenty-yard stretch, there and
back, there and back—slowly, stopping now and again
to stare off into the distance, something of the late Ali
in the shamble if not the physique. Wearing a floppy
sunhat, a green T-shirt, baggy shorts and rubber Crocs
over Christmas socks pulled up to his knees, he moves
with the stuttering confusion of the mentally ill—or of
someone badly, irreparably treated for being mentally ill.

— — —

Three months. Three months of walking. If he managed
eight miles every day, that's over seven hundred miles. If
he'd gone in one direction he could've walked to Chicago.
Instead he criss-crossed Staten Island like a tiger in a
cage. Somehow, it didn't drive him nuts but drove him
sane, liberated him from the madness. Perhaps the
greatest achievement of RZA's peregrinations was not
that he dreamt of ways of escape, but that he eventually
made a plan to expedite that escape. After all, anyone
can fantasise, but rare is the person who can make that
fantasy real. It's a process which requires resolve, self-
criticism, a certain steeliness of character. As Gros points
out, 'while walking, you hold yourself to account: you
correct yourself, challenge yourself, assess yourself'.
When RZA did so, he realised that he couldn't function
alone as Prince Rakeem, that he was weakened while
pursuing a cheque solely for himself. He couldn't do it as
Wu-Tang (at that stage just him and Ghostface Killah).
He wasn't strong enough as All In Together Now (him and
his cousins, Genius and Ason Unique/ODB). Nor could
he achieve any more as D.M.D. (Dig 'Em Down—himself

and the Park Hill crew of Meth, Raekwon, Deck and
U-God). See it as solidarity, an elementary union.
Treat it as alchemy, a fusion of elements. Celebrate it
as community, a single purpose. Princes and geniuses
dig down together now to form one Clan.

— — —

The pool looks much the same as any outdoor pool
anywhere in the world—that strange glow to the light
beyond the gates caused by chlorinated water refracting
the pale blue of the tiles beneath. The gates themselves
painted a bright sky blue, the prongs you push through
multi-coloured. The only thing to distinguish this from
any summer's day morning anywhere in the world is the
NYPD patrol car parked up in the shade of the driveway,
the silhouettes of the two figures sitting in it.

— — —

In *The Tao of Wu*, RZA praises Afrika Bambaataa while
implicitly criticising him for making music which was
'funkier and more dance-oriented', and it's true that
old skool hip hop grew in a club or party environment
and its first purpose was to move a crowd. By the early
1990s though, hip hop was shrugging off this particular
imperative in favour of a more downbeat tempo and
a grimier aesthetic, one whose aim was to reflect
life rather than to offer transcendence or temporary
respite. You could argue it was becoming true to itself as
an art form. 'I felt there was an actual sound to hip-hop
culture then,' writes RZA, 'a spirit that existed on its
own plane, in the streets and parks, in the air. I wanted
to be a vessel for that sound.' Saying this, he sounds
like a walker, someone who figured this out not in the
studio but marching through daily life.

The music on *Enter* tends to hover round a tempo of 92 bpm (beats per minute). That's a fast walk, almost a yomp, but it's certainly not primarily conceived for dancing. There's even something about the way RZA constructs his music which suggests bipedal movement, the swing in a tune like 'Method Man' pivoting on the four notes of a piano refrain which actually sounds out the beats of the bar while the drum rhythm shuffles round it. The bassline on 'Shame on a Nigga' does the same. You can hear the rhythm of a rolling, purposeful forward stomp in every tune, RZA often emphasising the first and the third beat of the bar, when you're swinging your left foot forward. The Wu-Tang are on the march.

— — —

Even the changes are changeable. Suburbia lies just off a steep, scrubby hill, its pavements cracked and the crumbling houses covered in diesel particulate. A turned corner and a few paces lead to perfectly mown lawns and neat, well-maintained properties, the fantasy homes of the American middle classes. In other places, the transition is more gradual. A long road morphs infinitesimally, the houses beginning to fall apart, a stop-frame animation of decay, the same rickety pulse you find in a RZA beat. Further back into the island there are no sidewalks beyond the main road—not through a lack of amenity but a surfeit of it. No one is supposed to walk, gawky, among these mansions, a riot of styles, the air suddenly quiet and clear. The hills have value. The beachside too. The poor live in between.

— — —

RZA sees this process of walking towards the Wu-Tang Clan as akin to a revelation. 'Like most meditation, those walks on Staten Island didn't create something; they revealed something—something that was already floating over the island, ready to take form.' There's an element of the mystical sneaking in there, which perhaps lessens the impact of the fact that he came up with this plan, this way of operating, all on his own, in complete isolation. But he's right in a very real sense. All the pieces were already there. But there is nothing floating above Staten Island, no mystery-god moment. RZA sees what was already around him by being down there among it all, by being a part of it all. He can only walk the path by becoming the path. As well as giving him the room to imagine, plot and invent, walking also narrows the conceptual gap between himself and his surroundings until it vanishes. He becomes the island, the island becomes Shaolin. He doesn't have to build a shining palace on a hill—Disneyland, Graceland, Neverland—he imagines it existing in the hardscrabble around him. Augmenting Clarence 13X's theo-geography of New York (Harlem as Mecca, Brooklyn as Medina), Staten Island is re-conceptualised as a Chinese temple, the landscape an extension of the kung fu fantasies running through RZA's brain. And what is a temple anyway, except the cranium of a god?

— — —

A clear plastic box sits on the ground, butted up against the wall, between a shop and someone's front door. Inside it, flowers are dying—slowly, inevitably—drying out, wilting, desiccating, their petals dropping one by one onto the backs of bleached, defeated-looking cuddly toys. There are three A4 sheets of photos behind the perspex, the same fading man enclosed in ovals and hearts, surrounded by family and friends. A battered picture of Winnie the Pooh in hiking gear (Disney-version), flaking from a wooden backing, lies on top of the box and beneath a small, inverted Marcus Garvey flag, the position of the red and green reversed around the thick central band of black.

— — —

On the very first Wu single, 'Protect Ya Neck', RZA says 'stroll with the holy roll then attack the globe'. The first step to liberation (and global dominance) is quite literally *the first step*.

17TH CHAMBER
FAKING FOR REAL

The thing about the skit at the start of 'Wu-Tang:
7th Chamber' is that it sounds so *real*. It begins with
Raekwon complaining about his missing VHS of the
martial arts movie *Master Killer* (aka *The 36th Chamber
of Shaolin*), which Method Man appears to have mislaid.
But before we get too far into this dispute, we hear
Ghostface hammering on the door and bursting in with
U-God to tell the assembled Wu members that 'Shameek
from 2-12' has been shot in the head and is out on the
street, 'fuckin' lyin' there like a fuckin' newborn baby'.
Ghost and U-God have come to get a weapon so that they
can go and take revenge. Raekwon is ready to join them.
Meth continues to explain that someone probably took
the tape from his place during a party.

The moment the whole thing takes flight is when
Method Man asks Ghostface if Shameek is dead. Both

U-God and Ghost are outraged—almost offended—by the stupidity of the question and they make their feelings abundantly clear. 'The n***a layin' there with…' Ghost says, struggling for words, '… all types of fucking blood comin' out of his fuckin'…' He trails off, before U-God takes to imitation in a low, singsong voice: *'Is he is he is he dead?'*

Of course, to see it on the page doesn't really do justice to the delivery, the sheer disbelief in Ghost's tone, the way the voices bounce and flow over each other, the density of the slang, the utter pizzazz of the whole thing. The scene fizzes with energy, with life, which is why it's so easy to believe you're eavesdropping on reality, even when it's obvious, if you take a moment to think about it, that you're not. Listen to the quality of that knock on the door if you doubt it's a construct— the product of a very disappointing Foley room. Think through the mechanics of a live recording. No, the skit is as fabricated, as constructed as anything else on the record, though the cadence and timbre of the delivery give it a kind of expressive truth. That's why so many rappers have ended up working as actors—not because they're expert at *making it up* or *pretending* but because they have a highly developed technical control of their voices, just like singers—except their singing is human speech.

It's not even clear, anyway, that when you hear the skit you're thinking of reality at all. Possibly you're thinking of another fabrication. What the feistiness of the delivery—and in particular, Ghost's indignant, *Is he fucking dead??!*—actually recalls is the work of Martin Scorsese and, more than any other movie, *Goodfellas*. It's an obvious reference. The film came out in 1990, three years before *Enter*, and its milieu wouldn't have been unfamiliar to residents of Staten Island, which boasts a huge Italian-American community and a long history of Cosa Nostra connections, both real and fictional. The borough was given its media-mafia imprimatur as early as 1971, when Francis Ford Coppola chose to use a house there as the location for the Corleone compound in *The Godfather*. The head of the Gambino crime family, Paul Castellano, meanwhile, was resident in the Todt Hill area—in his own, not-entirely-tasteful version of the White House—when he was shot in Manhattan in 1985 by gunmen sent by his rival, John Gotti. According to RZA's own account of his childhood, his mother worked for a numbers racket, and Dan Charnas explains that 'Linda Hamlin and her mother, Ethel, ran a restaurant across the street from the nearby Stapleton projects that served as a front for a mob-run numbers operation. While Ethel cooked in the front, Miss Linda tallied the daily wins and losses in the back, under the protection of a neighbourhood enforcer nicknamed "Fat Larry."' So yeah, some of the rhythms and inflections of speech are shared between these two New York subcultures, plus perhaps a broader cultural affinity, highlighted by Scorsese himself: 'Some of the best entertainment I had was listening to guys on street corners tell stories—the oral tradition!'

Only a lunatic, though, would presume that a Scorsese movie is a documentary (unless, of course, it's one of his documentaries). Indeed, the director specialises in 'a hallucinatory realism' in which speech, action, even colour are heightened and stylised. *Goodfellas* itself was based on the non-fiction book *Wiseguy*, written by Nicholas Pileggi. Remembering one particularly striking sequence in the film—a two-and-a-half-minute single shot tracking Henry Hill as he leads his wife-to-be through the kitchens and to a prime table in the Copacabana nightclub—Pileggi recalled, 'If you read the script, and you read my book, it's just three sentences. That's the idiot I am. I missed it, he knew exactly what to do with it.'

'Hallucinatory realism' as a term works rather nicely for the Wu-Tang, too, but as we've seen, there's a tendency to treat what they do as *real* and, to the extent that it's shown not to be real, as *fake*, or at least to judge it primarily by these standards. What's the difference between these two art forms so that one only has to be true to the spirit of the story and its protagonists and the other has to be literally true to the facts?

An easy place to start would be to argue that one of our examples—a feature film by Martin Scorsese—is self-evidently *constructed*, while the other—a debut album by the Wu-Tang Clan—is not. While this obviously doesn't make much sense, it's actually a commonly held view when attributed to books, which we divide between the categories of fiction and non-fiction. On this reading, non-fiction is built solely from fact, while fiction is everything else—all the lies and stories that the writer makes up in pursuit of higher truth or higher sales (the author of the article from which we quoted Pileggi says that 'any changes from the book come because Scorsese favors the story while Pileggi the author was bound to journalistic accuracy'). You don't need to get too deep to see the problems with this outlook and the porousness of the boundary presented. Non-fiction, too, is a construction in which the author chooses which 'facts' to highlight in order to make an interesting or compelling narrative, or just because of his or her own prejudices or weaknesses. 'Any narrative account is a form of fiction,' David Shields famously claimed. 'The moment you start to arrange the world in words, you alter its nature.' The less radical version of this argument is that a narrative at best represents one possible truth based on a partial presentation of available evidence. In the hands of Shields, though, this observation becomes a polemical ground zero for a call for the use of fictionalisation within non-fiction: 'We are all in flight from reality. That is the basic definition of Homo sapiens.'

The strange thing is that these arguments, while seeming cutting edge, often rely on a greater essentialism than can be found in the work they're attacking—the idea of the deeper or higher truth rumbling into view once again (and who is to say for sure whether it's up or down?). Shields, of course, is involved in a polemical slash 'n' burn, but even the gentler, less macho pronouncements of someone like John D'Agata end up somewhere similar. 'What I love to read in non-fiction often exists between those poles of what is verifiable and what's simply not,' he writes. 'I love the in-between, which is where I think the *most truthful* struggles with reality exist' (italics added). While this call for a kind of hybrid form is attractive, it remains a type of realism, understood as 'the conviction that art has the potential to truthfully reproduce the real world'. Because without this basic conviction, why would we even care about the truthfulness or otherwise of a work of art? It seems less convincing as an argument for fictionalisation than for saying that if you have the privilege of being the teller of a story, then it's your responsibility to be clear about your own assumptions and the decisions you take.

We're trying to drag a conceptual sled over a bog.

Is he is he is he dead?! Does Shameek exist to begin with so that he can die, gunned down on the streets of Staten Island? Is the skit real, a re-enactment or a fiction? And what does it mean that Method Man's character in *Belly*, the 1998 feature debut from Hype Williams, was called... Shameek?[15] We feel ourselves beginning to sink between notions of realism, fact and fiction, truth and falsehood. And where, outside of discussions of art and literature, does 'realism' mean anything other than settling for less than you'd hoped for? In what circumstances do we say that something is 'the truth' except when accused of lying? As for the broader underpinning we're relying on for our verifications, in the words of D.H. Lawrence, 'Heaven knows what we mean by reality.'

The hip hop album is an extremely subtle interleaving of truth, storytelling, bragging, name-calling, exaggeration and outright lies. It's a hybrid form of considerably more ontological sophistication than your standard novel or biography. The vinyl LP itself broke through as a format in 1949 with the release of the original cast recording of *South Pacific*—that is, a musical narrative. If we think of the Beatles as the first pop group to fully grasp the potential of the LP then it's also interesting to note that when Lennon and McCartney were interviewed by *NME* in 1963, 'both expressed a burning desire to write a musical'. It's as if the narrative potential of the 'album' was built into the format, a condition of its increased length. However, it was only with hip hop and the birth

15   Joining the dots, the actor Frank Vincent appeared in both *Goodfellas* and *Belly*, as well as in the video to Nas's 'Street Dreams', itself directed by Hype Williams as a pastiche of Scorsese's *Casino*. Incidentally, Method Man's character, Shameek, only pretends to be a gangster in the film.

of a new 'carrier',[16] the CD, that this potential was fully unleashed (a fact perhaps proved in reverse by the success of the 'rap-musical' *Hamilton*). And like hip hop itself, the narratives thus created are fractured, collaged, self-consciously constructed, indeed actually celebrate and revel in their constructedness and artificiality. But, for some reason, we read in them only truth or falsehood.

We are forced now to enter essentialism's very own Fortress of Solitude, the place where truth, fiction and realism go to do the do (or die). We need to talk about *authenticity*. Until now we've been circling it from high above, scared to land on treacherous terrain. It's a strange concept, one of those ones that gets pulled in all kinds of directions, losing touch with itself in the process. We know exactly what the word means in relation to a banknote or the provenance of a work of art, less so in relation to the self or the effects of that work of art. Like our earlier protests declaring realism or the truth, it's a largely negative or reactive property. As the writer and academic Miles Orvell notes, 'the concept of authenticity begins in any society when the possibility of fraud arrives'. We could, with Wittgenstein, say that the meaning (i.e. the use) of the word 'authentic' has a tendency to get stretched, tempting us to 'misuse language'. The question then might be why.

In his book *The Real Thing*, Orvell delineates how in America 'the problem of authenticity, of naming "the real thing," begins to take on significant proportions' from the mid-nineteenth century onwards. Orvell

---

16　'At the time we developed the compact disc, the LP market was saturated and the cassette was beginning to slow down so we needed a new carrier'–Norio Ohga, President of Sony. The use of the term 'carrier' suggests music as plague.

claims that this new obsession with authenticity is 'partly a response to a change in the technological environment, centering on the meaning of the machine', which is a rather elegant way of pointing a finger at the Industrial Revolution, a period in which society became hugely more complex, traditional social structures broke down and, with mechanisation and mass production, old notions of craftsmanship, of what is an original and what a copy, became increasingly confused. Orvell ties this trauma to the birth of consumerism. 'It was as if there were some defect in everyday reality,' he says, 'that had to be remedied by the more authentic reality of the object to be consumed.' But in America it also became knotted up with the end of slavery. And here the difference between authenticity and fakery became confused all over again.

The roots of minstrelsy are traditionally traced back to 1828, when Thomas D. Rice blackened his face using a cork, took a song and dance he claimed to have seen performed by an old, deformed African American man, and toured it across America and Europe as the 'Jim Crow'. The act and others like it rapidly became a craze. 'Minstrelsy swept the nation in the mid-1840s,' writes Robert Toll. 'Everywhere it played, [it] seemed to have a magnetic, almost hypnotic, impact on its audiences.' It maintained its central role in American popular culture until almost the end of that century, and its influence continued long after (arguably to this day). And not everyone understood that it was faked. Many people seeing minstrels for the first time presumed that they were *actual* Black people, rather than White people pastiching, faking and lampooning African American culture. 'Some Northerners, probably a substantial number of the gullible public that had seen few Negroes and were still unfamiliar with minstrel conventions, mistook minstrels for real.' A further level of confusion was to come later, when African American performers also 'blacked up' and performed minstrel routines, in effect disguised as White people disguised as Black people. 'Minstrelsy provided,' argues Toll, 'a nonthreatening way for vast numbers of white Americans to work out their ambivalence about race.' In fact, rather than 'working out' their ambivalence (which suggests some therapeutic benefit), minstrelsy provides an example of 'acting out' and heightening that ambivalence—and part of that enactment must have gained its power from the way in which the play between *authentic* and *fake* mirrored, echoed and amplified the audience's ambivalence.

A key driver of this orgy of misrepresentation was the idea that Black people—viewed as primitive and uncivilised—were supposed to have access to the heart in a way which 'civilised' Whites did not. Even the Fisk Singers—deliberately as sophisticated and elegant as possible in their renditions of slave songs—were fitted into this paradigm. 'There is little evidence of culture in their singing,' wrote the critic for the *New York Times* of one of their performances. 'But it has a spontaneity, a verve and a natural enthusiasm... Art has done little for these people and nature a great deal.' So it was that a music which most of White society had only learnt about through a deliberately demeaned counterfeit came to be seen as a bedrock sound of authenticity. 'The perceived purity and wholeness of the slave songs,' suggests the ethnomusicologist Ronald Radano, 'signified what was missing in whiteness as a consequence of civilization itself.'

We don't need to be experts in twentieth-century history to know that purity, when applied to humans and their culture, is another of those concepts we should always treat with suspicion. As Hugh Barker and Yuval Taylor have pointed out, 'the story of African music in America is', in actual fact, 'one of incessant miscegenation'. The pair emphasise the hybridity of so much Southern music—the interaction of influences from Africa, Scotland, Ireland and beyond—a hybridity which was attacked or ignored by the emergent Northern record companies in the early part of the last century, who wanted to fit all their releases into either the 'race' (Black) or the 'old time' (White) category. This process was accelerated by none other than Henry Ford, who, as well as being an engineering genius and creator of the production line, was also a virulent anti-Semite and racist, one who used his own newspaper, the *Dearborn Independent*, to run headlines like 'Jewish Jazz—Moron Music' and to promote what he saw as more wholesome (and Caucasian) fiddle music and square dances—which would eventually be celebrated under the rubric of country music. The result was that, over a relatively brief period, the idea developed that 'the most authentic American music was that which evidenced a clear and absolute divide between black and white'. Black people should play the blues, White people should play country—all connection and overlap between the two was studiously ignored or decried as inauthentic. Instead, there was a rush towards the fiction of 'the most racially pure music'.

This is not, however much we might like to hope, a fiction we have entirely shaken off. As Ted Gioia points out, it's there in most early writing about jazz, even from critics who considered themselves enthusiastic and supportive of the form. 'They saw the jazz artist,' he says, 'as a creature of inspiration who, in his own rough and unskilled way, would forge a statement that was of the heart and not necessarily of the mind.' Barker and Taylor trace the continuing fascination with this idea into the blues revival of the sixties, but, with very little re-working, their words would be as suitable for hip hop:

> Both the front-porch and outlaw images of blues musicians were romantic fictions that fit perfectly with... [the] conception of authentic black music as uncivilized, 'uncontaminated by white influence'— not to mention the conventions of minstrelsy. These images perpetuated stereotypes of blacks as poor sharecroppers to be pitied or untamed savages to be feared, as folks uneducated and isolated in their own peculiar world. In the fictions of the blues, there was little room for hardworking crowd pleasers, sophisticated innovators or musical miscegenators.

As well as the skit at the start of '7th Chamber', there's at least one other superb example of the factual/ fictional subtlety of hip hop on *Enter the Wu-Tang*. As a whole, it's not a record in which many verses are devoted to narrative, to the straightforward telling of first-person stories. In fact, only 'C.R.E.A.M.', 'Tearz' and, to a lesser extent, 'Can It Be All So Simple' fulfil this function (the last is too fractured, though, to be read in a completely linear fashion). 'Tearz' was one of the first two tracks recorded by the Wu-Tang Clan under that name and, indeed, was on their very first single, so it occupies a vital place in the cosmology of the group's creation. As we've already seen, RZA's verse here tells the tale of how his little brother got shot while going to buy bread at the local store for his mother. It's heavy with emotion, with regret, with lost innocence. It is utterly sincere. And it's a complete fiction. In his semi-memoir, *The Tao of Wu*, RZA recounts the story of his eight-year-old self being robbed by older kids while going to the shop, but there are no guns involved and the version presented in 'Tearz' is perhaps best understood as a metaphorical re-telling of the murder of a young boy's innocence.

RZA's words on 'Tearz'—as well as the skit at the start of 'Wu-Tang: 7th Chamber'—completely short-circuit or implode the desperate need of the audience for authenticity, for rap to be literal and true without artifice, for it to be primitive, to be dangerous or noble, but most of all, for it *not to be art*. To understand any hip hop album in these terms is to miss the point, but nowhere is that clearer than with *Enter*, where myth and reportage become so intermingled, so reliant on one another, that even to try to separate them is a category error. The Wu-Tang's conception of authenticity is much closer to what the photographer Wolfgang Tillmans is talking about when he says that 'for me, my pictures are authentic in that they "authentically" reproduce my fiction of the moment'. The Wu-Tang are authentic because they make it so, not because it is so.

18TH CHAMBER
PRIMARY COLOURS

However you look at it, it's a great jacket, a classic of its
kind. The top half and arms a solid, bright, egg-yolk
yellow, the lower dark-night blue. The fleece inside
the collar a block of blazing red, echoed by oval elbow
patches and the big, bold letters on the front, one word
above the other, justified, blocking out the whole
black panel of the doc-pocket: SNOW BEACH. Is it a
place name or a juxtaposition? You barely have time
to think it over. Everything about the jacket is angular
and immediate, pulsing, worn large so even its shape
mimics an advertising hoarding, pop art turned back
into product, product turned into sales pitch, sales
pitch embodied as product. And then that fleece lining,
the detail of the red pocket inners, hinting at a creamy
luxury, some kind of premium price tag. It's beautiful
in an utterly ugly sort of way and ugly in an utterly

beautiful sort of way. And that's what makes it perfect for its role.

In early 1994, Raekwon the Chef was to film a video, along with Ghostface Killah, for 'Can It Be All So Simple'—the fourth single to be released from *Enter the Wu-Tang* and the one with the biggest budget so far (the young Hype Williams shot the promo, just at the beginning of the run of music videos that would make him the dominant visual force of 'urban'—i.e. Black—music in the nineties). On the morning of the shoot, Rae went out shopping for clothes, looking, as he later told Karizza Sanchez, for 'something that I felt could relate to my culture'. The original plan had been a pair of Nike Air Force 1s, a baseball cap and some new jeans, but cruising down Fulton Street in Brooklyn, the Chef was smitten by the sight in the window of A&S: the Ralph Lauren Polo Snow Beach pullover jacket, a glimmering vision of bold colourways and radical prep-chic: 'The first thing I thought,' Raekwon recalled, 'was, "Yo, this ain't something I seen before. I could be the first one to rock this. When people start talking about it, they gon' eventually say, *Only one I seen with that jacket on was The Chef*."' He went into the store to find that they only had one XXL jacket left and—sensing some kind of fate in this exclusivity—he bought it there and then for a few hundred dollars. 'I jumped on it and wore it in the video,' he explained, over twenty years later. 'Next thing you know, the jacket became famous.' Today, examples of the Snow Beach pullover jacket in mint condition can sell for up to five thousand dollars on eBay. It really is a very famous anorak.

In the mid-eighties, two gangs in Brooklyn (Ralphie's Kids from Crown Heights and Polo USA from Marcus

Garvey Village in Brownsville)[17] merged to form the 'Lo Lifes—some kind of super-organisation for the collection and display of the best pieces of Polo clothing they could lay their hands on, often acquired in meticulously planned and fearlessly executed shoplifting raids on the city's major department stores. It's a movement which has been lovingly documented in books and on film over the last few years, and the central reason given for its power is that it provided a kind of home for its participants, a way to be in the world. As Thirstin Howl III—one of the founders of the 'Lo Lifes, now equally well known as a rapper— puts it, evoking some of the same superhero archetypes which played such a big role in the development of wider hip hop culture, 'a lot of us came from broken homes and had a lot of problems so the clothing helped us to get through a lot of hard times. Cats would never know what you were going through when they saw you dressed in the 'Lo. The garments gave us new identities.'

The identity it gave to these inner-city African American and Puerto Rican kids was confusing to a lot of people. In the words of a 1986 *Time* cover story on the Polo phenomenon, Ralph Lauren was a brand built almost entirely on a kind of high-end, WASP exclusivity. 'Watch polo matches in Palm Beach,' the article suggested, perhaps a trifle sarcastically, 'trim in a crested blazer and trousers of crisp linen. Sip cognac by the fireplace of a Sun Valley chalet... clad in a Nordic apres-ski sweater and wool twill slacks. Go on safari in Kenya wearing a bush jacket and khaki shorts... Sip tea at London's Connaught Hotel, draped to perfection in

17 Marcus Garvey Village was where RZA lived before moving to Staten Island and is considered one of the toughest neighbourhoods in New York City.

a chalk-stripe suit.' To put it more bluntly, as Margaret Carlson did almost ten years later in the same magazine, Ralph Lauren's advertising at the time consisted mainly of 'Aryan youth on sailboats'.

There was, then, a certain amount of consternation at this brand—and other purveyors of luxury, outdoor or even blue-collar workwear aesthetics—finding themselves so enthusiastically adopted by 'urban' youth. In 1986, *Time* could report that Lauren's 'Polo purchasers are typically professionals and other upscalers who feel they have more important things to follow than fashion trends'. By 1993, brands like Polo, Timberland and North Face had been enthusiastically appropriated by a whole new audience. 'The youth market came after us,' the director of marketing at Carhartt famously declared, a week or so before *Enter the Wu-Tang* was released. 'Fine, they like to wear what we make. But we will never go after that market aggressively,' he claimed (and if he meant what he said, he probably didn't stay director of marketing at Carhartt for long).

Raekwon's decision to wear the Snow Beach pullover is, from this standpoint, the moment at which the 'Lo phenomenon went mainstream. And it wasn't a fluke on Rae's part. On 'C.R.E.A.M.', he references both the *'Lo goose* (a goose-down Polo jacket) and, later, having to wear *the same damn 'Lo sweater*, two of the few explicit clothing brand references on the whole record. The album's release also coincided with the period when 'Lo Lifes stopped stealing and started to buy their gear, easing mainstream (i.e. White) America towards an acceptance of this new feedback loop of aspiration, appropriation and marketing—or, at least, of the money to be made from it. As such, it's hard to imagine a more prescient example of 'relating to my culture' than Rae's choice of top, voted second in *Complex* magazine's 'Fifty Greatest Fashion Moments in Rap Video History'.[18]

With a bit of distance, of course, it's hard to see what all the fuss was about when young Black men started decking themselves out in Polo. After all, Ralph Lauren's real name is Ralph Lifshitz and (like hip hop itself) he grew up in the Bronx, the son of 'an Orthodox Jewish immigrant from the Soviet city of Minsk'. Seen in this light, those 'Aryan youth' fantasies are exactly as authentically American as any other method of selling, and indeed in many ways much less authentic than the pride and sense of validation that young inner-city kids took from wearing his clothes. Indeed, in that they were selling nothing but only trying to be the freshest, the most stylish among their immediate circle, it's arguable that they were the most authentic aristocrats ever to wear Mr Lifshitz's garments. And among their number, none was more aristocratic than Raekwon, with that rolling walk and rubber-ball physique, the slight lisp caused by the gold fronts on his crooked teeth.

If you think of hip hop as a culture of creative misuse or re-referencing, then the story of its relationship to Polo/Ralph Lauren—and, indeed, high-end clothing brands in general—makes a lot of sense. You could see the appropriation of Ralphie's clothes as a form of sampling, and in fact Thirstin Howl makes this connection concrete. 'We made our own custom garments from stuff we stole,' he recalls, 'like XL shirts made out of 3 or 4 $500 silk scarves. There was a lot of creativity.' In some ways this is no different to what

---

18 It was only beaten into second spot by Run-DMC rocking not just unlaced but *laceless* Adidas shelltoes in the video to 'Walk This Way'. Fair enough.

predominantly White working-class football 'casuals' were doing with luxury brands in Britain at around the same time, and it even bears some similarities to the zoot-suit craze of the forties. 'For those without other forms of cultural capital,' the historian Kathy Peiss has explained of the zoot-suit phenomenon, 'fashion can be a way of claiming space for yourself'—and this idea of claiming space runs as a strong current particularly through graffiti and b-boy culture (what do the windmilling legs of a b-boy do other than claim space?).

The main difference between hip hop and other street fashion crazes, though, lies first in how systematic the act of appropriation becomes in hip hop culture, and second in how this very systematisation becomes a form of delirium—or at least in how difficult it is to distinguish between these two apparent poles. 'We all lived hip hop,' says Howl, 'and so the Polo just helped us describe ourselves as hip hop. Polo became our religion.' In actual fact, what the Polo craze is most reminiscent of is not religion but the blind faith which functions as the driver of our economic system. 'With its ceaseless boom and bust cycles,' writes Mark Fisher, capitalism is 'fundamentally and irreducibly bi-polar, periodically lurching between hyped-up mania (the irrational exuberance of "bubble-thinking") and depressive come-down. (The term "economic depression" is no accident, of course.) To a degree unprecedented in any other social system, capitalism both feeds on and reproduces the moods of populations. Without delirium and confidence, capital could not function.' Much as the DJ extends (and hence intensifies) the rhythmic mania of the break, one of the functions of hip hop generally is to extend (and hence intensify) the systematic mania of capitalism.

The question becomes, if the looping of the break also creates a qualitative change in the music thus treated, what qualitative change might hip hop create in capitalism?

19TH CHAMBER
RESPECTING VIOLENCE

White men kill and maim Black men and go
unpunished.

As a subway train left 14th Street station in Manhattan
on 22 December 1984, Bernhard Hugo Goetz was
approached by the young men who would become his
victims. Aged 18 or 19 and from the South Bronx, they
said they asked for five dollars to play video games, more
in jest than anything else. He said they demanded five
dollars, with implicit threat. Either way, Goetz stood
up and shot them, one after another, with a .38 calibre
pistol pulled from a quick-draw holster and filled with
illegal hollow-point 'dumdum' bullets. Having fired four
shots and downed the teenagers, Goetz stood over one
of them, Darrell Cabey, and said (or at least, claimed to

have said),[19] 'You seem to be all right; here's another,' before shooting him again as he lay on the ground, permanently paralysing him. A conductor pulled the emergency cord and the train stopped just before reaching the next platform. He walked up to Goetz and asked him if he was a policeman. 'No,' responded Goetz. 'I don't know why I did it... They tried to rip me off.' Then he climbed down from the carriage and disappeared into the tunnel.

Goetz hid for nine days before handing himself in to the police, during which time he ascended to the status of folk hero—a tall, ungainly, bespectacled White man who had not allowed himself to be bullied or brutalised. The four boys he'd shot lay in hospital. 'My intention was to do anything I could to hurt them,' he was recorded as saying during his eventual police interview. 'My intention was to murder them, to hurt them, to make them suffer as much as possible... If I had had more bullets, I would have shot them again and again and again.' None of this stilled the city's fervour. New Yorkers put up signs saying 'God Bless You, Bernie.' Bumper stickers were sold reading, 'Ride with Bernie— He Goetz 'em!' It was generally held—and without irony—that Bernie had struck a blow for ordinary, law-abiding folk who had been terrorised on the subway for too long.

In certain legal cases in the United States, a grand jury—usually made up of 23 members of the public— is assembled to assess evidence and decide whether a prosecution should proceed. The recently appointed

---

19   The words are taken from Goetz's own account of the shooting, but no one else remembers him speaking and nothing in his life story suggests a strong correlation between his assertions and objective reality.

Chief Judge of New York State, Sol Wachtler, famously claimed in January 1985 that such a panel, skilfully manipulated by a prosecutor, would 'indict a ham sandwich... Most of the time when you want to get a prosecution and you want to indict, you use the grand jury and you can get the damnedest kind of indictments.' All of which suggests some ambivalence (or incompetence) on the part of prosecutors in the Goetz case. The first grand jury to assess his actions indicted him only on counts relating to illegal firearm possession. A second grand jury was finally persuaded to add charges of attempted murder, assault and 'reckless endangerment'. However, the judge assigned to the case, Stephen Crane, dismissed these new charges. It was only after a trip to the Court of Appeals that the extra indictments were reinstated and the case sent to trial. This trial ended, though, with Goetz convicted for the firearms possession charge alone. The jury decided that he was justified in acting in self-defence, the fact that he perceived a threat deemed to be enough. As a member of the jury later put it, 'the fault in failing to convict him lies not with the jury, nor the judge nor the prosecutor, but with a deficiency in the justification laws. The law, I think, is not specific enough about the alternatives Goetz should have been required to seek before being allowed to fire his gun as a legitimate act of self-defence.' After appeal, he was finally sentenced to a year in jail in January 1989, four years after the shooting. He would eventually serve eight months.

On his solo track 'Clan In Da Front', GZA/Genius ends his first verse by stating that 'Bernhard Goetz what he deserves', an odd statement for a young Black man from New York to make until you realise that his suggestion is that, with the Wu-Tang coming through,

Goetz *will* get what he deserves. But did he? In 1996, he lost a civil suit brought by lawyers on behalf of the paralysed Darrell Cabey and was ordered to pay $43 million in damages. He declared bankruptcy a week later and, when asked in 2004, said, 'I don't think I've paid a penny on that,' before going on to say that the shooting 'was just what the doctor ordered for New York City. Not for me but for New York City.' Despite being involved in a dispute over how to hand-rear squirrels, plus being arrested for selling thirty dollars' worth of marijuana, Goetz continues to live in the same apartment in Manhattan. In his defence on the latter charge, Goetz said, 'This type of hysterical war on crime, which I helped start 30 years ago, is just no longer appropriate.'

Over thirty years later, the question still remains valid. Does any White man in America 'Goetz' what he deserves when it comes to attacking and/or killing Black men? And, as a subset of this, is the 'hysterical war on crime' appropriate?

On 17 July 2014, Eric Garner was stopped by the NYPD outside a beauty supply shop on Bay Street in the Tompkinsville district of Staten Island. Garner had a long rap sheet for selling single cigarettes and the police were keen to crack down on the practice in the area, still working to a blueprint laid down by police commissioner William J. Bratton in the mid-nineties which says that targeting small crimes results in lowering the rate of major crime (a theory which has never been adequately proved).

Two plain-clothes policemen, Officers Damico and Pantaleo, pulled up in an unmarked car and set about trying to arrest Garner. Garner was unhappy, feeling he was being unduly victimised, and when they tried to take his arms to cuff him, he pulled them away: 'Don't touch me please. Do not touch me.' What happened next is history only because Garner's young friend Ramsey Orta filmed it on his phone. As backup arrived, Officer Pantaleo put Garner into a chokehold (banned by the NYPD), and the pair of them staggered back into the glass window of Bay Beauty Supply before Pantaleo wrestled the much bigger Garner to the floor. He and other officers appeared to pile onto Garner, pushing his face into the pavement and kneeling on his back as they cuffed him. Then they held him there, ignoring him as, on eleven occasions, he uttered his now famous words: 'I can't breathe.' At 4.34 p.m. Eric Garner was pronounced dead. As with Bernhard Goetz thirty years earlier, a grand jury was assembled, but they decided that Officer Pantaleo had no charges to answer. He was moved to desk duties but not punished in any other way, with newspapers reporting on his substantial salary increase and forthcoming wedding. Garner remained dead.

Leaked files seem to suggest that prior to killing Garner, Pantaleo had a history of disciplinary problems. The leak, from a source at the New York City Civilian Complaint Review Board (CCRB), appeared to show 'seven disciplinary complaints and 14 individual allegations lodged against him. Four of those allegations were substantiated by an independent review board.' One of the cases substantiated, in 2012, was a stop-and-frisk and the punishment handed out by the NYPD was 'instruction'—the lowest penalty it could give, basically some re-training. As Jonathan Moore, the lawyer who represented Garner's family, points out, 'What happened on July 17th with Eric Garner was a bad stop and frisk.' To put Pantaleo's disciplinary record into some sort of context, the website which received the leaked information, ThinkProgress, analysed CCRB data for serving NYPD policemen. By their calculations, only 4.9% had received eight or more complaints. Furthermore, as very few of these complaints tend to be substantiated by the CCRB (witnesses, unsurprisingly, aren't so keen to testify against police officers), Pantaleo is one of an even more select band. Only around 2% of serving New York cops have two or more substantiated allegations against them.

You might wonder, then, how it was possible that Officer Pantaleo was still on the streets. A brief look at his colleagues at the 120th Precinct perhaps offers a clue. The 120th polices the North Shore of Staten Island and is renowned in the borough for its heavy-handed tactics and use of stop-and-frisk. According to a report in the New York *Daily News*, the precinct was ranked 11th in the whole city for substantiated complaints to the CCRB between 2009 and 2013, despite being 33rd in terms of size of population. On top of this, in 2014, the narcotics squad in the 120th had seven of the city's top ten most-sued police officers and fourteen of the top fifty. Brett Klein, a New York lawyer specialising in civil rights and police brutality, summed up what he saw as the attitude of the 120th. 'There's a culture in Staten Island, and particularly this precinct,' he told the *Daily News*, 'where you break the rules and serve your own interest and don't have to worry about getting into any kind of trouble.'

Nor was Eric Garner's the first death of this kind. Not even on the 120's patch. In May 1994, only six months after the release of *Enter*, Ernest Sayon, a small-time drug dealer known locally as Kase (or possibly Case), died outside Park Hill Apartments in the course of being arrested. 'A coroner's report says that the cause of death was suffocation because of pressure on his chest and neck while he lay in a prone position with his hands handcuffed behind his back. The report adds that he had bruises and a three-quarter-inch gash on the back of his head.' Shortly before he was killed, K/Case could be seen in the background of a music video for a local group who were starting to take off. The video was 'C.R.E.A.M.'

This particular revelation—and the way in which it related to more recent events—came courtesy of the RZA when he was asked about the killing of Eric Garner. RZA was obviously angry about what had happened and, in particular, about the grand jury decision not to press charges. 'Not just the one cop, all those cops should have been indicted. Those are the guys who give us the non-value of black life.' But, in keeping with his increasing spirituality, he was eager not to draw wider conclusions. When the interviewer asked him if Garner's real crime was to be Black, RZA responded that 'racism is played out for me. I have seen the quality of people from every race, and the lack of quality from every race. Everybody do some bullshit, everybody do some goodness.'

Maybe RZA was struggling with the fact that at that time he was also promoting a record entitled *A Better Tomorrow*, an album that was supposed to foster a new optimism, both internally within the Clan and in society more generally. A couple of weeks earlier, Ghostface Killah gave an interview and he didn't sound so constrained by either spirituality or marketing considerations. 'It's like, enough is enough,' he told *Vice*. 'It's bad enough that we did 400 years of slavery. And y'all motherfuckers are still doing the same shit. Y'all still killing motherfuckers like it ain't nothing. Choking motherfuckers out. So I feel that whatever they feel out there, in Ferguson, in Staten Island, wherever, that's on them. Let them do whatever the fuck they want.' Pushed further, Ghost continues: 'If you ask me, I think it should be an eye for an eye. On everything. You kill me? Somebody kills you. My perspective is like Malcolm X's. You know what I mean? It ain't time to be marching around when people are dying. If it's on, then it's on. Let's strap up and do what we gotta do,' he concludes. 'These motherfuckers, they don't respect peace. They respect violence.'

20TH CHAMBER
A SHAW THING

The process of recording a hip hop song in the mid-nineties usually worked as follows. The producer, using whatever sampling and sequencing equipment he had in his apartment or home studio, would develop a rudimentary beat and either give it out to the relevant rappers on tape or have them round to work on their lyrics. A rough version would possibly be recorded, a demo, using a domestic-quality two- or four-track recorder. Then, when the money was available, courtesy of a record label or some saving up, the band would go to a professional recording studio to lay down the vocals and to properly mix the beat (perhaps re-sampling any particularly troublesome elements or adding extra layers where necessary). Even this was a step change from previous practice, when producers would turn up at the studio with a box of records and a clear (or less clear) idea of which sections to sample and how they might fit together, a remarkable process of mental or theoretic editing having already taken place.

Having recorded a whole album's-worth of material, the producer and possibly other members of the band (everyone turned up in the Wu-Tang's case) would go to a mastering house. Mastering is the last part of the recording process, the final polish. Originally this would have been the point at which the record was cut to vinyl, and the process was designed to manage any sonic elements which that format might find hard to cope with (very high frequencies tend to distort, stereo bass can make the needle skip and so on). By the mid-nineties, though, it served the joint purpose of preparing the music for LP and for CD and so the aim had become to balance out sonic discrepancies in general (both of volume and of tone), within particular tracks and across the album. The idea was to make the record overall sound as big and as loud—as 'good'— as possible. Of course, this is an aesthetic judgement and as such, different standards apply depending on the music being mastered. The issue of loudness—or the feeling of loudness—is affected by how much you want to give prominence to low frequencies, for instance. Emphasise the bass and the rest of the music will sound relatively quiet. Roll off some bass and you may get an impression of increased volume but at the cost of some of the recording's warmth. By the mid-nineties, mastering houses had sprung up that specialised in the raw, rhythmic sound of hip hop (or had reinvented themselves to do so). *Enter the Wu-Tang* was mastered by Chris Gehringer at the legendary Hit Factory.

On the day, RZA turned up with a stack of VHS cassettes of classic Hong Kong action movies, saying he wanted to sample them for interludes. Mastering engineers hate this kind of thing. Even to this day it would be considered above and beyond the call of duty, but in the mid-nineties there were technological problems with it, too. There were no multi-track facilities at a mastering house back then. The artist would arrive with the mixed-down DAT tape (and before that, an open-reel tape) and the engineer would work directly from that. Adding in further, overlapping sounds, then, was a difficult process, one relying on judgement and feel. All the same, Gehringer gave it his best shot, recording the relevant segments on to DAT and then cueing them in by hand at the appropriate moment as he recorded the mastered tracks across.

There are four movies sampled on *Enter the Wu-Tang*. There might have been more if not for the technical difficulties of adding them. Vocal samples ended up being used from *Executioners from Shaolin* (1977), *Five Deadly Venoms* (1978), *Ten Tigers of Kwangtung* (1979), and last but not least, *Shaolin & Wu Tang* (1983). In addition to these main vocal samples—at the openings of 'Bring Da Ruckus', 'Da Mystery of Chessboxin', 'Wu-Tang Clan Ain't Nuthing ta F' Wit' and 'Conclusion'—RZA makes liberal use of sword-fighting sounds and incidental music on 'Protect Ya Neck', 'Wu-Tang: 7th Chamber' and 'Shame on a Nigga', so that these films provide part of the aural backdrop across half the tracks on the album. Of these four films, three are produced by Shaw Brothers and the fourth is a Shaw Brothers production in everything but name.

Shaw Brothers' dominance of the Hong Kong movie industry has few comparisons in world cinema. For well over a decade, Hong Kong film was synonymous with the company, which pumped out over 800 films, 'razzle-dazzle musicals, death-steeped melodramas, *huangmei diao* Chinese opera adaptations, super-noir swordplay sagas, gristle-ribboned urban thrillers, and some of the greatest martial arts movies ever made'. The firm also built a movie complex of some 850,000 square feet, with twelve separate sound stages, labs which could process up to 48,000 feet of colour film per day, plus housing for the 500 resident staff, including fifteen screenwriters. Operating at every level of the industry, from running movie theatres, to distributing films, right down to opening an acting academy, Shaw Brothers kickstarted a renaissance in Hong Kong cinema. Even when a serious rival finally arrived on the scene in the form of Golden Harvest and its Bruce Lee movies, the new company was run by Shaw Brothers alumni.

The family behind Shaw Brothers had been involved in film for over thirty years before the birth of its most heralded company. In the mid-1920s, first son Runje Shaw started up Unique (Tianyi) Productions from the family base in Shanghai and put one of his younger brothers in charge of the theatres they owned in three territories: Shanghai, Hong Kong and Singapore. Almost straight off the bat, Unique was producing a film every month and by the start of the thirties would become one of the first companies in the region to start making films with sound. Film-making operations (and the valuable equipment required) were moved to Hong Kong just before the Japanese invasion of Shanghai in 1937, by which time, the second son, Runde, had taken over. In 1938 the company was re-named Nanyang Studio—literally *South Sea*, to reflect the economic importance to the firm of the overseas markets of the Chinese diaspora. Runde, in fact, was always more interested in the economic aspects of the business than he was in the romance of movie-making. He returned to Hong Kong after the war and continued to produce films, but combined this with a cost-cutting agenda which meant that in 1957 the youngest brother, Run Run, decided it was time to come home from Singapore and sort things out. A year later, he and his brother Runme started Shaw Brothers (incidentally, due to their positions among the Shaw children, Runme and Run Run were known as Mr Three and Mr Six).

In the words of Chang Cheh, the legendary film director who made many of Shaw Brothers' best-known films, 'Run Run Shaw... rewrote the history of Hong Kong cinema.' It was him who built Movietown in Clear Water Bay, from where Shaw Brothers produced 300 films in just twelve years. They achieved their dominant position by abandoning synchronised sound recording in favour of post-production dubbing (which would later have a definitive effect upon the aesthetic of their martial arts output), tailoring the amount of sex and violence in each film for different markets, and keeping as much of the business in-house as possible. This was old-school Fordism in action, capitalism as behemoth. Sometime Shaw director Ho Meng-hua remembered the weaknesses of the system as well as the strengths. 'Sometimes it borders on the ridiculous,' he said. 'Once a director was shooting a street scene and he needed a few dozen eggs. Instead of going to the canteen and get them himself, he had to get them through the procurement department. So the whole crew just waited there for the procurement people to get them those eggs.'

The films which most interested the Wu-Tang Clan fall into a very particular strand of Shaw Brothers output.

In October 1965, the company declared a 'colour *wuxia* century!' *Wuxia* films already had a long tradition in Hong Kong cinema—movies about knight errants, where *wu* means violence and *xia* means chivalry. These were Cantonese-language productions which had long begun to seem stuffy and old-fashioned. Now, influenced by the international success of the James Bond films, Spaghetti Westerns and ultra-violent Japanese samurai movies, Shaw Brothers decided to give a staid genre something of a Mandarin-language re-boot. Or at least Chang Cheh did. Of the four films sampled on *Enter*, two are directed by him and the others are directed or produced by the man who started out at Shaw as his stunt co-ordinator, Lau Kar-leung. Releasing more than ninety films in a career that lasted over forty years, Chang's influence on Hong Kong cinema and beyond is hard to overstate. The aesthetic he created is acknowledged as a formative influence by John Woo—who considered him his mentor—and, as Woo's work has gone on to influence the action genre globally, Chang's place in world cinema is assured.

The film critic Sek Kei calls Chang Cheh (Zhang Che) 'Hong Kong cinema's Mao Zedong'—not for his politics but for the radical way in which he altered movie-making in the territory. Starting out as a scriptwriter for Shaw Brothers, Chang claimed that he was responsible both for the decision to use post-production dubbing and, later, for launching the 'colour *wuxia* century'. As it happens, the two are connected. Post-production dubbing allowed for greater freedom both in the way fight scenes were staged and, crucially, in where cameras were placed. It liberated directors from the static shot and opened up a range of possibilities which the colour *wuxia* century would exploit, not least the use of handheld Arriflex cameras and zoom lenses. Indeed, Chang Cheh was a cinematic innovator, 'employing a repertoire of visual signatures including slow-motion, zooms, flashbacks and flash-forwards, canted angles, overhead shots, hand-held camera, black-and-white sequences amid glorious Eastmancolor'.

To this technical expertise, Chang Cheh added the belief that 'two things symbolise men—violence and sex' (though, in all honesty, he seems mainly interested in the first). His films are renowned for a *yang gang* (staunch masculinity) aesthetic so pronounced that the films are popular with 'martial arts mavens and text-explicating homo-erotica aficionados alike'. Packed with disembowelments and 'vertical death', 'the deepest impression one gets is the almost inevitable and ritual *danse macabre*'. The director himself tried to put a more poetic gloss on proceedings, stealing some of the garments usually wrapped around the other great director of the era, King Hu. 'I use dance to express pain, emotion, and death,' Chang said. 'The whole world is immersed in violence, how can cinema avoid it?'

The 'colour *wuxia* century' films weren't an immediate success. King Hu's *Come Drink With Me* did well in 1966, but it wasn't until July of 1967 that Chang Cheh's *One-Armed Swordsman* started breaking box office records. The timing is key. April 1966 saw the Star Ferry riots break out in Kowloon. Ostensibly over a rise in the price of tickets for the ferry—which at the time was the main point of connection between the two halves of the city on either side of the bay—in reality this was the first anti-colonial uprising for a decade. Only one protestor died in this initial flurry of violence, though tear gas was used and over 300 people were jailed. However, the pro-Communist riots which ran from May to December the following year claimed a further fifty-one lives. Amid the fervour of the Cultural Revolution, this was the most concerted attempt by Maoists based in Hong Kong to bring an end to British rule. As Maynard Parker reported in *The Atlantic*, 'the colony's Communist Chinese stores now plaster their windows with pictures of British police brutality, with crepe-draped portraits of slain Communist agitators, and with Maoist slogans urging the city's four million Chinese to "paint Hong Kong red from the earth to the sky".'

One-Armed Swordsman was released at the very height of the riots, in 'a fragile, unstable city', and the director's vision chimed with what was happening around him: 'Chang depicts a turbulent, chaotic world which provides no sense of security.' His characters are regularly dismembered and mutilated, and we 'find the hero's mutilation echoed everywhere'. Meanwhile, in Hong Kong, tied-up corpses were washing up from the sea. 'Within the last few weeks,' Parker's report continues, 'more than 1500 bombs have been planted. Although most have been duds, some have exploded, and civilian casualties from bombings have become a new fact of life in Hong Kong.' As Stephen Teo points out, 'in Zhang's *yang gang* universe, the patriarchy is either weak, corrupt, or in the process of decline'—a vision of an uncertain, collapsing world. Seeing the success of Chang's films, other directors and companies followed suit. Shaw Brothers themselves produced only four *wuxia* in 1966, but they were up to twenty-six by 1972. And everyone's *wuxia* 'became more violent and bloody', reports Law Kar. 'Suspense, rebellion, blood, violence, psychosis and perversity were poured in.'

It's not hard to see the parallels between Hong Kong

in the late sixties and New York in the late eighties. But the connections run deeper, somehow. Chang was criticised for an over-reliance on the violence (*wu*) of the *wuxia* equation rather than incorporating the balancing concept of chivalry (*xia*), and much the same could be said of hip hop at a time when the emphasis of the music was moving away from the more overtly politicised and *conscious* rap of the late eighties. Moreover, Chang stood accused of misogyny (a charge which he embraced with a little too much glee for it to be just a provocative stance), and in particular of airbrushing women out of his narratives. In an observation which could quite easily apply to *Enter the Wu-Tang*, Teo points out that 'Zhang's male bias has led to many situations where the female sex is largely absent... or where present, is immaterial'. But there's a broader point here, too. When Teo describes Chang's 'idiosyncratic personality (a mixture of romanticism, perversity and vulgarity)', he could equally be delineating a mainstream understanding of hip hop in general—and the Wu-Tang in particular—although that may be because the collision of romanticism, perversity and vulgarity serves as a definition for popular culture more generally.

Of course, if you were to ask RZA who his favourite director is, there's a good chance he wouldn't choose Chang anyway. Instead, he might opt for the director of *Executioners from Shaolin* (and the producer of *Shaolin & Wu Tang*), as well as of classics like *Eight Diagram Pole Fighter* and, of course, *The 36th Chamber of Shaolin*. Lau Kar-leung (Liu Jialiang) is the purist's choice because 'martial arts experts declare Lau's to be the most authentic combats ever staged for film'. That's as it should be. Lau was the son of an extremely able martial artist and started his own training very young. The family relocated from Guangzhou to Hong Kong in 1948, when he was eleven, and he and his dad immediately began looking for movie work. From the age of thirteen Lau was performing as an extra and during fight scenes, leading to a long-running series of Wong Fei-hung films[20] with his father. He moved into fight choreography in 1965 and—along with his partner Tong Kai—soon became the go-to man for Shaw Brothers in general and for Chang Cheh in particular.

In 1975 he finally fell out with Chang and branched out on his own, specialising at first in a kind of comic kung fu romp which, if not actively lampooning Chang's work, certainly let some air and light back into the genre (and created the space for Jackie Chan's rise later in the decade). If one theme holds his output together, though, it's his commitment to kung fu itself and, in particular, to 'stressing the training process as a necessary stage of growth'. It makes for an odd narrative structure in many of his films, where the entire middle act of conventional Hollywood diktat is devoured by a man trying to master a skill, or series of skills, at great length. In *The 36th Chamber of Shaolin*, for instance, San Te (Gordon Liu) starts training 36 minutes into the film and finishes 36 minutes from the end, the acquisition of the necessary skills to kick Manchu ass and avenge his father, teacher and friends having taken up just a little over 36 minutes in the middle (around thirty-eight or thirty-nine, actually). Then—just when you think the whole skills-improvement part of the film is over—

20 Wong Fei-hung was a real-life Cantonese martial artist and Robin Hood figure who lived from 1847 to 1924, and whose story has been told in full or has featured in well over one hundred movies.

he has to train some more, as well as plan and strategise for another ten minutes or so, in order to deal with what's perhaps best seen as a human resources issue. And it's the emphasis on training, on sparring, on acquiring the necessary level of expertise, strength, resilience and sheer *chops*—what has been known in jazz since Charlie Parker as *wood-shedding*—that seems to animate the Wu-Tang Clan's imagination. They're not interested in violence per se. They're interested in control.

21ST CHAMBER
36 SYNOPSES OF DOOM

1. A student rebellion is brutally put down and the sole survivor flees to a monastery in the mountains. Over the next seven years, he absorbs and masters all of the monks' fighting techniques but he can't forget what happened. When he's asked to begin teaching, he leaves instead to instruct ordinary people so that they can hit back against their oppressors—though his fellow monks find this pathetic. As the revolution gathers pace, he returns to defend the monastery and, that accomplished, is allowed to start teaching the proles within its sacred grounds.

2. An evil lord learns the secrets of two divergent fighting styles from a spy. He's no good at either,

though, so he arranges a punch-up between the temples who teach them in the hope this will lead to all-out war. Fingers crossed they'll all end up dead. Two childhood friends get chosen to fight each other, so the plan's going wonky even before they find out the lord killed the sister of one of them—who, it turns out, was the other's lover. It's complicated, of course, but it's simple, too.

3. The man's father and most of his brothers have been killed in an ambush and now he wants to become a monk—even if it means giving up his spear and learning to use a staff instead. He never meant to use his new technique in anger, but word reaches him that the men who killed his father have now kidnapped his sister. The monks know what's going to happen next.

4. He has to find five highly trained and dangerous men and work out which of them are good and which of them are bad. The bad ones kill one of the good ones and, when they reach their final confrontation, the baddest one also starts killing the other bad ones. He's that bad. The only good one dies helping our protagonist to kill another bad one and then the baddest. He's left on his own with all the money, determined to do something good.

5. A spoilt prince gives up everything to become a monk. He walks to another country, where people are suspicious because of the colour of his skin. The miracles he performs win them over,

though. He's got so used to pilgrimage that even
when he's dead his spirit goes wandering.

6. A boy wants to avenge his father but isn't very
   good at fighting. Eventually, an old man teaches
   him the importance of strategy as well as
   physical skill. Using this new understanding—
   and with the old man's help—the geek finally
   defeats his foe.

7. His father committed suicide because he couldn't
   win and now he's taking revenge for him.
   Unfortunately, when he defeated one monk, he
   didn't bank on the monk's friend managing to
   get the dying cenobite somewhere to be healed
   and trained so that he could come back and
   finish off this angry outsider.

8. The monk fights the white-haired villain twice
   and loses twice. He needs to learn a new, more
   fluid style or else this floating granddad with
   retractable gonads will beat him up again. In
   the end it all comes down to acupuncture.

9. The occupiers seem intent on humiliating our
   hero and his countrymen but he's not going to
   stand for it. If they give him a sign to wear he
   will make them eat it. If they mock him he will
   beat them. If one of his compatriots works for
   them, he will hang his corpse from a lamp post.
   And if they kill his master, he will kill theirs.
   He will end up being betrayed, of course.

10. A nameless man is brought before the king to tell him how he has killed the three assassins who tried to murder said king. The king says he thinks the nameless man has killed only one of the three, in order to get close enough to kill the king himself. The nameless man says he hasn't even killed one—he's faked all the deaths so that he can come and slay him. Unfortunately, the king convinces the nameless man that the only one of the three assassins who ever got near enough to bump him off was also philosophically correct—any perfect warrior has no desire to kill. The nameless man agrees. They execute him.

11. He's been poisoned and knows he's going to die. The only way out is to deliver the same killer blow he used many years before, the one that ruined his life. He does it, but without the force to finish off his opponent. Then he dies. The opponent declares him the winner.

12. He's meant to get the girl but he can't (who'd be a monk?). Instead, when he, the girl and their other ally finally kill the evil lord, he slips the ally the anklet which matches hers and proves they're destined to be together. That way, at least the girl will get married to a good man.

13. The Emperor is secretly poisoning his second wife, who is secretly having sex with her stepson, who is secretly having an affair with his half-sister, though the last two don't know they're related. The Empress, on the other hand, knows

she's being poisoned, so she plans the Emperor's overthrow with her eldest son (the Emperor's second). The Empress's daughter tells the Empress's stepson about the mooted rebellion and in revenge, the Empress tells her daughter that her lover is her brother. The Emperor has the girl killed. The youngest son then kills the eldest son before being defeated and whipped to death by his father. The second son leads the Empress's rebellion. He fails. The Emperor says he was his chosen successor and still can be if he helps him poison the Empress, the boy's mother. He refuses and kills himself. The Empress has burnt her bridges somewhat.

14. Having watched his father being killed by an ex-colleague bandit, the boy hides with a bunch of travelling acrobats and trains himself up to take his revenge. Even though his dancing is borderline-embarrassing, in the end the girl helps him.

15. The old champ has more or less given up on fighting but he can't let the local gang leader force the girl to marry his son. Once the son is dead the old champ has to deal with the consequences—and so does his former student, who the gang leader suspects.

16. Not only do they fight in different styles, they've spent years warring over which style is best. But now they're being invaded, it's time to unite and defend their country.

17. The problem with being a hitman with a heart of gold is all the collateral damage. Nevertheless, even the cop chasing you is impressed that you'd give up your eyes for the girl you blinded. The goodwill of law enforcement doesn't necessarily keep you alive, of course, but it guarantees you some kind of revenge.

18. If you're going to fuck people up it's best to kill them. Instead, four of the villain's victims get together, learn to compensate for their disabilities, and return to kick the living daylights out of him and his metal-fisted son. Though not without cost.

19. Workers of the world unite—but be sure that the martial arts monk who has offered to defend you isn't just a dodgy builder who promises more than he can deliver. Luckily, the builder feels bad, goes to the monastery, accidentally learns all the moves while doing some renovation work, heads back to town and kicks the boss's ass using the detritus of his day job.

20. Returning to help the snobs who chopped off your arm just so you can refuse to take over and instead become a farmer with your girl.

21. It's one thing being a bad student, it's another giving away all your school's secrets to the enemy, then inviting your fellow scholars to a party where they're going to be poisoned. Luckily, your headmaster turns up and knocks

heads together. You learn your lesson, they learn theirs. Good boy.

22. If you help a man who's been tricked, had his hands crushed, had his sister forced into prostitution, found himself making his living with a performing monkey, had the monkey killed and then had his sister killed, you'd better be prepared to show some commitment.

23. Wily foreigners are stealing priceless artefacts and only an inebriated boxer, a fishmonger, the fishmonger's apprentice and a girl who wants to get intoxicated too can save the day. Actually, mainly the inebriated boxer.

24. There are three reasons for our hero to go to the island. The first is the cover: to fight in the tournament. The second is the job: to help catch the drug-smuggler running the tournament. The third is personal: the drug-smuggler's henchman killed the hero's sister and he's fighting in the tournament. Our hero kills the henchman. Then, with the help of prisoners and fellow competitors, he kills the drug-smuggler's army. Last, the drug-smuggler.

25. A broken man rises again and eventually triumphs but it doesn't work out too well for anyone else. His master is massacred, his betrayer is blinded and killed, his new master is also murdered and then the murderer beheaded. The singer who loves him is slaughtered by the villain, the villain accidentally stabs his son to

death and then the villain takes his own life,
distraught. But at least the foreigners get what's
coming to them.

26. Daddy's been looking after him, buying off his
    opponents, but he ends up fighting someone
    whose father simply executes troublesome
    opposition. More or less everyone ends up dead,
    but the first rich, spoilt son beats the second
    rich, spoilt son, so that's all right then.

27. The doctor tasked with catching a social bandit
    finds out the social bandit is also a doctor—the
    one who's looking after him. The bad guys drug
    the social bandit's assistant and capture the first
    doctor's son. The two doctors go to the palace,
    both disguised as the same social bandit, and
    they rescue the boy. He and his father leave
    town, the second doctor and his assistant
    get married.

28. The most evil of the occupiers has poisoned the
    man's master and fitted him up for the murder.
    If the man kills the most evil occupier, the
    occupiers will invade the rest of his country. He's
    willing to die to stop that happening. It turns out
    that won't be necessary. Have cake, take cake,
    eat cake.

29. Poisonous goings-on.

30. He's a contrary one, this fella. He becomes a
    monk in order to exact revenge, fails to become
    a monk because of his need to exact revenge,

exacts revenge and then becomes a monk,
leaving the woman who saved his life and who
loves him—and who he loves!—to mourn her
now-dead father (his fault, really) on her own.

31. Two best friends are expelled from school. One
joins the army, the other becomes a rebel. The
soldier betrays the rebel. The rebel goes mad.
When he recovers his sanity he invents a new
fighting style and uses it to kill his old buddy.

32. A famous swordsman is sent to rescue a
kidnapped magistrate from bandits. Except the
famous swordsman is actually a swords*woman*,
and the magistrate's sister. A drunken beggar
helps her, but luckily he's not what he seems,
either. He tries to end things peacefully and fails,
she and her troop of female warriors end things
violently, with much more aplomb.

33. Should your loyalty be to your belief system or
to the man who saved your life? If your belief
system means your fellow cult members think
they can stop bullets with their bare chests, then
the answer should be obvious.

34. He loves the woman even though she's a violent
fugitive. Better with a paintbrush than a sword,
he helps set up the ambush, anyway, and she
kills her pursuers then heads off to a monastery.
When he tracks her down she hands over their
baby and says goodbye. Luckily, the people who
were after her attack the artist and the baby so
she has to come back to protect them.

35. The general double-crosses the monks, making it look like the northerners have killed the southerners in their sleep. They're all about to start killing each other when they realise they've been tricked. Against all but insurmountable odds, some escape to warn the other monks.

36. If a guy makes a fool of you at your own wedding and, in addition, slaughters your guests, you can either try to kill him yourself or befriend people who might *actually* be able to kill him. The latter isn't the most honourable course of action, but it's certainly the most effective.[21]

---

21 Plots taken from *36th Chamber of Shaolin/Master Killer*, *Shaolin & Wu-Tang*, *The Eight Diagram Pole Fighter*, *Five Deadly Venoms*, *Master of Zen*, *Mystery of Chessboxing*, *Legend of the Liquid Sword*, *Fists of the White Lotus*, *Fist of Fury/The Chinese Connection*, *Hero*, *Fearless*, *Martial Arts of Shaolin*, *Curse of the Golden Flower*, *The Fearless Young Boxer/Method Man*, *An Old Kung Fu Master/Ol' Dirty and the Bastard*, *Tiger and Crane Fist/The Savage Killers*, *The Killer*, *Return of the Five Deadly Venoms/Crippled Avengers*, *Return of the 36th Chamber/Return of the Master Killer*, *One-Armed Swordsman*, *Disciples of the 36th Chamber*, *Mad Monkey Kung Fu*, *Legend of the Drunken Master*, *Enter The Dragon*, *King Boxer/The Five Fingers of Death*, *The Prodigal Son*, *Iron Monkey*, *Fist of Legend*, *Legend of the Fox*, *The Shaolin Temple*, *Tai Chi Master*, *Come Drink With Me*, *Legendary Weapons of China*, *A Touch of Zen*, *Unbeatable Dragon/Invincible Shaolin*, *Last Hurrah for Chivalry*.

22ND CHAMBER
THE SUN RISES IN THE EAST

The Wu-Tang Clan didn't discover kung fu movies in a vacuum. They weren't even the first to relate them to hip hop (think of those early Grandmasters). The place of those films in African American culture had, in fact, been cemented at least twenty years before the release of *Enter the Wu-Tang*. As David Desser points out, 'the appeal of the genre for black audiences is not hard to gauge. Outside of the blaxploitation genre it largely replaced, kung fu films offered the only nonwhite heroes, men and women, to audiences alienated by mainstream films and often by mainstream culture. This was the genre of the underdog, the underdog of color, often fighting against colonialist enemies, white culture, the Japanese.' But even that doesn't quite do it, because Black America's love affair with the Orient goes back further still. Perhaps it began as a reactive tactic, a deliberate reversal of colonialism's half millennium of divide and conquer. After all, White America's Othering of the East had its own home-grown correlation in the Othering of Black America, and no one was more aware of this shared inheritance than Black Americans.

You can see it in the teachings of the Nation of Islam. The clearest, perhaps most literal sense of it can be found in the emphasis placed by the NOI on the 'Asiatic Black Man', a concept carried over wholesale to the Nation of Gods and Earths: 'The original man is the Asiatic Black Man, the Maker, the Owner, the Cream of the Planet Earth, the Father of Civilization, and God of the Universe.' In this key concept, all non-White peoples are classed as Black and the geographical opposition implied by that 'Asiatic' is central, a subversion of Western Orientalism. 'The people of Islam are the black people, and their numbers are made up of the brown, the yellow and red people, called races.' To put it even more clearly, Fard Muhammad 'saw Africa as a mere extension of Asia; blacks were Asiatics not Africans'.

The roots of this conceptual system come from even further back, in the founding stories of Drew Ali's Moorish Science Temple (where Fard Muhammad is held to have begun his religious journey). Drew Ali argued that 'the nationality of the Moors was taken away from them in 1774 and the word negro, black, and colored, was given to the Asiatics of America who were of Moorish descent'. This pan-Asianism was one of the key reasons for the FBI to investigate first Drew Ali's organisation in World War I and then the Nation of Islam in World War II. Elijah Muhammad even preached during this second global conflict that the Japanese had built a spacecraft which was orbiting Earth waiting for

the instructions from Allah before destroying the evil
White race (an off-kilter ancestor of the mothership
connection). 'The key of civilization was and is in the
hands of the Asiatic nations,' Drew Ali proclaimed. 'Asia,
the East, the place where the sun rises, is the place of
origin and home of the Moors.'

This is not just a strand within African American
religious thought, though. As Sundiata Keita Cha-Jua
has pointed out, the identification with Asia is a strong
current running through radical African American
politics from W.E.B. Du Bois to the Black Panthers.
Indeed, Du Bois' classic statement that 'The problem
of the twentieth century is the problem of the color
line' actually continues, 'the relation of the darker to
the lighter races of men in Asia and Africa, in America
and the islands of the seas'. The Panthers, meanwhile,
reinterpreted the struggle of Black people in America
as essentially anti-colonial, their lack of any possibility
of nationhood meaning that history had 'bestowed an
obligation upon us; to take socialist development to its
final stage, to rid the world of its imperialist threat, the
threat of the capitalist and the warmonger'.

Edward Said, in his classic work *Orientalism*, referred
to 'the main intellectual issue raised by Orientalism.
Can one divide human reality,' he asked, 'into clearly
different cultures, histories, traditions, societies,
even races, and survive the consequences humanly?
By surviving the consequences humanly, I mean to
ask whether there is any way of avoiding the hostility
expressed by the division, say, of men into "us"
(Westerners) and "they" (Orientals). For such divisions
are generalities whose use historically and actually has
been to press the importance of the distinction between

some men and some other men, usually towards not especially admirable ends.'

Is there a way to reconfigure Orientalism without falling into the trap outlined by Said? Melvin Gibbs argues that the Five Percent Nation (i.e. the Nation of Gods and Earths) offers one solution, by making the division in human reality a schism based on enlightenment. For the Five Percenters, he says, '"Asiatic" is a state of being as well as a physical description. The Five Percenters teach that those in whom knowledge dawns, rises and completes itself are "gods," are "Asiatic," are "suns."' Certain formal similarities have been elucidated between Five Percenter philosophy and Chan Buddhism (the Chinese form of what is more commonly known in its later, Japanese incarnation as Zen Buddhism). As Fanon Che Wilkins puts it, they 'share nonsecular interest through their professed atheism and radical engagement with the realities of the material world and everyday life'— or, to put it another way, both of them are practical philosophies rather than religions. Furthermore, RZA himself comes to see Chan Buddhism as something which melts division. 'I think all barriers of discrimination, of segregation are dissipated by Chan Buddhism. For anybody who truly understands what Chan is, they know that there are no separations.'[22]

Perhaps what distinguishes Five Percenter thought, though, is how radical its syncretism is—it's possessed not just of an ability, but of a hunger to fold in and swallow up other philosophies and teachings in much

22   In Chamber 19 we talked briefly about RZA's resistance to explanation in terms of race and racism. This Chan Buddhist dissipation of barriers is presumably what lies behind that resistance.

the same way as hip hop folds in and swallows up other musics. In fact, it's arguable that it's the syncretic character of each that made them such good partners, caught in a kind of symbiotic blurring of borders where it's unclear which is subsuming which and where the boundaries between them lie (it's possible to argue, in fact, that they're not partners at all, but facets of the same thing). In other circumstances this might be seen as a reflection of the autodidactic roots of both, but this urge or drive becomes something qualitatively different when enshrined as principle. 'One of the characteristics of Allah is that he absorbs and emits knowledge,' Gibbs goes on to explain. 'This allows for highly innovative and idiosyncratic religious expression. No one person's interpretation of the faith is accepted as valid for anyone other than himself.'

All of which is a long way of saying that the minds of the members of the Wu-Tang were primed on many levels to receive kung fu from the Shaw Brothers—and receive it they did, with all the force of revelation.

In *The Tao of Wu*, RZA recalls showing *The Eight Diagram Pole Fighter* (1983) to a bunch of his friends. *Eight Diagram* is another of Lau Kar-leung's movies for Shaw Brothers, once again starring Gordon Liu. A large family is betrayed by a treacherous general. All the sons are killed except two. One of the surviving brothers goes mad, and the other hides out at a Shaolin Temple high in the mountains and tries to become a monk—something his fellow monks aren't too keen on. Eventually, after his sister is captured, he goes back on the warpath and the monks finally help him. It looks beautiful, if slightly old-fashioned, all bright colours and carefully composed widescreen shots, more than a little kitsch even during the exquisitely choreographed fights. The final sequence in particular is superb, involving monks de-fanging the bad guys as they have learnt to do with the wolves of the mountains. The dubbing is, as ever, appalling, with people… pausing in the odd… est places. It's fun—good entertainment.

Now here's RZA's recollection: 'Before we were an hour into it, something strange happened… People got real quiet, some n***as even started crying.' This does seem strange, an extreme reaction to the film which is hard to understand. As to why they started crying, RZA's explanation is simple, if not completely convincing. It's 'because that movie is… a reflection of the reality we were all living,' he claims. 'We were living in a place torn apart by wars—neighbourhood against neighbourhood, dealer against dealer—a place where you see people get killed or go crazy every week, a place where the bonds you make are almost stronger than blood.'

What if we suggest that something other than plot made those viewers cry, something they didn't necessarily directly notice—not the similarity between their story and the one presented, but a connection buried in the aesthetic, in how that story was presented? Based in Hong Kong and making movies for the Chinese population spread out across the South Sea (the name of the second iteration of their company, Nanyang) and America, Shaw Brothers created a cinema of diaspora, with sets and costumes designed to evoke a 'lost China—destroyed by history and thereby permitted to flourish as myth'. In 1989, crushed in an impossible set of social relations, under daily attack, homeless at home in 'a place where you see people get killed or go crazy every week', some new myth would be the very least the 'bunch of dudes [who] came over to my crib to get high and watch flicks' might be looking for from the art they consumed. As the poet Geoffrey O'Brien continues in his 2004 overview of the Shaw Brothers oeuvre, 'the movie offered not just a story but an extension of place to alleviate the claustrophobia of exile'.

The African slave diaspora is perhaps unique among diasporas for the violence with which its victims were removed not only from their physical homes but from the home of their culture(s), giving double meaning to Huey Newton's emphasis on the 'lack of the possibility of nationhood'. Perhaps this goes some way to explaining the eager embrace by the offspring of that diaspora of other narratives and mythologies of diaspora, from the Israelites of the Old Testament onward. It could be argued, in fact, that to the extent that both hip hop and the Nation of Gods and Earths (Five Percenters) formalise or systematise this eager embrace of other narratives/mythologies/sounds, both are themselves distinctly slave-diasporic in character.

Beyond this, though, O'Brien points out many formal aspects of Shaw Brothers productions which would resonate with anyone with more than a passing interest in hip hop. First, 'in the manner of the storytelling tradition in which they are rooted, attention is sustained rigorously from instant to instant, with overall structure less important', while the overriding ambition is to fashion 'an unbroken intensity of spectacle'—which sounds very much like what the creators of a hip hop album aim for. Next, when referring to the many fight scenes the martial arts end of Shaw Brothers' output contains, O'Brien points out that 'every duel is partly verbal. The wily magistrates, unctuous monks, and rapacious bandits are all masters of both hypocritical courtesies and baroque vituperations.' Hip hop has never been great at courtesies, hypocritical or otherwise, but it compensates with a specialisation in baroque vituperation. Last, in an observation which perhaps shows why the films were embraced by a largely working-class audience (hence setting their status as 'low' or 'popular' art) and would appeal to and encourage rappers, O'Brien observes that 'these were movies in which skill was central, a skill not merely alluded to but constantly demonstrated'.

We can push all this further still. In his study of the cinema of this former colony, *Planet Hong Kong*, David Bordwell draws on Eisenstein's theory of expressive movement—the notion that an actor's job is to transfer emotional experiencing to the audience through his or her actions. Sitting watching, the viewer 'reflexively repeats in weakened form the entire system of the actor's movements'. These motor responses will condition the audience's emotional reactions. 'By impelling us to invest ourselves physically,' he claims, 'the movies prepare us to emote.' Bordwell argues that the skill of the martial artists involved and that of the editors working on Hong Kong action films together elevate the effects of expressive movement to new heights. 'The very cogency of the presentation has invited us to feel something of what supreme physical control might be like'.

As we've already noted, this 'supreme... control' might in and of itself be appealing to people who feel an absence of control as one of the defining characteristics of their existence. But going beyond this, the British academic and theorist Paul Gilroy has emphasised the *kinesic* nature of communication among 'post-slave populations'—largely because this was a way to communicate among peoples who both didn't share a common language and whose languages were, in any event, largely banned; a way to communicate, moreover, that wouldn't be understood by the slave masters or, often, even noticed. Gilroy quotes the Martinican writer Édouard Glissant: 'It is nothing new to declare that for us music, gesture, dance are forms of communication, just as important as the gift of speech.'

Perhaps this historical legacy makes a post-slave population more sensitive to the highly complex and stylised movement found in Hong Kong cinema—and hence more capable of being moved by it. The kinesically literate will *read* these films at a much higher level, will feel Fifth Son's anguish through his actions as he practises his pole fighting, lashing out at the natural world around him. RZA himself has developed a theory that makes this connection concrete, historical, though the result is much the same. 'Kung fu movies resonate well with us because of our natural resonance with them,' he says. 'It's been said that Damo [*sic*] was part of the Davidian tribe of Africans who migrated to South India. And the martial art forms that he taught and learned were originally from the continent of Africa. I think our original ideas, dance and culture makes us predisposed to communicate with the martial arts.'

There's another possible area of kinesic contact as well. Bordwell argues that Hong Kong action films are inherently rhythmic. This is something which goes back to their roots in Peking Opera, 'rhythmic theatre... [where] the orchestra is led by percussion', but also to the basis of kung fu itself. He quotes Bruce Lee, who said that the martial artist should 'move like sound and echo', a sentiment you could imagine RZA (or Lee Perry for that matter) agreeing with wholeheartedly.

'Directors,' he goes on to say, 'rhythmicize any scene they can', both through the action itself and through the use of cutting as a highly patterned intensification of this action. Returning to Bruce Lee, Bordwell tries to specify the rhythm type used and, drawing on the way martial arts movement breaks down into 'sets', talks about Lee's 'drum tap micro-rhythm of pause/burst/pause'.

Few producers have used the drop-out with as much élan as the RZA does on *Enter the Wu-Tang*. As the name implies, the 'drop-out' (or 'cut') is when the producer mutes all or most of the music on a track and allows the rapper's verse to flow on its own, usually for a bar. It was quite an old-fashioned technique by the time the Wu came through, having been extensively utilised by Marley Marl in his work for Big Daddy Kane, among others. But RZA employs it less for punchlines or end lines than to introduce. On 'Bring Da Ruckus' for instance, Ghostface Killah, Inspectah Deck and GZA are each welcomed by a two-bar gap in the beat, a chance for them to run through their first 'set' of moves and establish their characters. Throughout the album, RZA alters the line of attack through the patterning of these cuts, keeping the rhythms flexible and bouncing.

Possibly the best example of the use of the 'pause/ burst/pause' rhythm comes at the start of 'Wu-Tang Clan Ain't Nuthing Ta F' Wit'. The only percussive element in the first four bars is a loud, gnarly—and initially disorientating—finger snap, which sits on the off-beat between the second and third beats of the bar. When RZA takes the first verse, this finger snap is slowly joined by an initially quiet, fading-up snare hit on the two and four, but the drum break proper (together with the bassline which animates the whole tune) only

comes in after he's already been rhyming for four bars—
a third of the entire verse. The traditional notion of an
MC's 'flow' is enshrined in the term itself, suggesting
a certain fluidity, but RZA uses this four-bar build-up
to attack in a series of short, rapid, staccato bursts,
both intensifying and becoming more fractured as the
verse progresses, so that it reaches its height only at its
quickfire ending: 'Me fear no one/Oh no/Here come/
The Wu-Tang shogun/Killer to my eardrum.' There's
a gap between each sharp flurry as the RZA resumes
his 'stance' like a Shaolin master. Although it sounds
wild, aggressive and loose, it actually fits everything
together with the harmony and panache of a carefully
choreographed dance routine. And no one who wasn't
steeped in martial arts movies would even have thought
to try it.

— — —

Hip hop is a martial art. This is the key insight of the
Wu-Tang Clan. It is not *like* a martial art. It doesn't
share certain practices with a martial art. It actually is a
martial art. The dictionary definition of 'martial art' is
a sport or skill that originated as a form of self-defence
or attack. The legendary MC and thinker KRS-One
describes hip hop as 'a mental survival tool for the
oppressed', and once you begin to tunnel down into
what that might mean, the parallels become clear.

First we need to deal briefly with what we mean by
'hip hop'. Hip hop is a culture with its roots in a youth
movement—and in particular in that movement's use
of music, dancing, art and fashion—growing outward
from the South Bronx area of New York City in the
mid-to-late seventies. From very early on, hip hop was
conceptualised as consisting of four elements: DJing,

MCing, B-boying and Writing (graffiti). Although some graffiti writers have questioned whether their art form is indeed a part of hip hop, many more have been happy to view it as a strand within this larger practice. All four of these 'elements' have a martial aspect which we'll explore here. As Joseph Schloss puts it in his magnificent book on b-boying in New York, *Foundation*, 'Battling is foundational to all forms of hip-hop culture, and the articulation of strategy—"battle tactics"—is the backbone of its philosophy of aesthetics.'

We'll start with b-boying, where the martial element of the practice is clearest. B-boying (widely known as breakdancing or breaking) is the dance element of hip hop, that 'B' referring to the break, the section of rhythmic explosion in a record which hip hop DJs liberated and extended through their manipulation of vinyl records and two turntables. Starting as a competitive gang dance used as a prelude—or occasionally an alternative—to fighting, the form is bound up in its essence with a sense of competition. Indeed, Schloss states that 'breaking was a form of allegorical fighting that came very close to actual fighting, not only in its physical movements, but in its social and symbolic dimensions as well'. Drawing on the work of the anthropologist Thomas A. Green, Schloss even goes as far as to suggest a direct link between b-boying and African martial arts, all of which 'are commonly carried on to the accompaniment of percussive rhythms. Therefore, even sympathetic outsiders often described African martial play and practice as merely tribal dance.'

Even if this link back to pre-slavery Africa seems too essentialistic, it's undeniable that the very heart of b-boying lies in competition, that, in fact, b-boying is a dance form inseparable from its competitive element: 'battling is the best venue for b-boy style, and the best b-boy style is that which is most suited for battling'. To unpack this, the suggestion is that what is considered most aesthetically pleasing within b-boying is exactly that which will be most effective in a battle. This might sound limiting, a kind of utilitarian curtailment of human ingenuity. Anyone who has seen the baroque contortions and rhythmic grace of a b-boy in full flow will know that this isn't the case. Schloss concludes that 'regardless [of] where it came from historically, b-boying does serve martial purposes. It teaches many abstract aspects of fighting, including balance, speed, physical discipline, judging and controlling spatial relationships, reading an opponent's emotional state, and anticipating his actions.'

Graffiti might be the hardest element to make a case for as a martial art until you look at the context in which all these cultural forms gained pre-eminence. In the early seventies, the Bronx was convulsed by gang violence. The traditional narrative of hip hop has been that it grew up as an alternative to this violence, though Jeff Chang (considered the most complete historian of hip hop since the release of *Can't Stop Won't Stop*) argues that this was motivated less by some righteous reaction than it was by boredom with the cycle of fear, bravado and violence. All the same, if you see graffiti as, in the first instance, a marking out of territory, and hence a kind of *capturing* of territory, then it begins to operate according to many of the same sort of rules as the gang violence it replaced. While b-boying might be obviously, explosively confrontational, *writing* is a stealth art with something of the myth of the ninja about it. The point is for only your mark, your distinct tag, to be seen. Traditionally held to start with TAKI 183 bombing (i.e. painting) his tag on a train on every subway line in New York and hence going 'All City', the mystery surrounding this legendary figure became part of the glamour of the form. These were not warriors so much as assassins or snipers. It's notable that Inspectah Deck— usually considered the quietest and most understated frontline member of the Wu-Tang—started off in hip hop throwing up his REBEL INS tag.

But as more and more people caught the bug, the assassins began tripping over one another. There were enforcement crackdowns and disputes over space, a squeezing of the arena in which writers operated, leading to a second wave of increased competition in which *getting up* was, on its own, no longer enough. You now also had to look distinctive, to destroy *toys* (as amateurs were known) with the pure magnificence of your style. David Toop puts it well in his classic *Rap Attack*, writing a precarious history of the form as early as 1984: 'Each borough shout[ed] its identity with a distinct calligraphic style – bubble letters in the Bronx, a Manhattan style, a Queens style and a Brooklyn style called "Wildstyle". Artists formed into clubs, an extension of the established neighbourhood gangs... and bombings upped their daring from nervously scribbled tags into inconceivably detailed wall-size murals or completed trains, painted at night in the yards.'

Seen in this way, what else is graffiti but a martial, a *warlike* art—art concerned at root both with the conquering of territory and, at one and the same time, with the glorification of the conqueror? Placed in the context of a city where poor people—often

184

the generational victims of colonialism—owned
nothing of the landscape around them, this reverse
colonisation takes on a glorious, quixotic, middle-
fingered ebullience. Indeed, this claiming of the city can
be clearly seen reflected in the mirror of nervousness,
discomfort and anger among other subway users and in
the developing battle with these 'vandals', which found
its most violent reaction in the actions of—and then the
support for—Bernie Goetz.

We're not going to look too closely at battle rhyming at
this point. For now, we'll satisfy ourselves by quoting
Jay-Z, quoted by Adam Bradley in his *Book of Rhymes*,
more because of what he says than because of who he is:
'People compare rap to other genres of music, like jazz
or rock 'n' roll. But it's really most like a sport. Boxing to
be exact. The stamina, the one-man army, the combat
aspect of it, the ring, the stage, and the fact that boxers
never quit when they should.' Central to this practice
is the African American tradition of signifying—or
Signifyin(g)—which we will deal with in some detail
later.

For now, let's concentrate on DJing. We could
turn to the phenomenon of turntablism as another
pure example of the battle aesthetic, one which Mark
Katz, in his book *Capturing Sound*, compares both to
the signifying tradition and to the jazz cutting session,
where bands would battle for supremacy in displays
of 'vicarious violence' and Kid Ory, the legendary New
Orleans trombonist, would instruct his band to sing to
the opposition, 'If you don't like the way I play, then kiss
my funky ass!' But really, the battle DJ is only a small
subset in the world of the hip hop DJ, and what should
interest us most here is the DJ as exemplified by the

pioneers: DJ Kool Herc, Grandmaster Flash and Afrika Bambaataa.[23] What we learn most clearly from these three is that DJs in traditional hip hop are generals. They marshal their forces with the aim of building their territory through winning more and more supporters. They trade in mental geography, in size of army, in *reach*.

As we saw earlier, Kool Herc was the pioneer of hip hop culture. His parties were distinguished by a Jamaican attitude to soundsystem culture, including his rudimentary, Americanised toasting, and also by the quality of his soundsystem itself, which was reputed to be the loudest around. Grandmaster Flash, coming through after Herc, needed some innovation to tempt partygoers to his events. At first he focused on Herc's sloppy mixing. Although Herc was the innovator who began playing breaks on loop, he would do this by eye, lifting the needle and dropping it back as near to the start of the instrumental section as he could manage. It was messy, hit and miss, and Joseph Saddler (as Flash was then known) didn't like it. Instead, he apprenticed with Pete Jones, a disco DJ who could mix continuously and seamlessly. Saddler quickly worked out that Jones could do this because he had a switch on his mixer which allowed him to hear, through his headphones, the record which wasn't playing through the speakers. Saddler went away and built his own headphone switch and, using this, found he could extend the break perfectly, again and again and again—indefinitely, if necessary. As Jeff Chang recounts,

23   In 2016, Bambaataa was the subject of some very serious allegations of sexual abuse, allegations which he strenuously denied. These allegations don't alter his material role in the birth and growth of hip hop, which is all we will deal with here, though they may, in time, alter our attitude towards aspects of that birth.

though, his breakthrough wasn't the immediate hit he had expected. Rather than freaking out and dancing their asses off, the crowd just stood and stared, trying to comprehend what he had done: 'And I cried for like a week.'

Once he'd recovered, Flash realised that innovation on its own could be a handicap as well as an advantage. He began recruiting MCs as part of his crew. Their job was to tell the crowd what Flash was doing, to take the audience by the lyrical hand and lead them to the floor. He brought in b-boys, too, who through their brilliant, frenzied dancing would show onlookers an ideal of how they might move. He even recruited the young Grand Wizzard Theodore, who is generally believed to have 'invented' scratching.[24] And in this way, Flash both made it plain to the crowd how they were supposed to react to his innovations and rendered Herc's show haphazard and old-fashioned.

Bambaataa, meanwhile, had a readymade crew to draw on. A warlord in the Black Spades gang, when he started his own Universal Zulu Nation he had a pre-existing constituency spread out across a bigger area of the city than most of his competitors, who were constrained by geographic gang-logic. But, drawing on the example set a few years earlier by the Ghetto Brothers in the wake of the gang truce of 1971, Bambaataa opened up his parties to people from all gangs, on the understanding that there would be no fighting at the party, only 'peace, unity, love, and having fun'. It's hard not to see this as using the weight of an

---

24 While working at the Bauhaus in Berlin in the early 1930s, László Moholy-Nagy, Oskar Fischinger and Paul Arma experimented with 'running the recordings backwards against the stylus to scratch new patterns. The results, however, were largely unsatisfactory.'

opponent (violence) against itself, by taking the very structures which formalised and maintained that violence and using them to get rid of it. In keeping with this approach, Bambaataa also played a broader variety of music than most DJs, taking breakbeats from anywhere he found them, regardless of genre—as long as he could find an explosion of rhythm locked inside, the tune went into his set. With the labels soaked off so that rival DJs couldn't see what he was playing, he too innovated, expanded the parameters, demonstrated his philosophy through music—and mystery.

Both Bambaataa and Flash approached Herc's dominance strategically. They assembled what they needed, deployed it in a calculated fashion and accrued a tactical advantage as a result. This might, on the face of it, sound a long way from a standard conception of a martial art, but that's not necessarily the case. What it sounds most reminiscent of is the game of chess. RZA has long been renowned as a very keen chess player, and he states that 'chess is also a martial art. It's about combat and directing chi.'

The latter part of that second sentence points to a problem we will have to deal with. We can explain the 'meaning' of *chi* simply enough, though possibly rather vaguely. But can we understand what is meant by 'directing chi' without some internal involvement in the practices in which the attempt to direct chi is made? Or, to put it another way, can you sit outside hip hop and comment on it? Or is it only from within the practice of a martial art that you can understand that martial art?

23RD CHAMBER
SOUND TECHNIQUE

It sounds like the plot from a Shaw Brothers epic. The two young students have sparred with each other and impressed their masters and are told that one of them will get a chance to compete for real that night. They bide their time, celebrating their good fortune, revelling in the atmosphere of the arena. They're made to wait and then they're made to wait some more. At first the excitement of being there keeps them focused and they spend the hours plotting their moves, thinking up strategies, figuring out how it's going to work. But slowly, tiredness creeps up over them, the wine and the smoke make them feel muggy and heavy, their eyelids like lead shutters over bloodshot eyes. The noises of combat recede and… one of them awakes to find that the other has taken the very last slot.

This is the legend of how Masta Killa became the

ninth member of the Wu-Tang Clan, an appropriate one considering that his MC moniker is taken from the original US title for *The 36th Chamber of Shaolin*. The man left lying on the couch, wondering what might have been, was Killah Priest, who spent the start of his career styled as an 'unofficial' or associate member of Wu-Tang and who eventually broke out of the box and went his own way. Instead, the opportunity went to Elgin Turner, who had only recently decided he was even interested in rapping.

It's one of those strange certainties of Wu-Tang that it seemed inevitable and proper that they would and should have nine members. There's the whole theory that the 36 chambers of the title refers to the two ventricles and two atria in the hearts of the nine men in the group. There's the numerological significance of the number nine to followers of the Nation of Gods and Earths: 'Born. To bear is to bring into existence. It takes nine months to make a baby. Nine is the only number that multiplied by itself ends up with the same product.' And yet there were only eight MCs on 'Protect Ya Neck' and only eight members are listed on the back of the original album cover. Masta Killa was the one added to the eight to make the group complete, so late in the day that there's no mention of him at all anywhere on the art.

One hundred and fifteen words spread over sixteen bars of music, lasting just under thirty-six seconds, right at the end of 'Da Mystery of Chessboxin''. This is Masta Killa's total contribution to *Enter the Wu-Tang*, rated by some aficionados as among the best verses on the album. It's a well-structured, dense little burst of language, showing the influence of the GZA, who had been mentoring him. In the space of sixteen lines, Turner uses twelve words of three or more syllables (by their very nature often the hardest to rhyme with). The next highest on the track is Inspectah Deck, with seven. Ghostface, who comes through with a particularly wild verse, doesn't use any. Masta Killa peaks with the couplet, 'Evidence indicates that's his stature / Merciless, like a terrorist, hard to capture', the repetition of three-syllable words at the start of each line a good example of using relative complexity to generate a certain swinging momentum.

You can almost hear the novice rapper's nervous-ness at the start of his verse, when he struggles slightly over the 'penalty' at the end of his first line. He's come out slightly too hard, and like an over-eager horse at the first fence of a race, he stumbles, almost falls. Obviously if you're the potential ninth member you don't get too many chances to get things right—it's a one-take type of situation. It's arguable, in fact, that Killa pushes a little hard throughout, reaching for the barked Wu house-style rather than the slightly more mellow approach to phrasing he would later adopt. At the moment, though, his main aim is to prove he fits, that he belongs. He tops and tales his verse with kung fu references, beginning with an oblique nod to the Praying Mantis kung fu style developed at a northern Shaolin temple at some point in the sixteenth century, itself twisted into one of the standout boasts of the record when he describes himself as 'the Master of the Mantis Rapture'. Then, right at the end of his bars, he sneaks in a reference to the Centipede, one of the baddest of the quintet of bad asses who make up the *Five Deadly Venoms*. By the time he reaches these last lines you can hear a new poise, a confidence to his delivery. He's nailed it and he knows it.

Perhaps the standout section of Masta Killa's verse, though, is an extended metaphorical riff concerning his flow. Flow, as we've already noted, is that hard-to-pin-down concept in which rhythm, rhyme and cadence come together, occupying much the same place in rap mythos as the notion of swing does in jazz. Masta Killa claims that his flow—also referred to as a technique—attacks his victim's immune system, a metaphorical nod to the AIDS virus. While the terminology comes from that source, though, what follows is a little more science-fictional. The victim of this rap attack doesn't even notice the assault until it's too late. By then he is paralysed and screaming, his brain exploding with 'the pain these thoughts contain'—as elegant an expression of language as a system for the transmission of sensation as you're likely to come across, and an example of battle-rhyming at its most intricate.

A technique, of course, is a method of doing something, an art. Traditionally, despite their common Greek root, we are advised of the difference between a technique and a technology, as if one is something we do and the other is an object existing independent of our needs, wants and hopes. A technique is a skill, the experts tell us, technology an iPhone. But, in fact, as Jonathan Sterne has pointed out, a technology is nothing more than a collection of techniques, a 'social phenomenon'. Appropriately for us, he demonstrates this with the example of hip hop's use of the turntable. 'At what point is the phonograph a playback device and at what point is it a musical instrument? These are not questions that can be answered "scientifically" or through *a priori* reasoning. Rather, the analytical categories of "instrument", "playback device", and even "use", "function", or "role" are derived in reaction to the practices affiliated with the technology – the practices that essentially *make* the technology in the first place.' Sterne's aim, of course, is in some way to demystify our notions of technology, to show it as a human practice like any other. We choose to misuse him. Hip hop, as an intricate collection of techniques, is a technology (think again of KRS's 'survival tool'). Part of what we're doing in this book is figuring out what the exact purpose or use of this technology is.

Hip hop also operates, as Masta Killa suggests, in the same way as a virus, in that it is non-living and complex and can only grow and replicate inside (or between) living things. The set of techniques which constitute it can be taught and learned, hence internalised—and the act of internalising those techniques alters both how you view them and how you view the rest of the world. It changes you. Of course, by this definition, the technology of language is a virus, too—according to William Burroughs, one from outer space. In fact, Burroughs sees language as malevolent, much as in Masta Killa's rhyme. 'The word is now a virus,' he says. 'It is... a parasitic organism that invades and damages the central nervous system. Modern man has lost the option of silence... Try to achieve even ten seconds of inner silence. You will encounter a resisting organism that *forces you to talk*. That organism is the word.' That's the theory, anyway, though of course, in fact, viruses are not malevolent. They just are. It's only in relation to humans that we decide to give them some form of agency. And, in many cases, we could just as well find them to be helpful, beneficial to our well-being.

It's Masta Killa's final rhyme that runs all foes through. Turner flips syllables to bounce 'of a centipede and injure' off 'any motherfucking contender'—leading to the inevitable impalement of all comers. The truth with any rap is that you have to hear it to feel it, that it's a technique of the body ('Man's first and most natural technical object, and at the same time technical means,' wrote the French sociologist Marcel Mauss, 'is his body.') In this case, the New York accent makes the line run something like '*uh*f *uh* cent*i*p*ee*de *a*nd *i*njuh / *e*ni m*uh*th*uh*f*uh*king contend*uh*'—those repeated 'uh' and 'i' sounds syncopating the two lines with all the casual brilliance of a kick drum and snare rattling out the break, a sound to which we react entirely physically. If that doesn't, in Masta Killa's phrase, *erupt your brain* then you must be immune and nothing ever will.

24TH CHAMBER
THE DEUCE

It's not just what, it's *where*. Think about a book or a
film or a record that you love—one that you've loved
for a long time. Chances are, you can remember your
exact location, who you were with and what you were
doing when you first came across it—particularly if the
encounter came in those borderless teen years, before
you'd learnt to properly police the boundaries between
your thoughts and your emotions, the objects you
consumed and the place of their consumption. The whole
will remain tied together, twisted round each other in
your mind, for ever. To fully understand the importance
of the kung fu movie in the imaginative universe of the
Wu-Tang Clan, you have to know that they watched
many of those films for the first time on 42nd Street,
known as 'the world's most notorious street', also 'a hub
of sensational thrills, vice and excess', alternatively,

a 'cesspool of filth and obscenity'. This isn't incidental to their vision, but part of it. That's how love works.

The history of 42nd Street is the history of American entertainment, see-sawing back and forth across the line of transgression with all the vim of a street hawker, that old battle between puritanical self-control and mass consumption played out with neon light and body fluids. It could be argued, in fact, that 'legitimate' entertainment followed the innovations of 'illicit' entertainment in the growth of Manhattan, much as it has done more recently with the internet, the two knotted together, symbiotic, or one like a parasite preying on the other (but which?). In his history of the road, *Down 42nd Street*, Marc Eliot shows how a combination of patterns of construction and an evolving transport network gradually led, by the 1890s, to the area around 42nd Street becoming the centre of New York's sex district. 'By the last decade of the nineteenth century, brothels had become a familiar, if not welcome, fixture in every neighborhood in Manhattan, but nowhere were they more popular than in the streets that surrounded Long Acre Square.'

Long Acre Square was soon to be re-named Times Square, when the *New York Times* moved to a new building there in 1904, attracted in part by new subway links, as well as by its proximity to the Grand Central Terminal (opened in 1899). The arrival of the subway 'helped transform the all-but-deserted-after-dark stretch of sex and crime into a round-the-clock commercial boulevard of naughty gentility where every type of family entertainment conducted business alongside the hottest and most infamous brothels this side of Paris'.

By 1900, theatres were popping up, first Oscar Hammerstein's Victoria, then a whole host of others. The two sides of the entertainment equation (transgressional versus legitimate) fed off each other, merged into one another, sucked and slurped at each other's trade. 'The business of sex dramatically increased its visibility on the city's newest and most popular drag as its purveyors moved to compete for... newly available entertainment dollars.' Prostitution in Manhattan is said to have peaked in 1905, when 150,000 men a day were paying for sex in the borough. The number of theatres showing live entertainment peaked at around the same time, reaching almost eighty, a figure which dropped to around thirty after the financial crash of 1929 and hit zero by the middle of the Second World War. The theatres were cursed, destined for nothing but demolition, from the moment that D.W. Griffiths' racist 'classic' *Birth of a Nation* premiered at the Liberty in 1915. You can interpret that as karma or just the result of inviting in the very thing which will kill you, a dinosaur becoming friends with a mouse.[25]

Events conspired. The first *talkie* was shown in 1927 and the stock market crashed in 1929. A bunch of over-leveraged theatrical proprietors went to the wall and their theatres became the property of the banks. The banks sold them to anyone who would pay and the people who would pay started showing burlesque. From 1913—when Flo Ziegfeld launched his *Follies* at the New Amsterdam Theatre—right up until the Great Crash, sex was being sold on the main stages of 42nd Street, though

25   It has been claimed that key scenes in *Birth of a Nation* were filmed on Staten Island, specifically around what is now Park Hill. These claims probably aren't true.

always in respectable form. Once the Minsky brothers took over the Republic and premiered performances like *Panties Inferno*, respectability went out of the window. Those more traditional theatres left on the street spearheaded a campaign against burlesque, which was charging less than them and pulling in huge crowds. In the ensuing fray (burlesque was outlawed from the street by the time America entered the war) both sides took their eye off the real threat—cinema.

There are many economic advantages to showing a film instead of putting on a live show, but perhaps the key one for any single establishment is that you can fit in as many 'performances' as there are hours in the day. The Great Depression saw the birth of the grind house, cheap tickets and a rolling and continuous selection of films making it 'the rare business designed to prosper in hard times'. In 1936 the Rialto, for instance, was selling around 4,000 tickets a day. As the theatre only held 600, this worked out at just under seven full houses in each twenty-four-hour period. The audience for these cinemas began to change, too, away from the wealthy glamour-seekers flocking to the smarter cinemas on Broadway towards a poorer, more working-class clientele who were mainly concerned about price and less worried about the rest of the experience. This new audience developed even further after the Second World War, so that 'these became the theaters of choice for the culturally disenfranchised, the hipsters, students, cineasts, minorities, gays, the unemployed', says Eliot, 'anyone looking for a bargain-basement admission into the world of wide-screen dreams'. In particular, it was before the war that New York's African American community began its relationship with 42nd Street, where the movie theatres were more welcoming of their custom than the plusher establishments on Broadway.

The billing for shows on 42nd Street, though, was often far more lurid than the film itself could deliver on, and soldiers and sailors returning from Europe and the far East had often developed stronger tastes in sex and pornography. Bookshops began to move into the area, offering under-the-counter fare to fill this gap between expectation and reality. As city administrators tightened up zoning and drove some of the movie theatres out of business, real estate prices fell and more bookshops moved in. In 1957 and then again in 1966, the Supreme Court relaxed previous standards on obscenity, making it easier for pornography to flourish. In 1965, Martin Hodas bought some nickelodeons—booths which played short films when you inserted a coin. On a whim, he put 'stag' films in these machines and placed them in bookshops on 42nd. Within a short space of time he was turning over $40,000 a week in profit. The 'Bill Gates of 42nd Street porn' didn't last too long, though. The mob noticed how well he was doing and decided to move in. By 1973, the Gambino family controlled the whole business. And where the mob goes, things get ugly. As the seventies progressed, the Gambino family realised that the real money was to be made selling drugs and that pornography was merely the way to tempt the customer in. 'We looked around and found ourselves in the middle of one great big ready-made marketplace,' explained the anonymous Mr X when interviewed by Marc Eliot. 'If we could get them to come down to see naked girls, we could also sell them drugs.'

The 1985 assassination of Staten Island resident Paul Castellano was bound up with exactly this change in Mafia priorities. John Gotti, who ordered the hit, believed that the family's future lay in drugs and pornography—on 42nd Street. 'His immediate goal was to intensify the family's involvement on 42nd Street by increasing the output of hard-core magazines and videos and stepping up the street distribution of coke, heroin, and marijuana.' Castellano, an old school traditionalist, wanted to keep the emphasis on concrete, construction and extortion, a position which sealed his fate. The effects of this change in priority were instantaneous. As Bill Daly, head of the federally funded Midtown Enforcement Project, put it, 'by 1987 the street had degenerated even further than anyone thought it could go, into a place where everything and anything went down twenty-four seven. Prostitution, muggings, drugs, pedophilia, white slavery, bestiality, the more disgusting and degrading, the more prevalent.'

When an attempted clean-up finally began in the late 1980s, those leading it were shocked to find several minority groups protesting against the changes, arguing that it would destroy 'the city's only legitimate, if de facto, black and Hispanic entertainment "zone"'. An anthropologist was hired to prove that in fact Black children were the most likely victims of sexual abuse on 42nd and that Black adults were more likely to be robbed, stabbed or raped. There was a suspicion that the Gambinos were behind the protests. All of which ignored the reality of the situation on the ground. The fact was that since at least the sixties, the police had been treating the Deuce (the block of 42nd Street between Seventh and Eighth Avenues and the epicentre of Daly's degeneration zone) as a 'moral leper colony' which they largely refrained from policing. Considering the vexed relationship between the NYPD and the city's ethnic minorities, it's of little surprise that those communities might prefer to take their chances in this anarchic zone than deal with law enforcement's often violent prejudices. There's a lesson here which is obvious to the powerless, less clear-cut to the powerful: lawlessness is preferable to those oppressed by the law.

RZA first saw *The 36th Chamber of Shaolin* on TV in June 1983, when he was fourteen. He had already been interested in Shaw Brothers' kung fu output for the best part of five years, since he'd watched *Five Deadly Venoms* at the age of nine, though in different interviews he alters where he might have seen it. Sometimes he says it was on television, the yin to 42nd Street's yang, and indeed there was a lot of it about as the eighties trundled into view. From 1981, WNEW on Channel 5 showed kung fu in its 'Drive-In Movie' slot every Saturday night and, as Joseph Schloss puts it, 'pretty much every single hip hop artist that I've met from that era used to watch that show religiously'. But on another occasion, RZA states that 'in 1979, my cousin took me to 42nd Street to see some kung fu movies and I was blown away. We started going every weekend after that. There was a movie directed by Chang Cheh called *Five Deadly Venoms* and when I saw it, I was *totally* geeked out.'

In this second version, RZA was a regular visitor to 42nd Street from the age of ten to at least the age of seventeen, when he saw the third film in his holy trinity, *Shaolin & Wu Tang*. This was 1986, when the Gambino rule of the Deuce was at its height and the Street was living up to Police Captain Alan Hoek's billing of it as the 'anus of the country'. 'We wound up at this funky little porno theater on Forty-second Street and Seventh Avenue,' RZA recalls, 'one with a back chamber the size of a classroom, where they showed kung-fu flicks and bums came to sleep. That's what we were about to do, but as we walked in—cold, drunk, and tired—I caught the tail end of a movie that woke me right the fuck up.'

It's not a coincidence that RZA remembers the cinema being the size of a classroom. This is where he learnt. He learnt about 'discipline and struggle... the warrior technique... the brotherhood, the soul'. But perhaps most importantly, 'it was through these films that I was able to see and feel from a non-Western point of view'. His classroom, though, is the back room—the back *chamber*—of a porn theatre. This is a familiar theme—the education of the Black American in unpromising, unusual circumstances—which goes back at least as far as Booker T. Washington and also fits with RZA's own all-American Buddhist belief that 'living where shit floats... [is] a source of precious wisdom'. But in truth, for a sensitive, highly intelligent teenage boy, knowledge and wisdom must have become plaited with sex and drugs, lawlessness with morality, discipline with debauchery.

This background hum of the illicit—the way that righteousness French kisses criminality—is what animates the Wu-Tang Clan. If you only watch the movies you won't really get it. You need to imagine them being watched with 'hard seats, sticky floors, and menacing audience members'; you need to imagine 'a turgid waft of human sweat and canned Lysol that hung tough around the nostrils'; you need to see in your mind the crowd of 'young boys, young girls, grown men dressed as women, old men dressed as young boys—all openly hustl[ing] themselves out on street corners, while drug dealers s[ell] nickel bags... without any apparent fear'. If you can sense all this and mix it through the widescreen celluloid tales of young monks and warriors taking vengeance against their oppressors, shipped here from the other side of the world, then you might just be getting close.

Of course, this also places the Wu-Tang's music at a very specific point in time. In December 1993, the month after the release of *Enter the Wu-Tang*, Michael Eisner, the head of Disney, signed a letter of agreement with the New York city and state authorities to take over and revamp the New Amsterdam Theatre, where Ziegfeld's Follies had high-stepped across the stage—largely at the cost of those authorities. Within ten years, most of the strip had been re-built and little of the lawlessness of the legendary 42nd Street was left. If you walk the Deuce now, it's hectic and tacky and desperate, but the sex industry and its attendant ills are largely gone. It's worth thinking back to where we started, though, to the porousness of teenage consciousness, in particular to the way that sex can finagle its way into the most unlikely events or experiences. Perhaps the Deuce has reached some kind of adulthood, expressed in its more 'family-oriented' attractions. But if so, this wouldn't mean the sex is gone, just that it's just much better hidden, sublimated into Disney musicals, schlocky tourist attractions and the pixels of those Times Square advertisements in much the same way as the Wu could be said to sublimate it into gun talk and sword fights. After all, have Eros and Thanatos ever found a better place to make out than in the back row of a grind house on 42nd?

25TH CHAMBER
CASH RULES

The Wu-Tang Clan is a hierarchy not a collective. There
are ties of family and friendship operating, plus a
meritocratic belief that the dopest MC is worth the
most space (although this, of course, opens up a whole
other debate which isn't our focus here). There is the
issue of leadership, with RZA telling the story of how he
gathered the Clan together and persuaded them to give
him control of their careers for five years—a narrative
which surely owes as much to the inexorable logic of
fairy tales as it does to lived reality. Then there is the
issue of fate—who was there at what session, who flaked
out, who was prevented from attending. As we've seen,
only two MCs get a track to themselves on *Enter the
Wu-Tang*, and we can rank the whole Clan by the total
number of lines they have on the record (not including
choruses or introductions). The list runs as follows:

Method Man (143), Raekwon (122), Ghostface Killah (117), Inspectah Deck (103), The Genius/GZA (101), Ol' Dirty Bastard (85), Prince Rakeem/RZA (74), Masta Killa (16), U-God (12).[26]

Masta Killa isn't even listed on the back of *Enter* as a member of the group but he still has more lines on the record than U-God. There are good reasons for this. U-God was in prison for much of the recording of the album and so largely missed his chance to shine. The RZA, though, is very keen on using the machinations of fate as justification, so maybe that's how he wanted it. There's a backhanded criticism in RZA's assertion that U-God is 'the Four-Bar Killer because he can kill it in four bars'. In effect, it places him as a hook-writer, someone who can hype a crowd but doesn't necessarily have the skills to carry a listener's attention for longer. It's true, as it happens, that his line 'my hip hop will rock and shock the nation' sounds so good in his gruff, basso voice that it was used as the hook on an otherwise instrumental workout from British producer Luke Vibert. (It also echoes Sydney Brown's lyrics for the song version of Scott Joplin's 'Maple Leaf Rag': 'I can hypnotize this nation / I can shake the earth's foundation'.) His rhymes have an uncomplicated scansion which make them stick in your head and he has a good, distinctive voice (though arguably it's the altos, with their high, nasal deliveries, who really stay with the listener). His aim is less to dazzle with his

26 If you include choruses and introductions etc, RZA jumps up to second and GZA comes up alongside Ghostface, while Method Man stretches his lead. But is a repeated chorus worth as much as a verse? How about unrhymed shout-outs? And, anyway, who is deciding where the line breaks come? The major point is that this statistical analysis should be taken with a pinch of salt. But U-God remains at the bottom however you look at it.

brilliance and originality than to get your head nodding, and that's a noble tradition in hip hop, arguably truer to the form's roots in parties than the work of any wordy show-off.

Although it took him over six years to release his own solo album and another six years for the follow-up (and in all honesty the critical consensus on them wasn't exactly red hot), he made some crucial contributions to later Wu-Tang albums, including his verse on 'Impossible' (on *Wu-Tang Forever*). In fact, in that instance, you could almost argue that he's going out of his way to lose his easy-going reputation. Much the same could be said of his recent lawsuit, claiming over 2.5 million dollars in unpaid royalties. And this lawsuit ties in quite nicely with the central reason for talking about U-God here.

In his book *The New Analog*, Damon Krukowski (of the group Galaxie 500) traces how the introduction of the player piano in 1898 shaped the way in which royalties are paid on music to this day. The player piano—into which you inserted a perforated roll of paper so that the piano would bash out music mechanically without any great effort on your part—was a major catastrophe for the companies that printed sheet music and held the copyrights in most popular songs. The player piano market was growing rapidly and the manufacturers of these miraculous new machines didn't see why they should pay royalties to the sheet music publishers, as they didn't use their product. The latter took the former to court for breach of copyright and lost, a judge arguing that 'a musical composition is an intellectual creation which first exists in the mind of the composer... It is not susceptible of being copied until it has been put in a form which others can see and read.' As there was no copying of the sheet music involved in the creation of a player-piano roll, no one's copyright had been breached. Once this had gone all the way to the Supreme Court without producing a result the sheet music manufacturers were happy with, they turned their attention to lobbying Congress, which was eventually persuaded to pass the Copyright Act of 1909, which introduced a system of compulsory mechanical licences: 'Mechanical reproduction of music (i.e., piano rolls, gramophone records) could continue without permission of the [sheet] music publishers, so long as those publishers were paid a statutory royalty for each "mechanical reproduction" derived from use of their music.' It took until 1972 for this system to be applied to recorded music, but it means that 'mechanical royalties' are still paid out for compositions to this day.

In effect what this means is that recording an original song creates two copyrights (the composition and the specific sound recording) and hence generates two separate streams of income for musicians. First, there are the royalties generated by the recording company from the manufacture and sale of a particular recording. Then there are the royalties paid for the use of the composition. These will include mechanical royalties paid by the record company to the publishing company (as in the legislation of 1909); also performance royalties paid by radio and TV stations and even bars and pubs for playing the composition; synchronisation rights (when music is licensed by the record company for use in a particular setting, such as in a film or an advert); and print rights. Not every musician clearly understands this, particularly when they are starting their career, and this can cause all kinds of headaches, not least because money from the publishing side of the equation, for the composition, often outweighs what makes its way back to musicians from exploitation of a specific recording. And all the money relating to the composition goes to the songwriter, not the group.

You can take an example of this which seems completely clear and find ambiguity in it. Bob Dylan wrote 'Like A Rolling Stone' and receives all publishing income for it. Quite right. But a young session guitarist called Al Kooper happened to sit in on the day of recording and came up with the famous electric organ line which could be said to be a key part of the song, too. Once you begin to talk about bands—which might expand and develop songs collectively in the rehearsal studio, often from quite basic outlines—the situation becomes even more fraught. More groups have split over the distribution of these royalties than over any personal reason used as cover for this underlying cause. There is no resentment like the bass player's resentment as he turns up at the latest session in his battered old Ford to find the songwriter arriving in a Bentley. Some bands get round this by dividing their writing royalties equally. It's been cited as one of the reasons that U2 have never split, which just goes to show that economic and aesthetic justice aren't necessarily the same thing.

With hip hop (and most other electronic and dance musics), rules of thumb have developed as to how to divide songwriting copyrights. The basic rule is that the music (or beat) is worth half and the melody and lyrics (the 'topline') the other half. So a producer would normally take 50%, with the remaining 50% divided between the rappers who appear on a particular beat. The truth is, though, that the final split is down to the relationship between the writers and, more importantly, to power. As songwriter Helienne Lindvall has recalled, 'an artist once demanded 70% of a song I had worked on, if she decided to record it. As the song was a three-way co-write, that would've left the three of us who actually had written it with 10% each.'

It's long been part of the Wu-Tang legend that royalties are divided equally. 'By assuring that the most successful and the least successful group members all shared publishing revenue equally, RZA assured that Wu could, for the most part, avoid envy or infighting over money.' That's one way of looking at it, anyway, although other commentators have suggested that it merely reverses the polarity of that envy. The subsequent years of threatened and real litigation, bad blood, media slanging matches and diss-tennis have certainly taken the sheen off this idea, and in all honesty it always seemed unlikely, anyway. Perhaps there was some kind of understanding over recording royalties, but songwriting has a whole history of precedent for how money is divided. In fact, the idea that the Wu-Tang split their publishing royalties equally was largely scotched by RZA himself when he was sued in 2005 by Ghostface Killah for non-payment of royalties. In September 2009, it was reported that Ghostface had been awarded $158,000, but RZA stated he would appeal the judgement and went on to question the terms of the claim, which he said revolved around his own 50% share of publishing. 'When it comes to the beats of hip-hop,' he said, 'how it carries on to this day is that the producer gets 50% of the composition, and the lyricist[s], no matter how many, gets the other 50%... Trust me, when it comes to doing these records, I'm in the studio hundreds of days where they're here for 20–30 days.'

And yet, if you know someone who works for a company which is a member of a royalty collection society, you can get them to search on a database for you and tell you what the writing splits are on any particular song. And if you look up the songs on *Enter the Wu-Tang (36 Chambers)*, what you discover is that every last track on the record has its publishing split equally between the eight original members listed on the back of the record, regardless of whether they had any writing input at all on any particular song. The only other splits on the record are for the composers of the various samples used (though not all of them). This means that Masta Killa gets nothing for his sixteen lines of lyrics, but also means that U-God, on account of his full membership, gets as big a share of writing royalties as Method Man, even though the latter has over ten times as many lines on the record and, in fact, one track on which only he rhymes. It means U-God gets as much as RZA does, despite those 'hundreds of days' in the studio. It's hard to comprehend. It certainly isn't standard. But the Wu-Tang is—or was, for this brief, beautiful moment— a collective as well as a hierarchy, financially if in no other way.

26TH CHAMBER
IN AND OUT

A backward thought. Breath as the shadow of words.

Breath gives words form, depth, physicality. To hear a rapper's intake of air jammed between utterances is to hear that he is alive, is human. To hear the rapper's breath is to feel him as a body occupying space and time, a four-dimensional being. At a basic level, it's to partake in his humanity, to feel him embodied. But it is also to understand his craft, his control, the push involved in getting to the end of a double-bar line, his mastery of technique. As Gift of Gab from West Coast group Blackalicious puts it, 'it's all about making the breath part of the flow'. This works both ways, of course. The skilled rapper not only has the lung capacity to make it to the right point to breathe, but also structures his verse around when he will need to. These breaths are part of the form and rhythm of his verse, too. They have to hit somewhere and when they do they alter the possible scansion of the line. 'Breath control,' Adam Bradley notes, 'shapes rhythmic possibilities just as much as an MC's lyrical imagination.'

You might hear it best on *Enter the Wu-Tang* when the music drops out, in those gaps RZA leaves for the MC to show his moves, like when Inspectah Deck comes in on 'Bring Da Ruckus' and gasps in oxygen after 'ghetto bastards with biscuits' ('biscuits' is slang not for Hobnobs but for guns, in case you were wondering). Because the Wu, as a whole, rhyme hard and loud, the contrast between enunciated syllable and intake of air is greater than it might be with quieter rappers. It's perhaps clearest with Method Man, who favours a smoother style than some of the others, and who tends to grab some air at the end of each bar. Then again, maybe he does it louder, with a bit of bravado, to emphasise exactly how easy he's making it all sound, the regularity and symmetry of his rhyme-architecture, the way he flows on and on as if nothing could be simpler. Once you begin to tune in, though, you start to notice breath more and more, the air inside this chamber.

ODB likes to alternate between short, staccato phrases and small breaths and then long, complex two-bar wailing excursions at the end of which he hard-sucks a lungful before continuing. GZA favours short, quiet breaths, in keeping with his image as a cold-eyed rhyme assassin. Ghostface likes to disguise his breath by starting his lines with words he can still sound while inhaling (*I* and *and*, for instance). Deck, like ODB though for different technical reasons, alternates short and long. U-God, as with Meth, takes big, ragged breaths which are used in his lines as rhythmic punctuation and add a certain—literally breathless—charm to his delivery. Raekwon tends to be pretty regular in his approach, louder than Ghostface and GZA, but still relatively quiet. RZA hits his lines so hard that it's difficult to pick out his breaths and, anyway, the jaggedy shape of his phrasing leaves plenty of space for air. All of them, though, are *present*.

That's why the practice of 'punching in' vocal lines is frowned upon by more traditional MCs. The technique has become more prevalent with the move to digital recording, where multiple tracks can be used without the necessity of 'bouncing down' from tape, an activity which increases background hiss. At first, the approach was used to correct small mistakes in an otherwise perfect take, to remove that one stumble in a burning, beautiful delivery. But, as is the way with any new method, people noticed that they could push it further. Now, in certain cases, the rapper delivers each line, one at a time, on a separate track and the engineer stitches them together on computer. There's no need to worry about where your breath will fit in the line because you can do it off mic, between takes. You don't have to learn your verse, or practise it. You don't even have to *write* it in advance. Instead, you can fire off a line, stop, think of another, record that, then come up with another. The result is a kind of disembodied cybernetic rapping with all its physicality gone.[27] Similarly, sound engineers have been known to erase the rapper's breaths in an attempt to 'tidy up' a vocal performance. These people should be fired.

---

27 Hence its frequent deployment alongside some kind of autotune effect. You definitely show your age if you don't like autotune, and in fact when used in this way (not for tuning but for exactly the unearthly, robotic effect it creates as a side-product) it's a misuse of the technology and hence a valid hip hop strategy. All the same, it sounds horrible.

There seems to be a contradiction here. Hip hop is a music and culture of constant innovation, but there's an inclination to say that a verse on which every line has been punched in may be rap but isn't hip hop. Not only an element of contradiction, in fact, but an element of essentialism is sneaking in. *Embodiedness*, it seems— even on a recording—remains a necessary condition of the music. It ties back to Gilroy's notion of kinesics, as if the breaths contain as much information as the words they sit between. Also to the notion we took from Mauss (via Sterne) of 'techniques of the body'—rap is a technique of the body (with as many regional and personal variations as there are styles of walking), and we need to be able to feel that in some way.

RZA hints at why this might be important when he says that 'music is harmonious with life... How chi flows, music flows. That's one of the reasons I've been successful in music because of my martial application. It's something that can't be defined, but it can definitely be heard.' As a whole, chi (or *qi*) tends to be taken to mean something like *life force*, but at its simplest it just means *air*. On this reading, inhalation and exhalation is itself, in the most basic of terms, the flow of chi. The sound of that flow is the sound of life. And control of that flow rests in balance—you can't keep doing one without the other. When RZA talks about 'directing chi' he could mean something as simple as breath control, which is an essential part of the art of being an MC.

That isn't *all* he means, though. 'Tai chi translates as "the grand extreme,"' he says in *The Tao of Wu*, 'and breaks all ideas, forces, and objects into opposites, yin and yang. But wu-chi, which translates as "no extremes," came before tai chi. It's infinite, the source of all power, and it's all one.' Here, chi means 'extreme' or 'extremes', possibly something near to *power* or *force*. Maximum chi is to split into opposites, to make life a series of ones and zeroes, minimum chi the removal of opposites. Both could apply to breath, too, and by thinking about breath we understand that the two ideas aren't necessarily antagonistic. Inhaling and exhaling are opposites but they are part of one process, the process of breathing, and hence the process of being alive. 'Life,' in the words of Daoist sage Zhuangzi, 'is a mere gathering together of breath.' That's what we hear—life, living, survival, continuing—in each gasped intake. Without it there's only death.

27TH CHAMBER
WARRIORS COME OUT TO PLAY

Within the Wu-Tang, no member is more highly
esteemed than Gary Grice aka The Genius aka the GZA.
This could be ascribed to the fact that he is the oldest
member of the group, or because he was the first to
embrace the teachings of the Nation of Gods and Earths.
But actually it's because of 'the invincible dopeness of
his rhyme style'. More particularly because he is the
consummate battle-rapper of the group.

Whereas Raekwon, Ghostface Killah, RZA and
Inspectah Deck all deliver at least one narrative verse on
Enter the Wu-Tang, the other three 'headline' rappers—
GZA, Method Man and Ol' Dirty Bastard—don't. We'll
come to Ol' Dirty's function within the group later. The
remaining pair are the only MCs awarded solo tracks
on the record—in itself a huge honour when nine MCs
are competing for space. Method Man specialises in

good-natured braggadocio, his gruff voice combining with his rolling flow and good looks to make him the group's first breakout sex symbol. GZA, on the other hand, delivers only battle-rhymes. His approach is built for combat—clever but never clever for its own sake, cool almost to the point of coldness, mercilessly efficient. As RZA has it, 'GZA's the only one with a style that actually instilled fear in me.' And by that he means the only MC in the world, not the group. To understand the significance of this you have to remember Schloss's dictum that battle tactics are the backbone of hip hop's 'philosophy of aesthetics'.

Even when the GZA does deliver slivers of autobiography, this information is transmitted in the form of battle-rhyme. One of the senior members of the camp, he had a record deal before the Wu-Tang existed, with Cold Chillin', at the time a highly respected label, home to Marley Marl's Juice Crew, including Biz Markie and Big Daddy Kane. 'I felt good to be on that label,' GZA recalled, 'because they was the Def Jam of that era.' But the deal soon turned sour. When his album didn't sell, the label 'commissioned a single called "Come Do Me," with music and lyrics that had almost nothing to do with the talents and strengths of the artist they signed'. On 'Protect Ya Neck', The Genius decides to settle a few scores. As is often the case, he takes the last verse of the tune, as none of the other members is prepared to rhyme after him. He opens by pointing out that his new group is too good for 'these Cold Killin' labels'. He goes on to say that these 'labels' haven't had a hit in years, are stingy, and have misused and misunderstood his inventions, wasting what resources and energy they have on the wrong artists.

Finally, having softened them up, he delivers what

217

is probably one of the greatest music business disses of all time, something which must haunt the waking nightmares of a certain sector of professionals. 'A&R' stands for 'artist and repertoire', and these are the people (usually men) who sign artists to record labels, steer them through the recording process and then on to release. GZA, it turns out, feels very little respect for them. 'First of all, who's your A&R? / A mountain climber who plays electric guitar.' It's a brilliant couplet, simple and devastatingly effective, as it suggests in the clearest, most effective way possible that these are people who have no qualifications to be deciding on what is good or bad in hip hop and how it should be presented. Through what they do (climb mountains, play guitar) he presents them as utterly lacking in the correct credentials. And as this is a fear which lives in the hearts of all but the most arrogant, ignorant A&Rs (that they are out of touch, that they are unqualified, that they are in some measure fake; that they are, more than anything else, *White*), GZA utterly skewers them on their own insecurity.

This is the art of battle-rhyming in miniature, a laser-point channelling of energy, the most economical way in which to unbalance your foe (in this case the entire music business). Talking about b-boying, Schloss discusses the mood one should foster when battling. 'The ideal, it seems, is to be aggrieved, yet simultaneously restrained,' he says. 'One should be furious and yet totally in control.' This is the disposition the GZA brings to everything he does. Somehow the coolness, the restraint, gives the fury more power, not less.

We need to think what a battle involves. Most important is that there are *two sides*. The winner of a battle will be decided between the combatants or by the crowd or, in some more formalised cases, by judges. The question posed is this: of these two, who is the best MC? Who has the best rhymes and flow, the funniest come-backs, the most style? *Of these two*—this is not a decision taken in isolation, as it might be when a music critic is listening to a record in his vinyl-lined study. This is done face to face, with onlookers cheering or jeering. In expressing all your MCing skills, you also want to put off your opponent, so that they can't express theirs. This is, quite possibly, an easier, and hence more economical way to win than through having to constantly hit the heights of your own abilities. In a verbal battle, then—perhaps even more than in a dance battle—the way to win is to disturb your opponent, to throw them off centre, to queer their pitch. This is what the use of insults is all about—causing your adversary to slip. 'Self-control,' Schloss goes on to claim, 'is really the essence of the battle aesthetic, and the goal is to make the opponent lose his.'

The tradition of trading insults and boasts, often in rhyme, has a long history in African American culture through playing the Dozens and the practice of signifying more generally. As Elijah Wald puts it right at the start of his overview of the phenomenon, *Talking 'Bout Your Mama*, 'the Dozens can be tricky, aggressive, offensive, clever, brutal, funny, inventive, stupid, violent, misogynistic, psychologically intricate, deliberately misleading—or all of that at once, wrapped in a single rhyming couplet'. The Dozens often involves reference to the protagonists' parents, and particularly their mothers, but not always. Indeed, the exact rules of engagement vary over time and from neighbourhood to neighbourhood. It is always, though, a competitive word game, usually played in front of—and to some degree, for the benefit of—an audience. As the Black activist H. Rap Brown remembers of the kids in his neighbourhood when he was growing up, 'we played the Dozens... like white folks played Scrabble'. In Brown's recollection, the Dozens appears as a subset of Signifying. The former was always a series of insults aimed at your opponent, but 'Signifying allowed you a choice—you could either make a cat feel good or bad.' For the purposes of this chamber, our focus will remain with the Dozens, also known as sounding, woofing, joaning, screaming, cutting, capping, snapping, hiking, playing house, ranking, busting and so on. There is no shortage of nomenclature and no great agreement on what it entails, but it's hard to understand the vocal element of hip hop—and particularly the centrality of battling—without reference to the practice. Indeed, as Wald has it, 'while the dozens is part of the larger world of African American verbal art, poetry, and comedy, it is also part of the larger world of combat'.

Wald traces a long history of the Dozens in America through recordings, literature and sociological studies. He also notes examples of ritualised insult-trading from around the world. Specifically, he teases out a variety of African traditions, from the Gusii in Kenya, the Wagogo in Tanzania, the Ano-Ewe in Ghana, and, in particular, the Igbo and the Hausa in Nigeria. Henry Louis Gates Jr., on the other hand, traces the figure of the Signifying Monkey (who, in the rhyming and often obscene African American folk story, insults the Lion, says it's what the Elephant said, watches the Lion getting whupped by the Elephant, insults the Lion some more and then gets a whupping of his own) back to the Yoruban trickster god, Eshu-Elegba. This question of ultimate origins— the where—is perhaps not as important to us, though, as the reasons for doing so—the why. Wald lists six main explanations for the Dozens, running from a puberty ritual, to group therapy, to misogyny, to an expression of self-hatred, to a central art form for African American expression, to our current favourite, a form of training in self-control. Most of these—all at once—have something to recommend them.

Looking back on his seminal work *The Signifying Monkey* twenty-five years after it was written, Gates points out that 'the most prevalent manifestation of signifying over the last four decades is to be found in the corpus of hip-hop music. You might say that hip-hop is signifying on steroids.' Although he's definitely on to something here, the notion isn't completely accurate. Hip hop didn't add muscle through drugs so much as make a sudden leap in evolution through increased natural selection. As Wald has it, 'until the rap era there was no formal space for those duels, so dozens champions took their earnings in the ephemeral coin of street reputation and their creations were forgotten or entered the anonymous oral tradition'. He goes on to trace the origins of battling back to 1981 and Kool Moe Dee dissing Busy Bee Starski. 'Tapes of this confrontation were soon being traded across New York, and freestyle battling became a basic measure of rap skill, not only onstage but in parks and schoolyards.' With this more formal space and increased competition grew new rules about what was acceptable and what wasn't, in particular the notion that rhymes had to be original (something which only really happened once these rhymes began to be recorded). But the major difference from blues or jazz—from the African American tradition up to this point, you might say—was built into rap's very essence. 'Such combat was nothing new in African American musical culture,' Wald notes. 'But where in previous styles it was accepted and even common, in rap it is *fundamental*' (italics added).

We'll be expanding upon the importance of the Dozens and signifying more generally—and in particular how hip hop transforms them—in the next chamber. For now, let's focus on a practical example. On the second verse of his solo track 'Clan In Da Front', The Genius offers up a masterclass in battle-rhyming. It's so perfect, in fact, that it's tempting just to quote it in full. The basic theme of the verse is that the Wu don't really need to boast or show off because their superior technique makes them untouchable. It breaks down into three interlinked sections. First of all, GZA sets out the idea that reputation means nothing to him—that he wants to see what skills you have rather than hear about them. Don't bother boasting until you've shown him what you can do. The third and final part of the verse is an extended baseball metaphor, where GZA compares himself to the pitcher, with RZA as his catcher, and the unnamed MC who has dared to boast as the hapless batter, destined to be struck out by these major league operators. Throughout, he hits exactly the tone Schloss talks about—coldly furious, utterly in control. While other Wu members may huff and shout, sound genuinely angry and ready to do violence, The Genius stays calmly on the edge, where he needs to be.

It's the section in the middle that seals the deal. His competitor is becoming increasingly afraid, The Genius suggests, as he shows his style more and more clearly. 'What's that in your pants?' he asks abruptly, then, with the disgust clear in his voice, answers: 'Ah, *human faeces.*' He tells his opponent to chuck his soiled

222

underwear in the laundry hamper and then offers some advice. 'Next time come strapped,' he suggests, allowing the listener to think he's suggesting that his adversary needs to carry a gun, before finishing the punchline: '... with a fuckin' Pamper.' Whatever comes after these three and a bit lines is just throwing earth over the body, really. The opponent is already lying in a hole and he's not breathing. To be a great battle-rhymer is to be a great battle winner.

28TH CHAMBER
TORTURE

Depending on how you look at it (or perhaps on where you are), the Torture skit is either one of the crowning moments of a hip hop sub-genre or the bit that you turn down if your mum comes into the room. It's ridiculously funny or slightly disturbing, a brilliant little character study or blunted babble, gothic brilliance or male miasma. What everyone can agree on is that there's something compelling about it which means it's rarely skipped.

In terms of content, 'Torture' is very simple, fifty-five seconds at the start of the track 'Method Man' that involves Method Man himself and Raekwon threatening each other or some unknown third party with a variety of increasingly inventive forms of brought pain. Meth leads off by promising to stick a red-hot coat hanger up the target's rectum. Raekwon responds by saying he will place his enemy's testicles on a dresser and hit them with a spiked bat. Meth counters by suggesting he will stab his victim through the tongue with a screwdriver. Raekwon essays the possibility of hanging him by his penis from the top of a building. Meth finishes off by saying he will sew his opposite number's anus shut and 'keep *feedin'* you and *feedin'* you and *feedin'* you and *feedin'* you'. At which point the game, like the victim, goes pop.

It's the combination of baroque detail and ambiguity which makes the Torture skit what it is. For one thing, we don't know who the threats are addressed to. The fact that the two MCs take it in turns and use the same ritualised form of words ('I'll fucking, I'll fucking…') seems to suggest that this is a game between the pair of them, and that the threats are addressed to each other, but they could just as easily have a man bound and gagged on a chair in front of them, tearful and desperate. And then there's those little flourishes. Meth says he'll tie the object of his attention to the bedpost and describes spreading out his buttocks before hot-hanger insertion, Raekwon is very specific about the type of furniture on which he will lay out the poor, defenceless testes which are about to get mulched, the screwdriver isn't any old screwdriver but a *rusty* one and the wang-hang is done from the twelfth floor when even the most extravagantly endowed target could safely be left to swing from the first. These exaggerations and non-sequiturs also provide a clue as to how to interpret the skit as a whole, but we'll return to that. First, context.

The skit was still a relatively new phenomenon in 1993. RZA learnt its value from one of its pioneers, the

producer Prince Paul, who famously came up with
the idea for the game-show interludes on De La Soul's
debut album, 3 *Feet High and Rising* (1989). As RZA
has recalled, Paul 'schooled me on a lot of things', and
it seems like this was one of them. Paul remembers
listening through the finished tracks with the members
of De La in 1988 (around the time he met RZA).
'I realized we needed something to link it together,'
he says. 'We did it to fill that void, to give our album
some structure. It was just something we tried out and
it evolved. We never thought it would become a rap
album staple.'

RZA uses skits in much the same way—to structure
the record and build atmosphere and identity. The pair
were introduced through RZA's manager at the time
and both had a relationship with Tommy Boy, to which
De La Soul and RZA (as Prince Rakeem) were signed.
RZA, in fact, has claimed that Paul did some of the
drum-programming work on his single for the label,
'Ooh I Love You, Rakeem', while the demo songs for the
Gravediggaz (a group put together by Paul and featuring
the vocal talents of RZA, Frukwan—from Paul's
previous group, Stetsasonic—and Poetic) were finished
by early 1992. As well as a love for unusual samples, the
pair share an affinity for space in their compositions,
for sampling single instruments rather than whole
bands, for a certain eccentricity of construction. And
for those skits, used as a way of building an album's
rhythm and shape. After all, as Gabriel Alvarez, of
legendary hip hop magazine *Ego Trip*, puts it, 'skits
don't just fill the space, they set the mood'. The Wu's
mastery of the form is evidenced by Alvarez placing two
skits from *Enter* (plus three from Raekwon's solo debut
album, *Only Built 4 Cuban Linx*) in his all-time top

twenty. The Torture skit comes in at number 2.[28]

Perhaps the Wu's greatest innovation is the naturalness of their contributions which, Alvarez points out, sound 'like you're eavesdropping during a break in recording'. There's none of the staged, obviously comedic quality of De La Soul or, for that matter, N.W.A. These are not fake gameshows or hokey radio broadcasts. They're not commenting on the media, or stupidity, or greed, or sex, or indeed anything else. There's no gap between the performer and the performance. And paradoxically, it's this naturalness, which, like ski masks over the faces of the participants, leaves you uncertain, off balance, not quite clear as to their purpose.

We have come back round to signifying—or, as it has tended to become known since Henry Louis Gates, Jr. made the suggestion in an attempt to distinguish it from its technical use in certain literary discourses— *Signifyin(g)*. Maybe Signifyin(g) has come back round to us. If you think of the Dozens as a predominantly rhyming game of insults and boasts, the skit is where, 'instead of having to say it in rhyme form, you can cut to the chase'. It's notable that the 'first full-fledged rap-skit', from 1988, was West Coast rapper King

---

28 Bizarrely, Dr. Dre comes out top for the '$20 Sack Pyramid' skit from *The Chronic*, but hey, not even Alvarez has perfect judgement. It may seem as if the author has it in for the West Coast in this book. Not at all. The record companies' insistence on signing and marketing only a narrow slice of what that side of the country had to offer meant that the huge wave of innovation exemplified by the LA Underground scene centred around the Good Life and then Project Blowed was successfully buried, at great cost to the whole Hip Hop Nation. It could be argued that Kendrick Lamar has gone some way to healing the wounds between these two divergent scenes, though on the ground they'd probably argue that this divergence was exaggerated by fools like this one, anyway.

Tee's 'Baggin' on Moms'—basically an extended bout of '*yo mama*' taunting. The Torture skit fits quite comfortably into the Signifyin(g) paradigm. The repeated opening phrases, the emphasis on recherché detail, it has all the hallmarks of a word game being played out between two competitors, moreover one that is won by summoning up the verbal and imaginative extravagance, the gory detail, the turn of phrase which will stop the other player in his tracks.

But although this is a game it's also more than a game, and it's perhaps this which we sense. As Gates has it, 'Signifyin(g) is the black trope of tropes, the figure for black rhetorical figures.' Signifyin(g), Gates argues, is central to African American cultural practices. Critics have become too obsessed with the Dozens, with the 'aggressive ritual', and have tended to miss the broader practice and its significance, he says. Signifyin(g), for Gates, 'is synonymous with figuration', both the use of figurative language and a language concerned, at root, with figuration. That is, it's a mode of language which is more interested in form than in content, or perhaps more accurately, which uses form to disguise content, a kind of indirection. Or to put it another way (a Germanic/philosophic kind of a way, one not exactly dripping with figuration), 'do not forget that a poem, even though it is composed in the language of information, is not used in the language-game of giving information'. Gates's study focuses in on the story of the Signifying Monkey and he says that the essence of that story lies in 'the relationship between the literal and the figurative, and the dire consequences of their confusion'. When someone is Signifyin(g), the biggest mistake is to interpret their words at face value. It's arguable, then, that we are falling into the role of the Lion, guilty of taking everything far too literally, if we complain of the violence spread across the surface of the Torture skit. This violence, Gates would respond, is merely part of a game of verbal imagination and one-upmanship.

This does, though, open up another line of criticism. Are the torture examples actually *good enough*? Meth's opener does make you squirm a little, if you take it literally. His middle threat at least strikes at the very heart of the game, in that someone with a rusty screwdriver stabbed through their tongue cannot talk back. His third, what seems to be the winner, is the funniest because it's the most surreal, the most outrageous, the most obviously cartoonish, the point at which the threats clearly become jokes. Similarly, though Raekwon isn't really operating at the same level, we can see his move from smashing your balls to leaving you swinging from a building by your dick as a ramping up of ludicrousness. But we're missing something, not getting the full experience, when we look at it like this.

The truth is, the exchange loses its power unless you're willing to believe that there's some sense of threat, some incipient violence lurking within it. What makes it a great skit is its naturalness, the feeling that its participants aren't performing but *doing*—or both performing and doing. The understatedness itself demands you take what you're hearing seriously. That is, to fully enjoy the exchange, you have to view it literally and figuratively *all at once*. You must treat the threats as both real and a joke, at the same time. Or rather, you have to reject that binary distinction altogether—bake the cake, take the cake, eat the cake, too, with your crew.

'In hip-hop and in the streets,' RZA writes, 'a boast is a projection of strength—a threat that is itself an action. Labor unions act by *threatening* to strike.

Rappers act by *threatening* to destroy.' There is the literal action of sewing up someone's anus and then feeding them until they burst. But there is also the action of threatening to do so, *'a threat that is itself an action'*. Then there's the act of pretending to threaten to do so. The language of hip hop is self-consciously multi-layered, a subtle millefeuille of meaning-as-action and action-as-meaning which can and should be interpreted in a number of ways all at once. None of which should distract us from how funny the Torture skit is, or at least how funny it is when you're stoned, male, and/or aged somewhere between thirteen and thirty. Because a certain goofiness is baked right through this particular cake as well, just never at the expense of any of the other elements.

Gates famously appeared as a witness for the defence at the trial for obscenity of Florida rap group 2 Live Crew in 1990, in effect arguing that what he describes as the group's 'lamentably sexist and misogynistic lyrics' should be placed in a tradition of Signifyin(g). 'Taking their lyrics—like the dozens— literally,' he said, 'was to miss the point of this art form entirely.' Gates argues, in effect, that the obscene is not obscene if its purpose is not obscenity—that is, if it's being used in some way under or beyond its literal meaning. But this can't be quite right, because it ignores the critical thinking involved in choosing to use the literally obscene to convey another meaning, knowing full well that the transgressive power of the literal obscenity is exactly what animates this process. It's this ambiguity, this hovering between the literal and the figurative that gives the whole process life. As Paul Gilroy has pointed out, even 'leaving the question of misogyny aside for a moment, to collude in the belief that black vernacular is *nothing* other than a playful, parodic cavalcade of Rabelaisian subversion decisively weakens the position of the artist, the critical commentator, and the community as a whole'. It's also worth pointing out that Luther Campbell is an abysmal lyricist and even if he didn't mean exactly what he said, it's not clear he could exercise the linguistic control necessary to mean something else. At which point there's no balance, and the literal obscenity is doing all the work, so at the very best it's probably *bad* Signifyin(g).

Is it possible, then, that Gates is guilty of a certain literalism in relation to his theory of the non-literalism of rap and Signifyin(g) more generally, a literalism shown up most clearly by the hooded matter-of-factness of the Wu-Tang skits? Gates draws on the account of the famed weed dealer and sometime jazz musician Mezz Mezzrow to argue that Signifyin(g) is 'a form of rhetorical training, an on-the-streets exercise in the use of troping, in which the play is the thing—not specifically what is said, but how'. This training was given an end goal in hip hop, because it could be used to accrue wider renown and fame and, eventually, even monetary reward. But in the process, Signifyin(g) was also transformed from a cultural practice—from rhetorical training, from a game—into an art form in its own right, a practice in which re-referencing was no longer carried out to teach you to hide your true meaning from your oppressors but was done solely for the glory of re-referencing itself. The torture in the Torture skit lies not in the descriptions of violence but in walking the tightrope between the outlandish and the believable, between making a threat and making a threat ridiculous. If that's the case, then it's Method

Man—as the first to tip too far one way—who loses. Isn't all art, to some extent, about tiptoeing along exactly this boundary? And doesn't popular art, *American art*, from horror films to Disney, take whatever power it possesses exactly from this thrumming tension—torture-as-torture versus torture-as-titillation versus torture-as-joke?

29TH CHAMBER
PASS THE BONE

In one of the funniest lines in *The Wu-Tang Manual*,
RZA kicks off the 'Chemistry' section by stating, 'I don't
advocate the use of illegal drugs and the Wu-Tang
don't either.' This is a little like Donald Trump saying
he doesn't advocate grabbing that pussy, or Coca-Cola
claiming they don't advocate sugar—perhaps narrowly
true but only misleadingly so. RZA is quick to clarify.
'I don't mean to advocate it, I'm not advising it, but I
know that for us, making music, you got to have some
good weed in the spot. I think weed has been involved
in at least 85 percent of all our music.' The only surprise
in this statement is the fifteen per cent which remains
untouched. To say that the Wu like their green is to fall
foul, every time, of understating the obvious. Whether
they say they're smoking bones or blunts, built from
Dutch Masters cigars or White Owl papers, packed with

sess, meth, methtical, tical, buddha or skunk, a key part of Wu mythology involves the consumption of copious quantities of Mary Jane.

It's hard to write about cannabis seriously without looking a little bit like you've either missed the point or are a dewy-eyed sixties type who thinks it might change the world. It's probably true of almost all drugs that there's a yawning chasm between the experience of doing them and the experience of hearing—usually at great length—about someone else's experience of doing them. But cannabis presents particular problems. As Martin A. Lee points out in his comprehensive survey of the history of the plant, *Smoke Signals*, 'It is difficult to generalize about cannabis, given that its effects are highly variable, even in small doses. When large doses are imbibed,' he goes on to point out, 'all bets are off.'

At the risk of sounding not only stoned but pompous, too, the key in relation to the Wu-Tang lies exactly with weed's ambiguous, dual-faceted nature— the way that it not only affects each user differently, but affects them differently each time they use it, teetering on that fine line between elation and paranoia and waiting to fall one way or the other. This is what Lee characterises as 'the herb's capriciousness, its tricksterlike qualities... The marijuana saga is rife with paradox and polarity. It is all about doubles, twins, dualities.' In fact, so inconsistent and contradictory is cannabis in its effects that when the Office of Strategic Services (the USA's wartime precursor to the CIA) investigated its potential to act as some sort of truth drug, it concluded that 'the drug defies all but the most expert and searching analysis... and for all practical purposes can be considered beyond analysis'.

These two poles, of elation and paranoia, are present and correct on *Enter*. On the one hand we can turn to the most enthusiastic Wu weed-promoter, Method Man, and his versioning of Michael Jackson versioning the Beatles, where he declares that, among other equipment, he's got 'fat bags of skunk... [and] White Owl blunts'. For Method Man (named in honour of his copious intake), weed represents the unbridled rush of connection, helter-skelter linguistic puns, recycled catchphrases and screwed-up syntax, the cartoon pratfalls of the brain chasing itself. In one of the standout lines of the whole record, RZA goes even further, putting the case for weed as an aid to creativity when he says it's got him 'open like fallopian tubes'. The brilliance of the simile lies in the way that what sounds at first like a slightly crude sex rhyme (relying on the alternate meaning of 'open' as 'open to sex') is in fact a reference to mental fertility (plus, of course, the way that 'fallopian' syncopates its rhyme with 'open', making the whole line bounce and stick in your head with all the cussedness of the single sperm which makes it through to the egg).

But then again, there's the other side, the side Inspectah Deck refers to in his bleak lines from 'C.R.E.A.M.' when he wonders why he bothers smoking at all. 'I guess that's the time when I'm not depressed,' he suggests, before noting that, despite this, 'I'm still depressed, and I ask what it's worth?' In his classic work on/of Afrofuturism, *More Brilliant Than The Sun*, the artist and 'concept engineer' Kodwo Eshun devotes a considerable amount of time to the 'mythillogical' in hip hop, the moment when weed 'deregulates the means of perception, breaks down the walls of HipHop's fortified ego'. 'All drugs intensify paranoia,' he says, 'but Weed's special effect is to magnify the misperception inherent in everyday hearing, thereby turning HipHop into a perpetual paranoia of peripheral persecution.' Part of this paranoia blows back and effects an interesting change, though. '"Keeping it real" no longer means representing, because there's no defined reality left to represent... The street's rigid border between the real and the fantastic melts.' This is important, because our first thought might be that it's odd that a group so apparently concerned with self-control should spend their time getting baked. But what if weed provided exactly the kind of border-melting between the real and the fantastic that the Wu needed to make room for their own brand of myth-building?

Reality is something which has to be endured and, as Nietzsche put it, 'to escape from unbearable pressure you need hashish'. Cannabis seeds, it's believed, were first brought to the American continents in the sixteenth century by African slaves. In fact, cannabis's connection to the Black population in America has long been one of the reasons both for White America's fascination with the plant and for its suppression of it. By the twentieth century, this fascination and abhorrence crystallised around the jazz scene, whose musicians partook freely, with Louis Armstrong stating that 'we always looked at pot as a sort of medicine... It makes you feel good, man. It relaxes you, makes you forget all the bad things that happen to a Negro.'

From 1934 onwards, Harry Anslinger and his Federal Bureau of Narcotics (FBN) went after cannabis (together with jazz) as if it were the most dangerous substance on the planet. Working from the same racist playbook used with cocaine, one of the many unscientific, hokey and utterly lunatic reasons Anslinger gave for prohibiting cannabis was that 'marijuana causes white women to seek sexual relations with Negroes'. By threatening miscegenation as the result of this particular escape from the stresses and strains of everyday life, Anslinger used fantasy (and sexual fantasy at that) to rigidly enforce the borders of acceptable reality. A decade or so later, he changed his line of attack to the new demon of the day. 'Marijuana,' he now said, 'leads to pacifism and Communist brainwashing.' It remained a strange choice of drug to fear a revolution from, this 'medicine' which 'makes you forget' rather than confront 'all the bad things'.

To see cannabis as merely a vehicle for forgetting, a medicine to ease the pain, though, is to miss the point. Jazz musicians smoked pot in part because it changed how they heard their own music, opening up a different kind of space and hence new possibilities. Lee describes Armstrong recording the tune 'Muggles' (yet another slang word for marijuana) in 1928, in which 'several musicians... passed the bluesy melody around like a burning marijuana cigarette... This landmark instrumental signalled the transformation of jazz into an improvisatory art-form with wide-open opportunities for individual expression. No one had ever made music like this before.' Michael Veal, in *Dub*, says that the effects of cannabis 'on auditory perception are well known; when under the influence, the listener is acutely aware of changes in the perception of spatiality, movement, detail, texture, and time'. Although careful to avoid any totalising approach which equates dub with 'ganja music', he quotes Scientist, the legendary dub technician, who says 'the first time I smoke a spliff, I hear music differently'.

Perhaps most of all, THC (the active chemical compound in cannabis) allows the user to hear music as space, as landscape, crucially as non-linear. It adds a concrete element to listening and—'seen' rather than heard—allows for new ways to navigate. At the very start of Ralph Ellison's *Invisible Man* the narrator is given a cannabis cigarette and he smokes it listening to Armstrong's '(What Did I Do To Be So) Black and Blue'. 'Under the spell of the reefer,' he recalls, 'I discovered a new analytical way of listening to music. The unheard sounds came through, and each melodic line existed of itself, stood out clearly from all the rest, said its piece, and waited patiently for the other voices to speak. That night I found myself hearing not only in time, but in space as well.'

This idea surfaces again and again, across time, space itself, and musical style. Dub (the double) becomes a focal point. Recalling the special ambience of his Black Ark recording studios, Lee 'Scratch' Perry, a man with more than a passing interest in ganja, said that 'you could hear space in the tracks'. As he also describes Black Ark as a space craft, it seems that his reference is to space as something intergalactic rather than purely three-dimensional, but then again, what is a galaxy but three very big dimensions? And anyway, isn't he really talking about a kind of alchemy, of music transformed, of reaching for the infinite? 'I was getting help from God, through space, through the sky, through the firmament, through the earth, through the wind, through the fire. I got support through the weather to make space music.' Eshun is correct in his emphasis on the peripheral because, in one sense, there is no peripheral when you smoke weed. Every part of a piece of music separates out and assumes equal status. Either you lift up above the

landscape and survey it like a god, or you find yourself
with all the elements crowding in on you at once. To
return to the narrator of *Invisible Man*, 'I haven't smoked
a reefer since, however; not because they're illegal, but
because to *see* around corners is enough (that is not
unusual when you are invisible). But to hear around
them is too much.'

Either way, once you've smoked and listened to
music you can never go back, because, whether you can
hear them or not at any particular moment, you know
those further dimensions are all there, immanent. The
problem is one of perception—or delivery—and the only
question which remains for a producer is whether you
can find a technical way to open up those perspectives
independent of the listener's mental state. This is
what you hear in dub: the extension and reversion,
the re-editing of sound over and over again until, like
one of those magic-eye illusions, a sudden unlikely
three-dimensional vista jumps from the speakers or
headphones. The process is, on Veal's reading, akin to
a meditation, as demonstrated in the words he quotes
from an interview with Bobby Vicious, a Jamaican
soundsystem operator now based in the USA. 'They
might play five, ten version of the same riddim, all with
a different mix,' says Bobby, recalling going to a King
Tubby's session in his youth. 'In fact, they didn't call it
version, they called it *chapter*. And each chapter opened
your mind a different way.'

Listening to the RZA's production work, you quite
clearly hear—or feel?—that same sound of space, this
sense of music as three-dimensional. At the time of *Enter
the Wu-Tang*'s release, his beats were seen as crude and
rather lo-fi compared with the slick, bass-heavy product
Dr. Dre was pumping out on the other coast. In fact,

a careful listen reveals a plethora of surface detail, the level of workmanship and mark-making that has gone into creating this allegedly crude artefact. Drop-outs, the use of reverb and echo, those famous kung fu samples, the doubling up of drumbeats, plus the room that is left around the elements used, a less-is-more confidence perhaps born of limited equipment, but amply repaid by the results achieved. Added to this is what he learnt from trawling through Thelonious Monk records looking for samples—an alternate sense of space, one which makes the pianist's solos and even his comping an extended exploration of the unexpected (Monk's biographer notes that his other obsessions, besides music, were 'gin and reefer'). Rather than evoking the infinite, outward-looking spaces of dub (or Afrofuturism more generally), RZA takes the skewed, Escher-like perspectives of Monk—the sense of a man building a bridge across a void while simultaneously standing on it—and turns both approaches inward to make a series of rooms, each track a separate chamber of varying size and texture. A space for the MCs to do battle in. They don't rap on top of the beat so much as inside of it.

How much of this is down to the weed and how much just to RZA's particular take on the aesthetics of hip hop is of course open to question. What we can say is that it's not all of it, because otherwise everyone who had ever puffed on a fat one would make music that sounded the same. It's worth pointing out that Dr. Dre, too, was partial to a toot, as memorialised in the title of that slick, bass-heavy album *The Chronic*. But there is something strangely Caribbean about RZA's work, perhaps an odd assertion if by that you think of rum punch and Bob Marley rather than the twisted Old Testament fervour of Rasta-fuelled roots music,

240

where every echo stands like a crumbling pillar of salt.
Some of this is might be down to the odd, stretched-
out and warped influence of Marcus Garvey, a man
with a right to claim some kind of parenthood of two
of the foundational sounds of modern popular music,
reggae and hip hop. It was disillusioned Garveyites,
after all, who flocked to both the Rasta movement in
Jamaica and the Nation of Islam in America, the twin
wellsprings for much of the respective imagery of reggae
and hip hop. Malcom X's mother was a Garveyite. And
before Malcolm had gained his X, when he was known
as Detroit Red, he ended up in prison for dealing weed.
Indeed, Wu-Tang could be posited as the rejoinder
to Paul Gilroy's assertion that 'there has been no
contemporary equivalent to the provocative, hermetic
power of dub which supported the radical Ethiopianism
of the seventies or of the anti-assimilationist
unintelligibility of bebop in the forties'.

The mention of the hermetic—the airtight, the
sealed in—is interesting, and even more relevant if
we're arguing that the three-dimensional spaces RZA
creates are deliberately confined—enclosed, even. How
can the hermetic and the infinite co-exist? How can
the same substance cause euphoria and paranoia? For
the Wu-Tang, the answer lies in their street spirituality,
that mixture of millenarian Black Islam, kung fu, battle
rap and the geography of New York. Throw in the Rasta
sacrament—weed—and everything melds together,
melts into each other. Our first clue comes from Melvin
Gibbs, who points out that 'Five Percenter praxis is
relentlessly individualist', but it's Kodwo Eshun who
comes closest. 'The moment it drugs itself,' he says,
'HipHop becomes an inner-space music.' For the Wu,
the infinite lies within.

241

30TH CHAMBER
THANATASIA

What is *Enter the Wu-Tang* actually about? So far, we've talked all round this—about the social situation of its makers, what movies they watched, the laws they were subjected to, their religious beliefs, about hip hop, the Dozens, signifying and the nature of battle-rhyming, and all of these provide answers of a sort. But what about at surface level? Shouldn't we listen to what they actually say? What is it that preoccupies them? Whether literal or figurative or somewhere in between, how do they choose to represent themselves?

The quickest answer is as purveyors—and consumers—of death. Across the hour of music and skits that make up *Enter* there are over fifty references to guns and to shooting (some used metaphorically, some less so). In addition there are almost twenty-five references to swords, blades, chopping, stabbing and slicing. There are forty-four references to death, killing and murder etcetera (some, of course, overlapping with the shootings and beheadings) and eighteen uses of the words *dead*, *death*, *die* and *deadly*. Listen carefully to the album and you can feel yourself wading across a landscape of corpses. We have learnt, of course, that we mustn't take this too literally, and that when, for instance, Method Man rap-sings that the Wu are 'hitting cats on the block with the Gats' there's no need to dive for cover (unless, of course, there is). But all the same, even if you read every reference to murder and mayhem as metaphorical you're entitled to ask why they choose this particular metaphor in the first place.

The obvious way to answer would be to claim quite simply that the Wu-Tang lived in a world of guns. RZA himself nearly went to prison in 1991 for shooting someone (he claimed self-defence) and certain lines on *Enter* sit comfortably in the realms of firearm connoisseurship, for instance when Raekwon lists 'chrome TECs, nickel-plated Macs, / black AKs'. U-God's son, Dontae Hawkins, aged only two years old, was accidentally shot and critically wounded while playing with his mother and other children outside the Stapleton Houses early in 1994. U-God himself has talked proudly of how many firearms he owned at the time. In 1999, Ghostface Killah was sentenced for third-degree criminal possession of a weapon, and reports also surfaced that the Wu were being investigated for gun running. As recently as 2015, Ghost's son was arrested on two charges relating to unlicensed firearms. These may be metaphors but they are metaphors solidly grounded in the group's day-to-day life. The year 1993 itself was a highpoint for gun crime in the USA, with 18,253 gun-related homicides (down to 11,101 by 2011), equivalent to seven per 100,000 of population. Non-fatal firearm crimes stood at 1.5 million that year and would fall by almost two thirds by 2011. So yes, guns—and their use for killing, wounding and maiming fellow citizens (or even the self; most gun deaths were and are suicides)—were a daily part of life in 1993. They remain so to this day, in a country where you are statistically more likely to be accidentally shot by a toddler than killed by a terrorist, a nation where there are more guns than people. It's tempting to view the Clan's ongoing referencing of firearms as a kind of inoculation, an attempt to rob these weapons of their power through their invocation.

But the Wu's metaphorical armoury is much broader than just Desert Eagles and TEC-9s. In addition are the many sharp edges—swords, but also axes, knives, razors, etc.—which can be used to slice up one's adversaries, often deregulating the neck's relationship to the head. Indeed, as immortalised in the title of GZA's first solo album, Wu-Tang metaphysics sees the tongue as a *liquid sword*, and hence the metaphor of swordplay for rapping lies at the centre of their practice.[29] This love of and fetishisation of the blade is a timely reminder of the influence of *wuxia* on the Clan and, more generally, that we occupy not just a physical universe but an imaginative one, too. Though they entered adulthood surrounded by guns, it is the flash of sharpened metal which animates their rhyming.

All the same, why so much killing? We need to twine the allegorical through unadulterated truth,

---

29   RZA claims, in fact, that 'Wu-Tang... means "The Sword Style"'. The objective accuracy or otherwise of the translation is less important than what it signifies to him.

mash the Deuce into Shaw Brothers, the whole mulched together by weed. On the one hand, the Wu's raps are an evocation of a lived reality, the reality of growing up in New York during the 1980s, when crack was deregulating street crime and guns were readily available to all. On the other hand, it's unsurprising that regular competitors in a martial art called battle-rhyming should rely so heavily on the notion of *killing* when they talk about finishing off their rivals. Ghostface fires 'styles from my lethal weapon— / my pen', while RZA threatens to drive his 'Wu-Tang sword right through your navel / Suspenseful force being brought through my utensil— / The pencil'. Furthermore, not only do the MCs operate on both literal and figurative levels at once, they are well aware that they are operating on both these levels at once. Indeed, the play between these two levels is what gives their words a weight and reality of their own. The story that liberals like to tell about hip hop is one in which the rapper becomes a social victim, forgiven his verbal sins because of the situation he finds himself in. He (or she) is ground down and trapped by (in) reality. Gates's response is to point out that rappers don't always mean what they say but sometimes that's just not enough. After all, if they don't mean what they say, what *do* they mean?

A standard interpretation of the changes in hip hop moving from the late 1980s into the early 1990s would emphasise the split between the more 'positive', Afrocentric strands represented by the likes of Public Enemy and the Native Tongues movement, and gangsta rap, with N.W.A as its figurehead. On the most negative reading, the latter would be viewed as some sort of death cult, a collapse into extreme nihilism. Often, though, this rupture is overplayed and Wu-Tang undermine such a binary reading—or collapse or transcend that reading. Drawing on many of the same sources as the Afrocentrists, the Clan combine 'Black nationalism' with a slightly gothic fascination with death and killing, a harsh negativity, the lore of the mean streets so prevalent in the gangsta narrative. They live, after all, in a world where 'to be a black revolutionary is to be a dead revolutionary', in a world where the average life expectancy of a Black male in 1990 was seven years less than for a White male. From the outside looking in, though, it could seem a lot like they're worshipping destruction.

In his essay 'Thuggods: Spiritual Darkness and Hip-Hop', bassist Melvin Gibbs traces the use of the word 'thug' backwards from its place in contemporary hip hop (it could be said to have entered common parlance with Tupac's Thug Life group in 1994) to its roots with the 'Thuggee' of India, memorialised in a series of cheap novelisations as 'a fearsome cult of religiously inspired killers, for whom the act of murder was akin to human sacrifice' (in the words of the historian Mike Dash). Gibbs compares the original Thugs' devotion to Kali—often viewed as a goddess of destruction—to contemporary devotion within the Five Percent Nation, claiming that both are actually committed to 'the One Primordial Power of the Universe'. Furthermore, he sees the threat the Thuggee posed to British imperialists resting exactly in the idea of 'a dark goddess, worshipped by dark-skinned people with "dark" rites'. It's a provocative idea, but Dash's history of the Thug phenomenon casts doubt on how slavishly in thrall the Thuggee were to Kali, instead suggesting that the lip service paid to her and the rituals carried out by the Thuggee were in fact more part and parcel of a complex caste system than an inspiration for the killings themselves.

Perhaps the reason this rings some sort of bell is that earlier in this book we quoted Michelle Alexander describing the racist operation of the USA's criminal justice system as a caste system. Looking at the accounts of interviews with the Thuggees, what strikes the reader most is how matter-of-fact they are about the trade they have, for the most part, been born into (that of murdering thieves). This touches on one of Gibbs's key points, too. While the authorities have tended to view the Five Percenters as a gang, young African Americans use these teachings to 'overcome their caste status'. And the key problematic within a caste system is how you picture yourself beyond that system, how you imagine yourself—or even conceptualise yourself as an existing human being—outside that world.

— — —

The end of 1993 was a difficult time for Sean 'Puffy' Combs. Fired from Uptown Records in September of that year, it took him until early 1994 to get the backing from EMI to launch a new imprint, Bad Boy. By the end of 1994, Craig Mack's 'Flava In Ya Ear' had been a massive hit and the Notorious B.I.G.'s debut album, *Ready To Die*, had gone gold (it would end up quadruple platinum). But Puff Daddy's success wasn't met with universal acclaim. 'For some people in the hip-hop nation,' Dan Charnas recalls, 'Combs's flamboyance was fraudulence. The rise of Bad Boy seemed to usher in a new era in which authenticity and credibility were defined less by artistry and more by access to power, whether in the street or the boardroom.' The response to this change was encapsulated by the increasingly popular call to 'keep it real', a rejoinder to the apparently fake Combs and the root of a schism which would shape hip hop throughout the mid-to-late nineties.

The Wu-Tang were caught up in this culture war, held up as paragons of the grimy, *keepin' it real* tendency, contrasted with the slick, slightly hollow product Puffy was releasing, even while Biggie and Method Man, at the very least, were friendly (Meth was the only guest MC on *Ready To Die*). The contrast was bound to be drawn. There was no apparent gap in terms of personal style between the Wu and their fans, while their music seemed dirty, aggressive and uncompromising. Some of this was perception rather than actuality. Not only did Meth appear on Biggie's album, but one of the biggest hits the crew had was his single, 'All I Need', featuring the vocal talents of Mary J. Blige. Puffy had A&Red Blige's first album before he was sacked from Uptown. And we've already seen Kodwo Eshun's suggestion that weed undermines any notion of the 'real' within hip hop, anyway.

What if this whole reaction was misguided? Not, it should be noted, the reaction of disgust in relation to Sean Combs, who it's hard to see as anything other than a clever, energetic marketing man who lucked out in his association with The Notorious B.I.G. and never managed to produce a halfway decent record without him (the nadir was, without doubt, his 'tribute' to the erstwhile MC after he was shot, 'I'll Be Missing You'— The Police's 'Every Breath You Take' made even worse, in itself some sort of gargantuan feat). No, the derision still seems reasonable. But perhaps it was a mistake to interpret Puffy's offence as a lack of authenticity and hence to react by calling for favoured hip hop artists to *keep it real*. The result led towards a rather dour and uninspired purism, a belief in big samples of classic soul and lyrics about hip hop itself (boring!), a turning-inward as it became harder and harder to find the solid ground of the real to launch a critique from.

'Realism', as we already noted, tends to be a rather limiting concept, used to berate the imaginative for their naivety, a politically loaded notion whose main aim is to persuade us that nothing can be changed, that everything should be as it always has been (or even better, as it appears to have always been). The criticism of Puffy shouldn't have been for a lack of realism, but for embracing the wrong alternative to 'Realism', a wet dream of cut-price oligarch chic. To replace reality with such a weak and sickly myth, with such a *lack* of imagination, that was the sin. To put it in terms of caste, Puffy's error was to imagine being allowed to be nouveau-Brahman, to conceptualise conspicuous consumption as the fuel for some kind of social—never mind mental and spiritual—escape.

Perhaps the Wu-Tang's obsession with death should be seen within the context of them building their own competing myth, whose job is to in some sense destabilise the dominant paradigm of 'reality'. We have to remember hip hop's talent for reversal, for that act of re-wiring which makes the machines of history run backward. Perhaps in the same way that 'bad' comes to mean 'good', so 'death' in the Wu-Tang's world actually means 'life' and the gun fires the silver bullets which bring breath back to the lungs of the undead. The talk of death isn't an inoculation, but a frantic rite of reinvention. To be *ill* or *sick* is only the first step on the road to *def*. The violence they observe and/or advocate (the violence of the action of their rapping) is metaphysical—designed to rip them (and their listeners) out of the reality they find themselves trapped in. Death, on this reading, constitutes an escape from a spiritual prison, a re-awakening, symbolised by those endless beheadings. The skull represents conventional thinking, a vision of reality as immutable, the neck the way in which we are tethered to it. 'Thirty-six chambers of death / Three hundred and sixty degrees of perfected styles / Chopping off your motherfuckin' *dome*.' We are talking enlightenment, not slaughter, something similar to the *spiritual war* concept of jihad.

The point is made explicitly on the Gravediggaz album—released as *Six Feet Deep* but originally titled *N***amortis*—which RZA was working on simultaneously with *Enter*. Another Wu-Tang associate, Shabazz the Disciple, guests on the record, and makes the connections plain when he raps on the lead single, 'Diary of a Madman', 'Grew up in Hell, now I dwell in an Islamic temple / I'm fighting a Holy War in the mental.' As Prince Paul (called the Undertaker for the purposes of the record) puts it later on the album, 'As your soul enters the next stage / Reality becomes obsolete.' Speaking in the sing-song voice of a bardonic tour guide for the deceased, he finishes up by saying that 'life is nothing but a form of animated death'.

The problem was that the Gravediggaz were treated as a joke, a kind of parody act, rather than a vehicle for spiritual cleansing, as exemplified by the reaction of the journalist Havelock Nelson, who coined the term 'horrorcore' for what they did. Prince Paul recalls, 'I was like, "Please don't do that. *Please* don't do that."' But it was already done. The grave was dug, and there was no climbing out. It's tempting to think that, although *Enter* came out a year earlier, RZA foresaw the problems which would beset the reception of *Six Feet Deep* and embedded

the same rhetoric of death and re-birth much deeper
on the Wu-Tang's debut, deliberately making it hard to
grasp, so that it was also hard to misuse or misinterpret.
So that, to the uninitiated, the violence and guntalk
was indistinguishable from 'gangsta' storytelling. Once
again, the strength of *Enter* lies in its ambiguity, its
hybridity, its refusal to be just one thing or the other, but
to try to be everything at once, myth and reality all rolled
up together. Though, of course, this ambiguity is more
easily maintained within the sealed, controllable space
of the artefact than it is out in the brute actuality of
the real world.

31ST CHAMBER
JUMPING FREE

Inside *Enter the Wu-Tang*, Ol' Dirty Bastard is still alive. Inside *Enter the Wu-Tang* we can meet Russell Tyrone Jones and deal with him as an artist, making artist's choices, rather than as a salutary lesson. Outside *Enter the Wu-Tang* we enjoy hearing and telling stories of ODB lifting cars off kids, appearing on stage while on the run from rehab, being shot at by the police, changing his name to Dirt McGirt and then Big Baby Jesus and then Osiris, rushing the stage at the Grammys to declare 'Wu-Tang is for the children', cashing his food stamps on MTV and so on. But outside *Enter the Wu*-Tang, he's ashes in an urn somewhere and the Bastard's children have no father. So what are we doing when we indulge this appetite for outside? Are we celebrating Ol' Dirty or are we killing him all over again? (I really don't know.)

What we're going to do here is focus on the move Russell Jones made from being Ason Unique to being Ol' Dirty Bastard. We're going to think of it as the ratification, the naming if you like, of an already-taken formal decision. It's not exactly clear when this decision was reached, but it can be summed up by some words from that infamous MTV interview that Jones gave in 1995. 'I rap, but I sing, man—knowhamsayin'? And I don't know how to sing.' The statement isn't, of course, strictly true. Jones can sing, kind of, he just can't sing in the highly trained, technical manner of a soul man drilled from youth in a Baptist church choir. The standard assumption would be that his attitude to vocals is closer to punk rock—a rejection, implicit or otherwise, of *craft* as a barrier to entry. Or maybe he just really can't sing. He doesn't say that, though. He says he doesn't know how, which is slightly different.

Jones eases into it. On 'Protect Ya Neck' he contents himself with a crooned 'C'mon baby baby, c'mon baby baby, c'mon baby baby, c'mo-o-o-on' before he jumps into his verse, a line which could just as easily have been delivered by Method Man. The rap itself is delivered pretty straight. He extends 'shame' a little and pitches it up ever so slightly. He repeats the trick on 'fool' but only really lets go on his two uses of the word 'rolling', which he separates out from the verbiage around them, repeating the exact tonal attack on the second so you can be sure that the first was not a mistake. They sit outside the rest of the verse as if they've been punched in from a different performance, a different persona. It's almost as if he's working out what he can do, how far he can push it, edging towards something which scares even him (RZA: 'He scares some people, but other people just love him because

he'll do what they wish they would do but are scared.'
To put it another way, whether you love him or not, fear
plays a part in your decision.)

You can trace the development of Ol' Dirty Bastard
(as opposed to Ason Unique, let alone Rusty Jones)
through the rest of the record. He takes two short
verses on 'Shame on a Nigga'. The first is, once again,
reasonably conventional, but on the second he starts to
stretch his words and add a more singsong tone. When
he quotes the movie *Warriors* ('Warri-ee-ahs come
out and play-ay-ay') he seems to cut free of his own
inhibitions. He launches into an extended diarrhoea/
gonorrhoea riff, comes out of that talking about the shit
stains in his drawers (like a judoka reversal of GZA's
'what's that in your pants?' line), all of which allows him
to use the word 'fizzafunky' before dropping the quite
ordinary line 'I'll be like wild with my style'. Except that
ODB (because he is now, most definitely, ODB) takes this
banal little boast and makes it just as wild as he claims,
belting out *I'll*, *wild* and *style* in an identical lower-
register roar, so that they make the line bounce way
more than it has any right to.

The juju is thoroughly out of the box now and
there's no putting it back.[30] It's hard to be sure if Ol' Dirty
sounds more unhinged on 'Wu Tang: 7th Chamber'
or on the longer verse on 'Da Mystery of Chessboxin''.
The latter probably just about takes it for its rhythmic
innovations, the sense that he can barely be bothered to
make the lines scan, let alone hit them anywhere near
the metre. Rhyming a little way off the back of the beat

---

30   An asson is, in voodoo, 'the calabash rattle that is the symbol of office of the
houn'gan or mam'bo… Inside the asson are stones and the vertebrae of snakes
which give the asson its sound. These stones and vertebrae are considered bones
of the African ancestors.'

is a valid rap strategy. It gives your delivery a laid-back, swinging flow. But this is not rhyming off the back of the beat. This is something else.

Let's deal with 'Wu-Tang: 7th Chamber' first. ODB contributes one short verse to the tune, going last but one, after six MCs have already spat their hardest. He takes the first line in a relatively understated fashion, but when he comes to his name in line two, he lets it go, aiming for some Scooby Doo-styled bravado, as if the magic of his own chosen title has set him free. From then on it's all systems go: he hollers out 'piss' at the end of line four, emphasising the sheer ludicrousness of a simile in which he claims to be like a sorceress because his special power, too, is some weird kind of urine-shooting ability. He then runs through a rhythmically tricky couplet about wack MCs before naming himself once again ('the Old Specialist') and finally finishing off by exhorting his previous self (Ason Unique) to *drop that science* (a classic Five Percent Nation phrase) in a high-pitched, possessed screech. He hasn't delivered any two consecutive lines in the same style. It's a quite masterful display of imagination and control disguised as a chaotic brain-dump.

ODB's name is said to have been taken from a Hong Kong movie issued on video in the States as *Ol' Dirty and the Bastard* (or *Ol' Dirty Kung Fu* or, in its original iteration, *Mad Mad Kung Fu*). The film itself is, by all accounts, fairly disappointing, but is perhaps best seen as one of a host of movies to come out off the back of the success of *Drunken Master* (1978), starring Jackie Chan. ODB takes the drunken style to a new level, sounding like an inebriate staggering and jumping from stone to stone across a raging river. Somehow he is always just where he needs to be when he needs to be, and the way in which he keeps narrowly avoiding disaster intensifies our pleasure in his success.

Mistakes and all, 'Da Mystery of Chessboxin'' sounds like a high-wire comedy act, an exercise in sustained improvisation, in rescuing victory from the jaws of defeat. It has so much energy and verve, so many ideas in terms of melody and rhythm, it can hardly contain them. It's peak Dirty. He's reached the point where you can no longer see the joins between delivery and persona. Throughout he alters pitch with an uncanny sense of where you expect him *not* to go. And despite the apparently wild abandon of his performance, it's worth remembering this—it's very hard to choose to send your voice where no one is expecting it to go.

More than Rick James (who he would later disguise himself as) you can hear bits of Screamin' Jay Hawkins and Little Richard in ODB's vocal style. Hawkins is reputed to have been so drunk when he recorded his breakout hit, 'I Put a Spell on You', that he could remember nothing of it afterwards and had to learn the song all over again by listening back to his own recording. Dirty himself was 'straight alcohol', according to his friend Buddha Monk. 'Dirty was an Olde English motherfucker. I'm personally surprised they didn't endorse his ass.' Hawkins included so many grunts and screams on 'I Put a Spell on You' that the record company decided to edit them out after members of the public complained about the tune's 'suggestive and cannibalistic' overtones. An airplay ban only seemed to increase sales of the record and established him as 'the most outrageous performer extant during rock's dawn'. Bo Diddley summed up Hawkins' appeal when he said 'he was different. He was comical... and *scary*.' The scariness is what he added to the tricks he'd learnt from Little Richard. As we've already noted (much) earlier, Richard was the Beethoven of the grunt and the screech. But Richard could really sing, the rest was just the baroque 'n' roll flourishes he placed around this fact. For Hawkins, though, the thought process went as follows: 'One, I can't sing. Not to my knowledge. Two, I can holler, I can scream... I said, *Now, if you gonna scream, you gonna scream on everything. So that means you're never gonna be a good singer. You can't sing anyway. Make noise.*'

There's something slightly disingenuous—or at least self-protecting—in this. Inspired by Paul Robeson, Hawkins had wanted to be an opera singer. He had a good, rich baritone voice, perhaps just not exceptional enough for a Black man trying to break into an exclusively White world. The creation of *noise* is perhaps best seen as a reaction to this disappointment. When he first met Rudi Protrudi of the band the Fuzztones in the 1980s, the first thing he said to him was, 'I don't like White people.' Whereas Little Richard uses noise to increase and direct frenzy, Hawkins employs it as a middle finger, a fuck you, a deliberate, tactically deployed disruption.

Something of this could be attributed to ODB, too. He and his two cousins, Prince Rakeem and The Genius, had formed a group, first called Force of the Imperial Master, then All in Together Now. RZA mentions Dirty more than any other member of the Wu when he talks about travelling round the city of New York battling other MCs. Is it possible that, lacking the sheer technique and coolness of manner of The Genius, ODB opted for a high-risk, all-or-nothing battle technique, a kind of scorched-earth policy in which he would attempt to be so outrageous that his opponent would become distracted, falter or fall apart? That is, his own deliberate, tactically deployed disruption?

Let's focus less, though, on the grunting and shouting in ODB's performances and instead concentrate on the music he creates with his rap-singing, in particular the interval jumps that he makes throughout his most animated performances: unusual, precipitous switchbacks in his melodic flow which, along with his rhythmic and tonal shifts, leave the listener unsure what to expect next. The use of unusual intervals can, in fact, be seen as the signature innovation of his performances. It's what creates our uncertainty about where he's going, which is, in turn, what generates our exhilaration when he goes there. And it's here that we see, most bloody-mindedly, Dirty *choosing*. It's in the nature of these unusual intervals ('*I don't know how to sing*') that they don't come naturally. In that they seem random—unresolved and unresolvable—they're not where your mind and hence your voice would, left to its own devices, choose to settle. To hit these notes, then, is a sustained act of will. In an interview with Jaime Lowe in 2004, Lowe asked the rapper, 'Do you feel like your life isn't based on your decisions?' ODB responded, 'Nobody's life is based on something they decide.' And yet, note by note, syllable by syllable, only ODB could be said to have consciously chosen where and how his vocals land.

The problem with this technique is that it pisses people off. It makes you sound crazy at best, wilfully and deliberately eccentric at worst. Although in many ways a person of a completely contrary character to Dirty, the multi-instrumentalist Eric Dolphy is acknowledged as a pioneer of the 'wilder use of unexpected intervals' in jazz. As with any pioneer, his innovations weren't allowed to pass without garnering a certain amount of abuse. In 1961, the writer John Tynan famously attacked Dolphy and John Coltrane for 'the musical nonsense' they were peddling. 'Coltrane and Dolphy... seem bent on pursuing an anarchistic course in their music that can be termed anti-jazz.' Three years later, Miles Davis was played a Dolphy tune in one of the 'blindfold' tests the magazine *Down Beat* carried out with famous musicians (where they were played records and asked to comment without being told what they were listening to). Davis, never a man to hide his contempt for a fellow professional, responded, 'That's got to be Dolphy— nobody else could sound that bad! The next time I see him I'm going to step on his foot. You print that. I think he's ridiculous. He's a sad motherfucker.' Tynan, meanwhile, finished his attack by quoting the composer William Grant Still on developments in contemporary classical music: 'It is mainly the exclusive use of dissonance, formlessness, and stunts that I deplore.'

In that the interval leap involves a jump, it makes sense to characterise it as a stunt (to its detractors, at least). What is it about this stunt in particular that upsets people so? The deployment of odd or unusual intervals in music has a long and controversial history. The tritone (three whole tones above the root) has been called the *Diabolus in Musica*, the devil in music, and has been both used and avoided for the uneasy, queasy power it generates. You can hear it in everything from the opening guitar chords of Jimi Hendrix's 'Purple Haze' to the timpani at the start of Wagner's *Siegfried*. It's perhaps not a complete coincidence that on 'Wu-Tang: 7th Chamber', the first tune on which ODB really cuts loose as a vocal stylist, RZA fashions a tritonal chord leap straight from the Thelonious Monk playbook. As Geoff Dyer has put it, 'a logic was operating, a logic unique to Monk: if you always played the least expected note a form would emerge, a negative imprint of what was initially anticipated'. At the other interval extreme, Stravinsky uses a chromatic run (made up of all semitones) in the *Firebird* to signal the arrival of the evil enchanter Koschei, and Bernard Herrmann famously came close to twelve-tone composition to express Norman Bates' madness in Hitchcock's *Psycho*.

None of this is set in stone, though. Different cultures have different ideas about what works harmonically. Indian classical music as well as Spanish flamenco both rely on quarter tones, for instance. The ethnomusicologist Alan Lomax developed the theory of cantometrics in part to explain this. Lomax suggested, among other things, that the freer and more egalitarian a society was, particularly in its attitudes towards women, the larger the intervals in that society's sung scales would be. As societies became stricter and more hierarchical, so the notes they used would begin to clump together. He accounted for the unique sound of the blues by pointing to the way in which the wide interval gaps of traditional African tribal music were married with 'blue' notes (predominantly flattened thirds and fifths), as a response to slaves finding themselves stranded at the bottom of the strict hierarchy of American society. 'Big leaps give a sense of freedom,' Lomax claims, 'but the narrowing or blueing of the intervals tinge them with irony and sadness.'

Seen in this light, the interval jump, whether employed by Dolphy or ODB (or for that matter, the West Coast group Freestyle Fellowship, working contemporaneously, though with a very different set of influences), is not eccentric at all, but a leap towards freedom. Not only is each note chosen a decision consciously taken by the artist in question, it's a decision which strikes at the musical—and hence the social—status quo. No wonder it makes people so angry, so eager to declare its exponents mad or idiotic. Dirty is usually branded the fool or court jester of the Wu-Tang Clan, as if his aim was to provide a commentary on his surroundings—America as a whole, the world of hip hop, the world of the Wu-Tang—and yes, he may have done this to some extent, but it's not clear that this was his intention. His purpose was, in fact, much more fundamental, much more radical. His was a liberation music. But there's another narrative, too, which developed over the eleven years between the release of *Enter the Wu-Tang* and Jones's death—overweight, lost and broken—shortly before his thirty-sixth birthday, and in this one ODB was just stone-cold crazy, strung out on crack or any other form of cocaine he could get hold of, an agent of chaos eaten up and spat out by chaos.

You can see how the two played into each other, the way that choosing this form of deliberately willed expression might lead inexorably to getting trapped into a wider social perception. It's the fate of visionaries without power to end up as dead visionaries or broken visionaries (remember, once again, Hoover's threat about Black revolutionaries). And the line between acting crazy and actually *being crazy* is a very fine and subtle one, not immediately obvious from the outside. Or, after some time, from the inside, either. Brian Cohen—head of marketing at Elektra Records when ODB's debut album was being prepared—is quite clear about who he was dealing with. 'My impression,' he says, 'was that he was not crazy, *at all*.' Even right at the very end of his life, his close friend and associate Buddha Monk noted, 'Dirty was a mastermind. Everybody thought he was crazy but if he wanted to get something, he knew where, if he wanted to get somewhere, he knew how.'

And that's why we should stop. Let's stop before everything went so wrong. Let's hold time still. Let's remember him as he was on *Enter*—not crazy *at all*, only brilliant and brave, the most radical member of a radical Clan, whose apparent lack of control was predicated on the most complete control. Let's remember him whip-thin, his head tilted, gold teeth showing, his eyes aggressively wide, wiry dreads moving away from his scalp like spilt lines of paint or the tentacular extrusions of his brilliant Black mind. Let's let him win. Let's remember those vocals, uninhibited by any rules except those he chose. Let's focus always on the exhilaration, the feeling we had when we first heard him, the disbelief, the laughter which bubbled up like it does in children. Not the laughter of mockery, but the laughter of pure joy, the laughter of disbelief and amazement, the laughter which is all you can manage when confronted by the undeniable, surprising beauty of the world. Let's let him breathe.

32ND CHAMBER
THE LAST BATTLE

Musically, 'C.R.E.A.M.' is one of the more conventional pieces of music on *Enter the Wu-Tang (36 Chambers)*. Looping up a sample from the introduction to The Charmels' 1967 single, 'As Long As I've Got You', it serves as a simple, soulful, almost elegant base for the words of the MCs on the tune. Nothing is supposed to distract from what's being said. The title itself is an acronym, which expands into Method Man's repeated phrase, 'Cash rules everything around me', and the lyricists paint a striking picture of capitalism at its rawest and most unregulated as part of the New York drugs trade: 'we got stick-up kids, corrupt cops, crack rocks and / Stray shots'. Reification is the name of the game here, the way in which money becomes real, a concrete prison trapping us—the way we become money, interchangeable notes in a variety of denominations.

The effect is amplified by the use of Barbara McCoy's falling vocal run, disembodied and thinned out until it's the sound of a ghost moaning—a world in which cash is more real than the humans who use it.

The lyricists on 'C.R.E.A.M.' spell out money's effects in vivid, fractured lines. Marx, channelling Shakespeare, says that one of the properties of money is as 'the visible god-head' but, unlike the gods of NYC, it creates nothing, merely transforming whatever already exists—a kind of cheap conjuring trick: 'the transformation of all human and natural qualities into their opposites, the general confusion and inversion of things'. You could see it as a god of chaos, of mischief and trickery, but if so it's one completely lacking a sense of humour, implacable, utterly systematic in its cruel magic. Raekwon takes the first verse, a brilliantly animated, ghoulish piece of first-person storytelling, ending with the revelation that the combination of 'cracks and weed /... made my eyes bleed'. The second verse is by Inspectah Deck and it's a tour de force—not just reportage like Rae's, but also a compacted outline of the band's belief system. It's a bleakly beautiful study in alienation which we've returned to again and again throughout this book, but the despair it spells out is followed by a revelation of sorts. Asking his mother why he shouldn't just give up, Deck reports that her response is that 'working hard will help you maintain / to learn to overcome the heartaches and pain'. The question remains, though: working hard at what, exactly?

There's a strong argument to be made that Inspectah Deck is the best MC on *Enter the Wu-Tang*. If you had to pick a verse as the emotional core of the album, you'd struggle to improve upon his contribution to

'C.R.E.A.M.', but at the same time, his lines on 'Wu-Tang: 7th Chamber' are a miniature masterclass in creative boasting. He's immaculate throughout, but the funny thing is how often you don't notice you're noticing him. It's only when you devote some attention to it that you begin to realise how many of your favourite lines are his, how often he says just the right thing at just the right time.

This isn't an accident. It's the result of a deliberate tactic on Deck's part, a kind of self-abnegation. 'My whole thing with being the Inspectah,' he recalls in a wide-ranging interview with *Halftime Online*, 'was that you had a whole lot of characters that were loud. Dirty is a loud cat, RZA is loud, and Meth is wild... Everybody had a crazy personality... I'm the laid back n***a.' Seeing the showmen in the group, rather than trying to compete on their terms, Deck deliberately opts to contrast himself with them. If you're going up against loud and wild opponents you can try to go wilder than them, but your best chance to wrongfoot them and gain an edge might be to come through understated and analytical and see how they respond. It's not dissimilar to the aesthetic decisions taken by Miles Davis at the start of his career when, knowing he couldn't compete with Charlie Parker technically, he opted to emphasise a controlled sense of space and timing in his solos (and it's worth remembering that Deck's father was himself an accomplished jazz trumpeter).

It is, in Deck's case, something of a selfless decision, though. If there were more fireworks, a bit of showmanship in his performances, he would be as revered a figure as the other key members of the Clan. Instead, beyond the aficionados, he's largely ignored—and the aficionados talk about him mainly in terms of his being ignored, which is almost as bad (possibly worse). Of the core MCs, he was the only one not to release a solo album during RZA's original five-year plan, ostensibly because a flood in the producer's basement studio destroyed all the beats which had been set aside for his project. And yet it's his voice more than any other member's which glues together the Clan as an ensemble, which makes the whole thing work. There is a humility to this, an old-fashioned belief in craft over charisma, which is somehow reminiscent of Staten Island itself. Deck makes one of the last plays for hip hop as proletarian music, concerned with substance and skill, with an unassuming representation of self and community. And it's a play which works out better for the group as a whole than it does for him as an individual.

This tension between communality and the importance of the individual is one of the threads (or fault lines?) that runs through *Enter*. In 'Wu-Tang: 7th Chamber', for example, the word 'I' is used twenty-seven times, while 'we' only appears twice and there are just three references to the Wu as a group.[31] If you use this rough statistical measure across the album the results are even more stark. GZA's ratio of references to the self as opposed to the Wu collective is the lowest, closely followed by RZA and then their cousin, ODB. Method Man refers to himself the most (but then he does have a tune on the record devoted to his persona), but Ghostface Killah's ratio is worse because he only refers to the Wu once throughout the whole record. It's a rather

---

31   And perhaps something of this appeal to a wider community–even an imaginary, a utopian collective–is represented by the 'we' which appears throughout this book even though the author largely wrote it in a room on his own.

small sample from a statistical point of view (and also partly depends on what kind of songs each MC appears on), but it does point to interesting geographical/familial splits at this early stage, with RZA's immediate relatives most committed to the Wu-Tang concept, the Park Hill crew hovering in the middle and the one member from Stapleton the least obviously enthusiastic.

Although the collective power of the Wu-Tang is essential to their success, they operate as a group of highly skilled individuals carrying out individual actions, much like a cricket or baseball team. You can't lose yourself in the collective when it comes to hip hop— this is not a choir, where the voice of each individual is subservient to the sound of the whole. And if you think of hip hop as the renaissance of a post-slave culture, in which individual subjects were previously reduced to an undifferentiated object, then this emphasis makes sense. Individualism, it seems, is hardwired into hip hop—so the problems of individualism must be hardwired in, too.

Deck makes a lot of very sound points in that *Halftime Online* interview, all of which feel a little out of place for a member of Wu-Tang. He says this, for instance: 'We got n***as who think they're gangsta because they shot two n***as they grew up with and got away with it. You ain't *gangsta*, n***a. *Gangsta* was Harriet Tubman, who got away from slavery and went back to go help n***as. And kept going back. Risked her life to get away and went back to face certain death and did that shit like forty times. *That's* gangsta.' Deck also talks about his respect for Chuck D, saying that his tag name, Rebel INS, was inspired by Public Enemy (the original rebels without a pause). He goes on to suggest that 'it's time to go back to the sixties. Them n***as fought for their community… It's time to go back [to] when Martin [Luther King] was like, "Fuck that, we are gonna start marching on shit and demanding to be heard."' The reason none of this sounds quite like Wu-Tang (or Martin Luther King for that matter) is because it's political. And the Wu don't seem that interested in following Public Enemy by expounding a political philosophy, beyond their role as a collective with an emphasis on individualism. Or, as the Rebel INS puts it, in a phrase which has echoed through this book, 'I bake the cake, then take the cake / and eat it, too, with my crew.'

There's individualism, of course, and then there's individualism, and this is something Deck explores in a story he recounts about close Clan-associate (and, after ODB's death, unofficial ninth member), Cappadonna. Deck remembers being round at Cappadonna's house and Cappa rapping in front of a full-length mirror, 'like he's battling himself'. Deck had no idea what Cappa was trying to do and so he asked him. Cappadonna responded, 'Who is the illest n***a who can fuck with you? It's you. That's the only n***a that can fuck with me so I have to go toe-to-toe with *him*.' Cappadonna, it transpires, was battling his own reflection, using the mirror not to admire his latest finery, but in order to take himself down, to learn, to practise. To work. Deck goes on to explain how seeing this helped him train for battling—getting his stance right, helping him to *fix his face*—but in this case he's missed the point.

The main difference—the big difference—between the Wu's individualism and that promoted by the high priests of conspicuous consumption lies in the central emphasis on battling and, beyond that, in what battling is, at root, all about. Since the mid-nineties, the RZA

268

has been training with Sifu Shi Yan Ming—a genuine Shaolin monk who defected and sought asylum when the Chinese government brought members of his monastery to New York to demonstrate their skills. The key lesson absorbed from the monk, RZA says, is 'that kung fu was less a fighting style and more about the cultivation of spirit'. Or, to put it another way, battling is a spiritual pursuit—and, as with all spiritual pursuits, the main fight is with yourself. Cappadonna was on to something more important than just a way of getting your stance right. Instead, his primary concern was with getting his spirit right.

This is not a fight that the Wu have always—or even often—won. You only have to think about ODB to know that. In fact, to suggest that, at its core, *Enter the Wu-Tang* is an album primarily concerned with spirituality (rather than with guns, drugs, cars, swords, and how absolutely brilliant the Wu-Tang Clan are, for instance) might be to open yourself up to a certain amount of ridicule. Then again, if you collide a heretical sect of the Nation of Islam with the popular culture of the Chinese diaspora, throw in enough weed to stun a horse, and pass the whole thing through the intestines of hip hop culture, then whatever spirituality you can distil from what comes out of the other end is going to be a distinctive, possibly explosive brew.

Maybe it's not even a fight that's supposed to be won. Yeah, enlightenment must be lovely and all that, but it's probably dull, too. The point is to fight, to fight yourself, to keep fighting. And to do it all in a world which is simultaneously trying to crush you. That's why it's called work. And it should be said, for the sake of clarity, that *Enter* isn't *only* concerned with spirituality.

Right back at the start, on the short documentary made for the release of the album, The Genius explains the genesis of the group as follows: 'brothers from the same projects that got together to work on one project—to escape the projects. Not only move out, but escape the things they were subjected to.'

In rap, the initial form of escape is provided by rapping itself, the fantasies it allows you to exercise: of revenge, of domination and of transcendence. The feelings you're running from, though, never completely fade. At best you stop the wound from hurting for a while, but the throb of it is even worse when it returns. The obvious next step is to make a hill of money and get out of there. Pack up, buy a big house out in Jersey, get Moms the place next door. And this is not only an important step but often a necessary one, because the local youth of whichever project you start in may turn out to be ambivalent, at best, about your success. But as The Genius has already noted—and as many a rapper has discovered, even as they show the cameras of *MTV Cribs* around their property—just escaping from the physical reality of the projects isn't enough. You have to escape from 'the things [you] were subjected to', as well. You have to escape, in some way, from what the projects have done to your soul (and by the projects we mean poverty, racism, crime and drug abuse, among other things—what we mean by 'your soul' is less clear). This is what the Genius is hinting at when he remembers the effect of those kung fu flicks upon the members of the Clan. 'All we did,' he says, 'was apply the morals of the stories to our everyday life basis—the brotherhood, the trust, the respect, the honour, the discipline. And we just applied that to everything we do, man.' Discipline. The discipline. It's the same thing Ghostface says he learnt from those movies. A work ethic in which you're both worker and what's worked on.

But discipline isn't enough, because discipline becomes tiring, boring even. You can't keep escaping for ever. You're drinking. You're not just smoking weed, you're smoking woolas (weed with coke) or digi (weed with PCP) and, yes, that gets you out of it but when it wears off it throws you right back in—and hard. You're struggling to keep your dick in your pants. You think someone's going to try to kill you. You think a lot of people are going to try to kill you. You're stuck in a world which, rather than becoming less hostile, has become more hostile. (Do you think the country club wants a *rapper* for a neighbour? Do you think your friends are pleased for you, or jealous? Do you think law enforcement officers appreciate why you might deem it necessary to wear a bulletproof vest? Do you think you should've *known your place?*) Your costs have gone through the roof and people at the record company keep telling you about the internet, as if their sob story is the same as yours—or actually takes precedence. There's a whole ecosystem depending on you to eat. You realise eventually, exhaustion washing over you, that you can't escape. It's not possible. And that's when it comes to you.

In the end, you have to escape from escaping.

33RD CHAMBER
WHOSE PROBLEM?

As we've moved through these chambers we've found
ourselves returning again and again to notions of
race. The history of race, the bizarre shapes it creates,
the circumlocutions and downright lies that are told
in its name, these are the torture instruments lining
our walls. They are warped and warping. Most of all,
they don't make any sense. 'According to an estimate
derived from decades of census reports, some 24 percent
of Americans listed in 1970 as "white" probably had
African ancestors, while more than 80 percent of those
listed as "black" had non-African ones,' Karen and
Barbara Fields point out. As they go on to explain, this
'implies that there were nearly twice as many white as
black Americans of African descent'. Yet we seem to treat
our racial categories as normal, as *real*, based on some
scientific fact, and it's only when confronted by Yakub

and his breeding programme to create white devils that suddenly we find them ridiculous.

As Ta-Nehisi Coates has pointed out, 'Americans believe in the reality of "race" as a defined, indubitable feature of the natural world' (and Americans, though the subject of this book, are not alone in this). But there is no scientific basis for this, none at all. You'd think that if there were, the unravelling of the human genome would have cast such a reality into sharp contrast, but the opposite has happened and geneticists have lined up to say that 'racial classification does not make sense in terms of genetics... Historical racial categories that are treated as natural and infused with notions of superiority and inferiority have no place in biology.' If there is no place for racial categories in biology and biology is supposed to lie at the root of our notion of race, then there is no place for racial categories at all. After all, the field of human genetics was founded by a racist, Francis Galton, 'who sought to demonstrate white British dominance over the colonies using biometrics'. As Coates points out, 'race is the child of racism, not the father', and genetics is too. That it has rejected the assumptions its foundations were based upon is as clear an example of good scientific method as you could hope for.

There are, of course, people who deny this reality, this scientific truth. They are not denying it because the evidence supports their case, unless that evidence is partial, misunderstood, misused, misinterpreted or plain false. They are denying it for devilment, or profit, or from some deep, ugly hunger. Importantly, most of the people who ignore or distort or cherry-pick the science in order to argue for some notion of genetically distinct races are united by a second characteristic.

They 'have been brought up hopelessly, tragically, deceitfully, to believe that they are white'.

It would be comforting to be able to report that 'race' is an ancient idea which will begin to fade away now that science has shown us the error of our ways. In fact, it's a relatively recent innovation. In the second volume of his long, detailed and magisterial study, *The Invention of the White Race*, Theodore W. Allen lays out how the notion of 'whiteness' was magicked into existence in the aftermath of Bacon's Rebellion of 1676. The origins of this clash in the colony of Virginia seem to lie in attitudes towards a Native American attack, but when Nathaniel Bacon gathered men to oppose the authorities, he included African Americans among their number, as well as English bond-labourers, at which point proceedings took a more liberatory turn.

The answer to the growing fear of a rebellion combining lower-class Europeans (themselves subject to a kind of servitude in their position as bond-labourers) with African slaves lay in 'racism, to separate dangerous free whites from dangerous slave blacks by a screen of racial contempt'. As Allen is keen to point out, the 'hallmark' of this system of racial oppression 'is the insistence on the social distinction between the *poorest* member of the oppressor group and any member, however propertied, of the oppressed group'. A land-owning 'yeoman' class had been developed to act as a buffer between the ruling class and dispossessed peasants in England. But in Virginia, where it was too expensive for freed bond-labourers to acquire slaves of their own, the status quo was maintained both by an emphasis on the innate superiority of White people and by the granting of certain privileges of citizenship which only pertained along racial lines.

These privileges—including the right to vote—are why Edmund Morgan, among a wider group of historians, believes that 'the subordination of class by "race" at the beginning of the eighteenth century is the key to the emergence of the republic at the end of it'. Or, to put it even more plainly, 'the founding fathers' emancipatory ideology depended on slavery as a condition of its possibility'. It wasn't a coincidence, this argument runs, that George Washington owned slaves while railing against English attempts at 'enslaving' newly emergent Americans. On Morgan's reading, slavery in effect created a 'racial' yeomanry and hence got rid of the troublesome poor European working class so that a socially homogeneous 'white' society could extol its belief in freedom and the rights of (White) Man. Allen's position is subtly different. He feels that Morgan's argument—that it was in the interests of a poor White working class to oppress Black slaves in pursuit of their own freedom—is incorrect because that White working class remained poor and without a true economic stake in society. Instead, the rhetoric of 'race' only served to distract both parties from their mutual class interests.

Allen would presumably say that it still does, that racism serves no one's interests beyond a ruling elite whose exploitation of the powerless is made easier by them fighting among themselves. Patrick Wolfe argues that 'though born of slavery... race came into its own with slavery's abolition', a ghost unchained. This was the point at which the presumed superiority of one group over another was expressed less through the ironclad certainties of law and more through belief in some 'innate' set of characteristics. Wolfe summarises particularly succinctly the way in which, with the end of slavery, race was re-thought in terms of 'science' while at the same time relying on an almost magical notion of the power of Blackness, as enshrined in the notion that one drop of Black blood would make a child Black: 'Black blood took on a mystic hyperpotency.' It would be reassuring to agree with Allen, to see this as a classic case of false consciousness, but, somehow, that doesn't quite account for the hunger with which people devour this myth, the centrality they've given it in the space where their souls should be, the hatred which has been allowed to flow through it. Perhaps that shows a lack of understanding of the idea of false consciousness, where every frustration in your life is channelled into this one small pipe until the pressure it contains becomes unbearable.

Do we want to play this game, the one in which we say that the only thing left for a disenfranchised White working class is their belief in thwarted superiority?— a superiority which all the facts contradict, suggesting instead that these are the stupidest, the blindest, the most self-pitying and over-sensitive people the planet has ever known (beyond the incessant dog-whistling and even the occasional lusty shout of 'Here, boy!' is it any wonder these people should flock to Trump, the most self-pitying and over-sensitive president the USA has ever known?). Do we want to ascribe false consciousness to Dylann Roof, who gunned down thirteen people as they prayed in the basement of a church, killing nine of them? Or do we want to say only that he was pathetic, spineless, stupid, pumped up on the banality of his own hate? Is it best to see him, too, as the victim of an ugly history or, as Ghostface suggested in the context of Eric Garner, to make him respect violence by visiting it upon him? It's so tempting to opt for the latter, but when we do, aren't we taking an eye for an eye and giving up humanity for humanity? Or is that easier to say when it's not your humanity under attack?

Money and race are similar concepts. Neither has any objective, scientific reality beyond the people who use them. Both are ghosts we all believe in, even when we say we don't. And there is something sticky and intimate in their relationship to each other: 'race is inextricably linked to economics'. Or, as Wolfe notes, 'colonisers – in this case planters – did not set out to create racial discrimination. They set out to create wealth.' Cash Rules Everything Around Me.

We've explored the idea of 'race' as a method of social control in an economic system built on slavery. Slavery, in turn, is a system for turning subjects into objects, people into commodities. The anthropologist David Graeber argues that 'there is every reason to believe that slavery, with its unique ability to rip human beings from their contexts, to turn them into abstractions, played a key role in the rise of markets everywhere'. He goes on to put forward the suggestion that 'some of the most genuinely archaic forms of money we know about appear to have been used precisely as measures of honor and degradation: that is, the value of money was, ultimately, the value of the power to turn others into money'. This notion, central to his study of the way in which our society has been shaped by debt, also feeds back into our examination of the Wu-Tang Clan, who, as we saw, took from the Shaw Brothers movies they watched as teenagers a sense of 'the brotherhood, the trust, the respect, *the honour*, the discipline' (italics added). And when you think about it, the notion of honour is central to hip hop, running through each participant's sensitivity to a potential 'diss' (an act of disrespect). While this notion of honour was found in *wuxia* films for the Wu, it also lies at the heart of hip hop's adoption of Mafia themes. Graeber points out that Pierre Bourdieu has likened honour to '"symbolic capital," analogous to but more important than economic capital, since it is possible to turn honor into money but not the other way around'. Stripped of both dignity and wealth by the depredations of racism, this obsession with the fragile capital of honour makes a strange, off-kilter kind of sense.

Money is, in the words of Felix Martin, a 'social technology', by which he means we should think of it not as a 'thing', as notes and coins with some intrinsic value, but as a system of transferable credit. The description is as well suited for 'race': a complex collection of simple techniques for distributing inequality. In fact, remembering our earlier discussion of technology, we could lose that 'social' (all technology is, after all, social). And if you think of money, as David Graeber does, as debt, then both it and race are technologies for distributing inequality, different but intimately related. As Martin goes on to point out, 'there is a paradox at the heart of money. It is a social technology which depends on other people. Yet it is a social technology which isolates us from other people, by transforming the rich and varied ecology of human relationships into the mechanical and monotonous clockwork of financial relationships.' Perhaps slavery is the model, the ur-story for all our objectifications.

So far we've talked mainly of African Americans as a slave-diasporic people who use the re-referencing or re-wiring (or *signifying*, if you prefer) of cultural systems both to transmit their own culture and, with the advent of hip hop, as an expression of their own culture. But there's another way to think about this, hinted at but not yet clearly stated, which is as a creative misuse of technology. Take the example of the adoption of the saxophone by jazz musicians in the 1920s and '30s. Invented in 1841 by Adolphe Sax, the instrument was far from a runaway success. Although Sax managed to get it adopted by military bands, between 1844 and 1919 only twenty-seven symphonic or orchestral compositions were written with parts for the instrument, mainly to add tonal colour. As late as 1931, it could be stated that 'the saxophone is not a soloistic instrument'. By the end of the First World War, the ability to mass-produce saxophones cheaply—and the ease with which a novice could get a note out of them—had made them into the novelty instrument of the day, with over half a million sold in the USA between 1919 and 1925. It was jazz musicians who realised the way in which this 'toy' instrument could become 'a kind of amplification for the human voice with its great flexibility, many subtleties of articulation and dynamics, and nuances of pitch'. In turning the saxophone into the ultimate solo instrument, these musicians transformed jazz and, by extension, contemporary music as a whole.

Another example which we've already touched on is, of course, the use of the turntable—a delivery system for pre-recorded music—as a musical instrument. Nor were digital samplers developed for the kind of musical collaging that hip hop used them for. In fact, the idea behind the Fairlight CMI was to create a synthesiser with more 'realistic' sounds, while its main competitor, the Synclavier, was marketed as a tapeless studio. To take another example, if you think of the Dozens as a game technology developed to teach young African American males how to control their emotions when under attack (a situation most of them will find themselves in every day for the rest of their lives), then rap itself is a creative misuse of that technology. Even the obsession with the accumulation and maintenance of honour can be read as a creative misuse of the technology of capitalism itself.

It's arguable, in fact, that the notion of race contained in the teachings of the Nation of Islam is exactly such a creative misuse of technology— the technology of race. It's a creative misuse of the technology of the Qur'an and the Bible, too, in the latter case a turning on its head of the various assumptions of White, Western society, an attempt to use the power of that collection of techniques (stories, linguistic underpinnings, philosophical assumptions, etc., all the impedimenta of the pre-conscious grammar of our thinking) against that collection of techniques. And if you accept that idea, then what the Nation of Gods and Earths is involved in is nothing less than the creative misuse of the technology developed by the Nation of Islam.

Of course, you can see martial arts as a technology, too, and the temptation is to treat it as a technology not of war or fighting, but of self-control (just like the Dozens). That's more or less what RZA appears to be talking about when he says kung fu is 'less a fighting style and more about the cultivation of spirit'. But perhaps that's to miss the point, too (or perhaps the point just keeps moving). Perhaps it's actually a technology of transcendence—and what you're supposed to transcend is exactly what you thought you were learning to control. Perhaps martial arts are designed as a journey towards the dissolving of self. What's the purpose of Chan/Zen Buddhism, after all—to the extent it can be said to have a purpose—if not as a series of techniques for undermining our reliance on the notion of self? 'We generally believe that we as individuals have enduring identities, and that the values that determine our relationship with the objects around us are immutable,' writes Sheng-yen, the Chinese Buddhist monk and religious scholar. 'Yet these attitudes are really self-conceived and do not have any reality apart from that which we give to them... It follows that if we can see through our notions of self, we will consequently see through our attitudes about existence as a whole.'

It's worth thinking about what a radical gambit this would be. 'As property,' Wolfe reminds us, 'slaves had no personhood, no basis for rights.' It's this lack of personhood, this removal from any and all social relationships, which leads Graeber to suggest 'that the slave is, in a very real sense, dead' (and this, in turn—echoed and mimicked in the functionings of the US penal system—could be cited as another reason for the Wu's death-drive). The history of the civil rights movement in America is the history of attempts to reinstate or establish the personhood of African Americans, in effect to resurrect them, hundreds of years after they were dragged, in chains, over the Kalunga line. Fundamental to this proposed resurrection is the notion of self. But the same notion of self also underpins America's traditional battle between puritanical self-control and mass consumption. And, as we've seen, the notion of the juridical self with rights (to life, to liberty and, of course, to property) is underpinned by slavery. It's like dead people trying to become zombies or phantoms instead of searching for life. How can you wake up and breathe when the energy to become the very thing you aspire to be is generated by the blood from your own corpse? Perhaps it's time to short-circuit this whole complex of ideas, not so much drive a stake through its heart as transcend it, float up and away from it, following Cliff Smith's preacher-man exhortation to *RELEASE YO' DELF*. That, ladies and gentlemen, would be an exorcism.

34TH CHAMBER
LEVELS OF DEVILS

Etymology is a knotty, compacted, messy business, and
language carries power and conflict—our conflict—
deep inside it. Method Man takes his name from Wu
slang for marijuana, meth (in itself confusing, as for
most people meth would suggest crystal meth—that
is, methamphetamine). But that title is itself surely a
bastardisation of a jazz term for high-grade marijuana
with its roots in the 1930s: mezz. Mezz was so named
for Mezz Mezzrow, a renowned marijuana dealer
who counted Louis Armstrong among his most loyal
customers. And Mezz was White. Or so the records say.
He himself might disagree. Indeed, the co-writer of his
autobiography, Bernard Wolfe, said that Mezzrow 'came
to believe he had actually, physically, turned black'.

Milton Mesirow was born in 1899, the son of Jewish
immigrants, on the Northwest Side of Chicago. Arrested

for stealing a car, he was sent to reform school where he met a group of young, Black jazz musicians—and began smoking weed. He liked the music and the drug and took up both enthusiastically, puffing and playing clarinet, the former with more élan than the latter. When he moved to New York in 1929, it was selling marijuana which supported him rather than music. Having found a Mexican connection who would sell him 'real golden-leaf', he set up on a Harlem street corner, claiming later 'that mellow Mexican leaf really started something in Harlem—a whole new language, almost a whole new culture'. He spent the next decade as a dealer to jazz royalty and beyond, in the process becoming yet another slang term for the product he was pushing. The opening two lines of 'If You're a Viper' (performed by Fats Waller amongst others, a viper being slang for a cannabis smoker) are, 'Dreamed about a reefer five foot long / A mighty Mezz, but not too strong.' When Mezzrow was arrested and sentenced to three years on Riker's Island in 1940, he begged to be placed with the Black prisoners. He got his wish, but not without a short spell in a 'White' cell block first. 'There I could hardly listen to the talk of my cellmates, their language and mannerisms and gestures were so coarse and brutal, they spoke with their lips all twisted up, in harsh accents that jarred on my nerves. I realized again how well off I'd been these last few years, being able to live far away from all this grimy, grating white underworld, up in Harlem where people were real and earthy.'

— — —

If anyone is in any doubt as to why the populations of the world beyond might think of the people of Europe as white devils, they could do worse than read twenty or so pages from Sven Lindqvist's masterful *Exterminate All the Brutes*. In this short section, the Swedish essayist teases out the technological developments of the Industrial Revolution which allowed 'the backward and poorly resourced Europe of the sixteenth century' to become a dominant global power. 'Our most important export was force. All over the rest of the world, we were regarded at the time as nomadic warriors in the style of the Mongols and the Tartars. They reigned supreme from the backs of horses, we from the decks of ships.' Lindqvist spells out how an arms race between small, warring coastal states led to the placing of cannons on boats and how these boats upset the global balance of power, doing untold damage first in India and China and then more widely.

The American input to this particular story came in the form of Robert Fulton's steamboat, which made its maiden commercial voyage up the Hudson from New York Harbor in 1807. So successful was the vessel that when the British threatened to attack New York in 1812, the money was found for Fulton to build *Demologos*, the first steam-powered warship. This innovation was swiftly copied back in Britain. The advent of steam-powered boats made it easy for heavy artillery to be taken into the interior of foreign countries, increasing European military power. 'The "gunboat" became a symbol of imperialism on all the major African rivers,' notes Lindqvist, 'making it possible for Europeans to control huge, hitherto inaccessible areas by force of arms.'

The last stage of this colonial dominance was achieved by the rapid evolution of handguns, particularly due to the development of mass-manufactured steel and nitroglycerine. In the middle of the 1800s, both sides were using muzzle-loaded muskets, which took a minute to load while standing up, which failed at least thirty per cent of the time even in dry weather, and which had a range of around one hundred yards. By the end of the century, a European infantryman could fire fifteen shots in fifteen seconds, without any smoke released to give away his position, all while lying down. His bullets—including lead-filled dumdums that splattered and spread on impact, causing horrible, gaping wounds—now had a range of a thousand yards. His opponents mostly still had muskets.

As Lindqvist goes on to point out, this technological dominance led to military dominance, which in turn led to 'a new epoch in the history of racism. Too many Europeans interpreted military superiority as intellectual and even biological superiority.' There was even a sense that superior armament/technology was a reflection of a superior morality. Imperial adventurers often castigated their opponents for their cowardice, exemplified in a refusal to fight, even though to 'fight' only meant to be killed at a distance with no chance of killing your opponent in return. Lindqvist's descriptions of the depredations visited upon the people of Africa by their conquerors—the contempt in which they were held, the holocaust these conquerors hoped to visit upon the people they had defeated—can leave the reader in little doubt as to the suitability of the term 'devil'. He ends by quoting a character in Joseph Conrad's *An Outcast of the Islands* who has lived through a naval bombardment. The survivor could just as well be talking about drone strikes as cannon on a ship. 'First they came, the invisible whites, and dealt death from afar.'

The Battle of Rorke's Drift provides a fine example of this dynamic. Having defeated the British at Isandlwana earlier the same day, around three or four thousand Zulu troops (or 'warriors', as we seem duty-bound to call them) crossed the Mzinyathi River into the British territory of Natal and attacked the mission station and hospital at Rorke's Drift. The compound was successfully defended by 150 British troops and the engagement became a celebrated example of redcoat heroism, resulting in the award of the Victoria Cross (the highest honour of the British army) to eleven soldiers, the largest number ever dished out for one battle. All of which rather overlooks the fact that the British were armed with Martini–Henry rifles ('the first really good weapon of the new generation: swift, accurate, insensitive to damp and jolts') while the Zulus had a few hundred unreliable muskets but largely rejected the use of firearms as cowardly. It's estimated that the British fired all but 600 of the 20,000 rounds they had stockpiled. Of the seventeen British soldiers killed, meanwhile, five were shot (usually at close range) by musket—an indicator of the relative per capita effectiveness even of a musket compared with a spear. Roughly 350 Zulus were killed during the action and up to another 500 wounded and/or captured and then massacred afterwards. Different accounts refer to a makeshift gallows and to wounded Zulus being thrown into mass graves along with the dead, with 'only three Zulu wounded... taken alive'. Rorke's Drift 'was the scene of an atrocity—a war crime, in today's language—which Britain covered up'. Indeed, much of the reason for the song and dance around Rorke's Drift, and, in particular, for the amount of VCs handed out, was to draw the attention of the British public away from the battle at Isandlwana, where 1,000 British soldiers were killed. Sir Garnet Wolseley, who became Commander-in-Chief of the Forces in 1895, said at the time that it was 'monstrous... making heroes of those who... could not bolt, and fought like rats for their lives'.

Unsurprisingly, not so much is made of this in the 1964 film *Zulu*, starring Michael Caine. In fact, not much is made of the Zulu perspective at all. As Jeff Chang points out, 'there are hundreds of African extras, but not a single Black role of any consequence'. Nevertheless (or maybe because of this lacuna?), Afrika Bambaataa cites *Zulu* as a major inspiration, and shows, once again, the formative and creative power of hip hop's re-referencing. 'I see this movie coming out,' Bambaataa recalled to Chang, 'showing Africans fighting for a land that was theirs against the British imperialists. To see these Black people fight for their freedom and their land just stuck in my mind. I said when I get older I'm gonna have me a group called the Zulu Nation.'

— — —

In his book *Why White Kids Love Hip Hop*, Bakari Kitwana—among many other achievements—skewers the notion that hip hop music is, or has ever been, predominantly bought by suburban adolescent white males. The fact that he can even question this particular perceived truth seems shocking at first, so ingrained has the notion become, so much a part of our cultural landscape. But as Kitwana demonstrates, there is no statistical evidence at all for this claim.

David Samuels was the first man to assert the 'fact'. As Kitwana outlines, Samuels published an article in *New Republic* in November 1991, exactly two years before the release of *Enter*, which argued not only that 'although rap is still proportionally more popular among blacks, its primary audience is white and lives in the suburbs' but also that, because of this fact, 'rap's hour as innovative popular music has come and gone. Rap forfeited whatever claim it may have had to particularity by acquiring a mainstream white audience whose tastes increasingly determined the nature of the form.' His argument is that in producing music for White people to vicariously consume as 'authentic' Black experience, hip hop has collapsed into a form of minstrelsy. 'The ways in which rap has been consumed and popularized speak not of cross-cultural understanding, musical or otherwise, but of a voyeurism and tolerance of racism in which black and white are both complicit.'

But while Samuels claimed to have derived his original statistical insight from the recently introduced Soundscan system, the data revealed much less than he claimed. Soundscan, a new digitised method for counting record sales using barcode scanning technology, was at that time used in fewer than 7,500 retail outlets, mainly big chain stores in suburban malls (by the time Kitwana was writing his book, Nielsen-Soundscan were up to 19,000 stores and still admitted that left 10% of sales beyond their reach). As Kitwana points out, this meant that Soundscan's 'data pool was lopsided to begin with' (something of an understatement), but this was only compounded by the assumptions that were made based upon this 'data'. Not least that sales in *high-income* areas (the only demographic distinction Soundscan made) necessarily meant suburban sales to White people—even though malls in high-income areas of cities would likely be frequented by people of all ethnicities.

If Samuels' basic assumption was incorrect, his argument began to fall apart, too—the idea that hip hop had become a form produced predominantly for a White mainstream. After all, he never came up with any evidence beyond the Soundscan data, anecdotal or otherwise, for this claim. We mustn't get too comfortable, though. While the proportion of sales might seem to be important, it's inarguable that hip hop culture has (and indeed had), on a number of levels, come to be consumed by a White audience alongside its traditional Black audience. You can't help but hear the element of truth in the argument of Bill Yousman, whom Kitwana quotes. 'White youth adoption of Black cultural forms in the 21st century is also a performance,' Yousman says, 'one that allows Whites to contain their fears and animosities towards Blacks through rituals not of ridicule, as in previous eras, but of adoration. Thus, although the motives behind their performance may initially appear to be different, the act is still a manifestation of White supremacy.'

Zadie Smith circles around a similar point in an essay for *Harper's* magazine, in part a review of Jordan Peele's film, *Get Out*. The central insight of the movie, Smith argues, is 'that to be oppressed is not so much to be hated as obscenely loved. Disgust and passion are intertwined. Our antipathies are simultaneously a record of our desires, our sublimated wishes, our deepest envies.' Then she goes on to reinforce Yousman's point. 'In place of the old disgust comes a new kind of cannibalism. The white people in *Get Out* want to get inside the black experience: They want to wear it like a skin and walk around in it.'

All of which was summed up by William 'Upski' Wimsatt in an article he wrote for *The Source* in May 1993 which, at the time, caused quite a storm. They cut his last paragraph, though, on the grounds that it was too mean-spirited. It began, 'Of course there are many ways to view whites' role in hip-hop, not all of them bad, and yes, we are individuals. But let me offer this advice to black artists: Next time y'all invent something, you had better find a way to control it financially, because we're going to want that shit.'

— — —

In the *Tao of Wu*, RZA offers up some spiritual comfort to the many white devils who, it may be supposed, have bought the book. Having talked about how recently humans have come into existence compared with the age of the planet, the producer and MC suggests we are all children, feeling our way to some sort of adulthood. He then states, 'I wouldn't categorically say that the white man's a Devil, the black man's a God, the woman's an Earth. I'd say those attributes are in their nature, but that everyone can choose what nature they express. They can change.' This is certainly in keeping with wider currents within Five Percenter teachings, largely because of the extent to which individuals are encouraged to develop their own understanding and interpretation of these teachings. The Nation of Islam position is clear, as expressed by Elijah Muhammad, who stated that 'the white race knows God. But they can't represent God as you or me' (and that was much more positive than earlier formulations). Father Allah, on the other hand, had been clear in his later teachings that the Nation of Gods and Earths was 'neither pro-black, nor anti-white'. Nevertheless, most gods are clear that a White man may not be a devil but cannot be a god. At best he can try to slay the internal devils of the way of thinking which constitutes White supremacy. The simple truth is that the basic purpose of the Nation of Gods and Earths is not to 'raise up' White people. And why on earth should it be?

To succeed even in this basic battle with your devils, though, to fulfil the RZA's criteria and change, it's necessary to understand what you are, to feel one's nature. Conscience is not a topic of much interest to many writers—too slow, too worthy, somehow, perhaps too old-fashioned—so we return once again to Lindqvist, for whom it's a central concern. In *Terra Nullius*, Lindqvist remembers a trip he made from Sweden to Iceland when he was still a young man. When the Icelandic ship he was travelling on stopped off in Norway, the Norwegians wouldn't speak to him, still angered by the free transit of German troops through 'neutral' Sweden which had led to their own country's invasion. Lindqvist was irritated by a question about it, saying that he was only ten in 1942. '"But big enough to share the booty," said the great-grandmother.' At first angry about this imposition of responsibility, Lindqvist the younger quickly came to realise that 'the great-grandmother was right. I'd had my share of the booty, so I had to take my share of the responsibility, too.'

— — —

Cultural appropriation has been defined as the 'taking—from a culture that is not one's own—of intellectual property, cultural expressions or artifacts, history, and ways of knowledge'. It's perhaps the most diffuse and insidious form of booty that can be carried off, and its history runs parallel to—hand in hand with—the colonialism that enabled it, whether it be thieving the

Parthenon sculptures from Greece, bringing home tea from China, or playing the music of the ancestors of African slaves. In fact, it's not clear that you can separate out issues of cultural appropriation from issues of colonialism. It's why Afrika Bambaataa's appropriation of the film *Zulu* (or the Wu-Tang's appropriation of names, attitudes and styles from Shaw Brothers films for that matter) strikes us in a completely different way to a White hip hop kid lecturing others on the philosophy of the Nation of Gods and Earths. It's to do with power.

The usual defence against claims of appropriation, mounted most graphically (and ridiculously) by the writer Lionel Shriver—while wearing a sombrero— is, in effect, that art allows anything and is its own justification. 'I am hopeful,' Shriver stated, 'that the concept of "cultural appropriation" is a passing fad.' Shriver's basic point is that writing fiction, in essence, involves imagining oneself inside someone else's head and that the notion of cultural appropriation is a threat to the very basis of that activity. This in itself is an arguable position, or at least thought-provoking. It could be expanded into Timothy Morton's observation that 'it is as if white Western thought is required to remain white, Western and patriarchal in order to provide an easy-to-identify target. The net effect is that nothing can change, because it would be wrong for someone in that lineage not to sound like that.' Instead, Shriver goes on to make a broader, more controversial point. 'Membership of a larger group is not an identity. Being Asian is not an identity. Being gay is not an identity. Being deaf, blind, or wheelchair-bound is not an identity, nor is being economically deprived.' She goes on to say that, 'both as writers and as people, we should be seeking to push beyond the constraining categories into which we have been arbitrarily dropped by birth. If we embrace narrow group-based identities too fiercely, we cling to the very cages in which others would seek to trap us.'

All of which is very easy to say, and sounds almost noble, if you don't think about the direction that those relations of power might run in—who is taking riches wholesale from a position of domination (for instance, 'a virtual "strip mining" of Black musical genius and aesthetic innovation') and who is stealing a bread roll from the master's table. Or, as Zadie Smith puts it, 'a people from whom so much has been stolen are understandably protective of their possessions, especially the ineffable kind'. And what, in the end, could be more devilish than to approach as friend, as admirer, as lover, only to finally steal the ineffable? Especially if that's all the person stolen from has left.

— — —

There can't be anyone left out there who still believes in the objectivity of the non-fictional or biographical account. We spoke about it in the 17th chamber. It's almost a cliché of modern non-fiction that you must acknowledge your mistakes, interrogate your assumptions, show yourself for what you are. There is always a point of view, and the failure to declare your point of view is dishonest. The people who refuse to do this are dinosaurs, believers in their own ability to transcend their time, their place, their class, their race, the way their identity colours their assumptions. They believe their standpoint is universal, which is the same as saying that they hold the power. The least a writer can do is acknowledge that fact, be open about it. Own it, in the parlance of the day.

Like I didn't own enough already. I am white, I am male, I am middle class, I am Oxbridge-educated, I am from England.

This is devil talk, of course. What could be worse, really, than inserting your White self into a story which has nothing to do with you, which is—definitively and absolutely—not yours to tell? And to try to do it in such a way that suggests it's *for the benefit* of the people whose toes you're stepping on? Isn't this, in effect, to appropriate appropriation? Nothing could be more dishonest, a more selfish notion, than including myself in this book. I shouldn't even be in the index. I should be invisible. I'm not needed, I add nothing, no value. My existence, in fact, undermines the whole thing.

That's the measure of my mistake, the true contradiction at the core of this project. I both have to be in a book I don't belong in and absolutely can't be in it. Whatever I choose will be wrong. The project collapses beneath the contradiction.

This book shouldn't exist.

— — —

What can I tell you? I wrote it, anyway, even knowing I shouldn't. I guess I'd gone too far before it finally became clear to me. And now I'm in it, even though I know I shouldn't be. I'm not sure there's an answer here, or a reason. All I can say is, you're reading so it's up to you to decide for yourself whether what I've done has any worth—just as it always is. I think the solution is probably about love, about whether writing a love letter is ever enough. Milton Mesirow might be the place to start, a Jewish man who persuaded the governor of Riker's Island to let him bunk with Black prisoners on a segregated wing. Did Mezz's deep devotion to

Black culture in any way excuse his larcenies from it? Personally, I don't know.

In his classic work on minstrelsy, Eric Lott calls this tension—addressed in his title, *Love & Theft*—'a nearly isotopic sizzle of historical conflict'. He seems to want these two incompatible tendencies to shape into some sort of dialectic, ready to be transcended in a synthesis which has so far stubbornly refused to come (and which may, just may, involve the overthrow or transcendence of capitalism itself). While we wait, it seems we are doomed to play out these same dynamics over and over again, history repeating itself first as tragedy, then as tragedy, then as tragedy again. We're all trapped. 'Every time,' Lott states, 'you hear an expansive white man drop into his version of black English, you are in the presence of blackface's unconscious return.'

We are all trapped, you see, but not equally so. The concept of race only works as a system of contrasts, and it's a system created by the people who have the power. You can't have Black people without White people and vice versa. The two concepts are locked together in an uneasy embrace, a dialectical smooch. Touching on the issue of this interrelation, Zadie Smith quotes James Baldwin. In footage used in the recent documentary *I Am Not Your Negro*, quivering with emotion (both anger and sorrow, it seems), Baldwin says that 'what white people have to do is try to find out in their hearts why it was necessary for them to have a n***er in the first place. Because I am not a n***er. I'm a man... If... you the white people invented him, then you have to find out why. And the future of the country depends on that.' We've seen this invention explained as a way to separate European bond-labourers from the African slaves they shared class interests with. We've seen it lying at the very roots of the American republic. But all of this is too easy, the structural formality of Marxist analysis, of class relations and political theory, the whole impedimenta almost designed to push the issue far away from what's in anyone's heart, from love and loathing (of both the self and the Other), from repulsion and fascination.

Smith goes on to argue that 'the real fantasy is that we can get out of one another's way, make a clean cut between black and white, a final cathartic separation between us and them'. There is, she says, 'no getting out of our intertwined history', a history which, she points out, is intertwined in her own body, her own family. This same intertwining underlies the theology of God and Devil, the most intense of relationships, antagonistic but mutually dependent. We can't have one without the other. In the Bible, Lucifer, son of the morning, needs something to rebel against. In the Qur'an, Satan (Iblis) is banished for refusing to bow to Adam after Allah has created man. Is this pride, though, or simply a refusal to prostrate himself to anyone but God—that is, a refusal to worship false idols?

And there's another intertwining going on, one which I've hinted at but haven't had the guts to name yet, not least because of the complications and contradictions it introduces to proceedings. Is it possible that the wonders of African American culture grow in large part from the pain inflicted on its practitioners? That its beauty is inseparable from oppression? It's an idea hinted at by Arthur Jafa in his remarkable film installation, *Love is the Message, the Message is Death*. A seven-minute montage of found footage (visual samples) set to an extended edit of Kanye West's 'Ultralight Beam', *Love is...* aims, in Jafa's own words, to represent 'the power, beauty and alienation of Black Music' in images and zigzags back and forth between footage of police brutality and Black spirituality, dancing, sport and music, 'verifications of what black people know to be true about our status in society, positive and negative'. The effect is quietly devastating, horribly moving, an extended thesis in compacted form, growing out of the twinned impulses of his artistic practice. 'Over the last few years of doing this, I've pushed… toward things that disturb me,' Jafa states, before going on to say, as well, that 'I've promised myself that I'll try to record the spiritual quality of the things that strike me'. Or, as Fred Moten recently put it, 'the music is a riotous solemnity, a terrible beauty. It hurts so much that we have to celebrate. That we have to celebrate is what hurts so much.'

There's one last point which needs to be dealt with here, and we might call it forgiveness, or warmth, I suppose, or even humanity[32] (which you can only maintain, perhaps, if you're not systematically fucking other people over). There are, apparently, plenty of White people who hate Black people. But—in almost twenty years working in hip hop, both as a journalist and for a record label—I never met a Black person who hated me for being White. As the other Allah, the original leader and founder of the Nation of Gods and Earths, put it, towards the end of his life, 'God and the Devil walk hand in hand.' Feel the generosity in that, the clear-eyed wisdom of this supposed madman—the love—and know, here and now, what a god truly is.

---

32   In the same interview, Jafa also says, 'I'm trying to make my shit as black as possible and still have you deal with my humanity.'

35TH CHAMBER
MASKED AVENGER

During the years I spent working as a music journalist,
I spoke to the RZA probably three times, the last in
1998, in some smart new hotel in downtown New York,
where he was giving interviews for his solo project as
Bobby Digital. Having met him before, I already knew
what he was like—quiet, quite shy, really, with that
lispy, nasal way of talking, but always interesting,
sharp as his chosen name suggested, picking up on
what it was you were after and giving it to you, filtered
by his own agenda. He had the intelligence and
imagination to take any idea you offered him and run
with it, in the process making it his own. Around that
time, I must have interviewed forty or fifty of the best
rappers and hip hop producers in the world—legends
and stars and up-and-comers—but RZA is one of the
few who stick in my mind, a man I was excited to speak

to both before the interview and, crucially, after.

I really believed in The Plan back then and that it consisted of more than just a bunch of rappers selling some CDs. I was devout and, I suppose, I dreamed of being let in. And he did let me in, at least for the length of the interview, or gave me the impression of doing so, anyway. He allowed me to think that the fevered thrashings of my mind were part of the Plan, too, that my beliefs about what he was doing were as valid as his own. In the circumstances, this was a considerable achievement. We were in the penthouse suite and the whole place had been dressed for the occasion to fit in with the superheroic theme of the Bobby Digital record, he himself in costume, flanked by a line of similarly dressed girls in short skirts. Richard Branson, who owned the label he was signed to, breezed in and made a loud, self-satisfied fuss of asking RZA if he had a honey-dipped spliff to share (the origin myth for Bobby D) and everyone who heard him felt a little bilious, compromised by his presence. But I couldn't allow this to get in the way. There was too much riding on it.

What I wanted to believe more than anything else—what I continued to believe right until I wrote this book—was that I was dealing with *Art* and that this *Art* was embodied in, personified by, the RZA (because as soon as you start thinking about *Art* in these terms the notion of *Genius* is never far behind, as sure as italics lead to more italics). It seemed to me then that any White guy with a guitar and a reasonable ability to shape a lyric was declared Leonardo, while Black hip hop stars were treated as if they were utterly disposable and interchangeable, unthinking fluke-meisters on the production line of pop. And this angered me, this was topsy-turvy—completely upside down—in a sonic

300

world where the guitar boys were re-hashing the same
tired clichés and hip hop kept innovating and making
sound new. This felt like an injustice that needed to be
addressed, I thought, even while there were bigger, more
urgent injustices littered all around me.

Not that long after writing my last piece based on
my last interview with the RZA, I began winding down
my 'career' as a music journalist, mainly because I
started a record label and most of my energies began
to be channelled into that. This was to have a number
of consequences for my life as a whole, and perhaps
the least of them was that my opinions concerning the
RZA became set, like an insect in amber, just at the
end of the initial Plan, so that I believed, along with
Method Man, that 'he the smartest motherfucker in
the whole Clan. He always on point—razor sharp. With
the beats, with the rhymes, whatever.' So that I believed
everything he said. So that I believed, most of all, in his
genius, his ability to shape and create *Art*. And this idea
didn't leave me, even when I began putting together
the book you're reading now. But, although I took this
for granted, something else was itching away at me,
making me feel uncomfortable, and it would take me a
good part of the process of researching and writing to
figure out what it was. For a long time my fretfulness
centred around the issue of appropriation, the question
of whether I should be writing this book. And that was a
big part of it—still is part of it. But there was something
more immediate, too. To worship the RZA—who was
supposed to represent my idea of the genius art-maker—
was to conform to a particular well-trodden narrative
(not least that of the genius art-maker). But at the
same time, the notion of art I was so in love with was
meant to be about undermining or challenging all such

conformities. Perhaps you can already see where this is leading. Though probably not how.

I was in New York when it happened, researching. One evening I met a very old friend for dinner. After we'd eaten we strolled towards the Village to grab a drink and on the way we stopped and smoked some weed. I was jetlagged and old and perhaps not familiar with the strength of fine US product in this dawning age of legalisation and/or decriminalisation. Nervy, standing out in clear view, I pulled in too much too fast and soon found myself with half my brain hanging out the side of my skull. I made excellent company as long as all you want from company is someone to nod occasionally and stare off into the middle distance. As for the notion which my friend had sold to me, that somehow weed growers could now breed the paranoia out of their product, I quickly disproved that. When I set off home I became convinced I was walking in the wrong direction. The road looked dark and unfamiliar and I began to believe that soon I would meet the Hudson, possibly walk into it and, relieved, be carried away, back towards Shaolin. And it was then that it happened. Ahead of me, at the junction, a man walked past. He looked completely normal, unremarkable, straight-backed but relaxed. Except he was *wearing a hockey mask*. And I knew, right then I knew.

We've travelled this far—almost to the very end—along the road of orthodoxy, solid in the belief that RZA was the guiding light behind the Wu-Tang Clan for at least the five years of The Plan, that hip hop is a technology of transcendence or escape and that to forgive is always, of necessity, a good thing. It's extremely sustaining to hold to such beliefs, if a little worthy, a trifle safe. But what if hip hop's soul lies exactly in the subversion of orthodoxies, all orthodoxies, even its own? What if a technology for misusing technology is only true to itself when it misuses itself? What if, as Fard Muhammad or Nietzsche might have argued, forgiveness is just a way to get slaves to absolve their masters? What if escape is always and forever impossible? What if my epiphany on the streets of New York was correct, or at least provocative? What if the central figure of the Wu-Tang Clan—not so much the head as the heart—is not the RZA?

What if it's Ghostface Killah?

There's no proof, only clues. When Method Man runs through the individual characteristics of his fellow group members at the end of 'Can It Be All So Simple', all he says about Ghostface is that 'he on some *now you see me, now you don't.*' It's not the most fulsome encomium, but there's a story you can tell based upon it, not a million miles from the Keyser Söze twist in *The Usual Suspects*. Ghostface is the sole member of the Wu-Tang Clan from the Stapleton Houses, and Raekwon—who many fans would associate most closely with him—has reminisced that when RZA suggested forming a group including Coles, 'it was definitely spoken on, like, "Yo, I don't really fuck with Ghost, he's a crook." We tell it how it is, you kna'mean?' So that, if the idea to bring together all the talents in one rap supergroup had been Ghost's rather than Prince Rakeem's, then he would've had to plan to do it just as it all turned out, with his friend as the figurehead. Because one thing is certain— none of the Park Hill crew would have joined if it had been his suggestion.

It's more than just some *now you see me, now you don't*, though. RZA himself says that Wu-Tang was originally just him and Ghostface (as evidenced by 'After The Laughter'/'Tearz', probably the first Wu-Tang Clan tune recorded, and included on the first single). Moreover, despite RZA being, in Ghostface's words, 'the chief of the kung fu flicks', Ghostface says it was him who got hold of a VHS of the seminal *Shaolin & Wu-Tang* and showed it to his friend (this film is sampled more than any other on *Enter*): 'I played it to RZA and he just fell in love with it.' Even more essentially, it was Ghostface, not RZA, who first conceived of the idea of reimagining their existence in terms of the Shaw Brothers movies which so obsessed them. Ghost was the one, after all, who began calling his favourite brand of malt liquor, Olde English, *Wu-juice*. RZA, joining in with the conceit, re-branded the other major make, Ballantine Ale, as *Shaolin*.

Beyond this, there are even more contingent bits and pieces which just add to the sense that there's something to the idea. The very fact that Ghost mentions Wu-Tang less than any of the other rappers on the record points to the same Söze-ish conclusion (admittedly in a way designed to infuriate empiricists). His widely acknowledged position as one of the finest, wildest lyricists on the record certainly helps, as does the fact that he remains the *only* member of the group— including RZA himself—to have made a classic album outside RZA's five-year plan (that record is *Supreme Clientele*, widely acknowledged to be one of the greatest hip hop albums of all time, and described in a long and brilliant review by Jeff Weiss, which I would highly recommend checking out, as 'the closest hip hop ever came to *Ulysses*'). Plus, there's something gloriously, bloody-mindedly contradictory about Ghostface, right from the fact that his rap voice doesn't seem to fit his body, a boy trapped in a bear, or Charlie Parker having swallowed his saxophone. And there is evidence at the very least to position Ghost as yang to RZA's yin. He was living at that house on Morningstar Road with RZA and various members of the Diggs family when RZA began going on those walks and developing The Plan. And when they were in Steubenville selling crack, the duo adopted code names: RZA recalls that 'Ghost was Moses and I was Jesus'. You know, at the very least, who's most likely to get Old Testament on your ass.

Ghostface is the first rapper you hear on *Enter the Wu-Tang*, and he comes with what RZA describes as 'one of the most famous darts in Wu-Tang history': 'Ghostface / Catch the blast of a hype verse / My glock bursts / Leave in a hearse / I did worse.' In those lines—delivered in his trademark front-foot yelp, each small package of words dropped with the rock-solid certainty and authority of Gospel—the Stapleton boy sets out his place in the Wu firmament by first using the gunfire of that 'glock burst' as his metaphor for rhyming and then making it a reality with the apparently throw-away admission that 'I did worse'. Immediately, the rhyme buzzes with ambiguity, with a capriciousness that could be Ghostface's calling card. On his verse on the first single, 'Protect Ya Neck', our mercurial poet comments on the form of his work: 'I come with shit that's all types of shapes and sounds', a statement which RZA glosses by saying 'that's really true with Ghost's lyrics: they are colourful and abstract, their sound and shape as important as their meaning'. It also acts as a deterrent or a block on the worthy interpreter. There's a hint here that his lyrics aren't even strictly *meant* to be understood so much as appreciated as organised sound and shape—that is, as music. And indeed, this is what he hints at in a quote that Weiss uses: the essence of good rap, he claims, is to get 'some official beats and say fly shit over them'.

Of course, fly shit doesn't necessarily equal meaningless shit. It just means that the way you say it, the panache with which you say it, is as important (more important?) than some dowdy *message*, hollow in itself for having no style. This, it could be argued, is the essence of hip hop itself, and the importance of this is that it begins to position Ghostface as more than RZA's opposite, but as a god of chaos in his own right. Ghostface exemplifies Keats's notion of Negative Capability, of a man 'capable of being in uncertainty, Mysteries, doubts, without any reaching after fact and reason'. Except that his is Negative Capability squared— and a negative number squared becomes positive. He's not just 'capable of being in uncertainty'—he goes out of his way to create it. He is *now you see me, now you don't*. As he puts it in one of the album's finest lines, 'I'm raw, I'm rugged and raw, I repeat / If I die my seed will be ill like me.' In fact, on the remix to this song, included as the last track on the album, the way the new beat bounces seems designed to emphasise this couplet in particular, to make it stand out, to make it the key take-home message from the whole hour of music. And that broadside should be interpreted both as a statement of the unutterable and inalienable flyness of Ghostface and his offspring, but also to say: you can kill me if you want (if you dare), but the next one of us will be along straight after.

Then there's the mask: 'when I struck I had on Timbs and a black mask'. Ghostface is the only member of the Wu-Tang to really take his name and the

306

mythology it implies completely seriously (except maybe Ol' Dirty Bastard). In the movie *Mystery of Chessboxing*, Ghostface Killer is the villain. But, as RZA points out, 'he was the best, best bad guy ever'. In keeping with his chosen title, early on in the days of Wu-Tang, Ghostface decided he should only appear with his true face hidden. He took to rocking a hockey mask at live shows and in photo shoots and appears in the video for 'Da Mystery of Chessboxin'' in a black stocking mask framed by white.[33] It has even been claimed—despite the evidence of the low-budget video the group paid for and filmed for 'Protect Ya Neck', plus the videos for 'Method Man' and 'Can It Be All So Simple'—that no one saw Ghost's face until the release in 1995 of Raekwon's *Only Built 4 Cuban Linx*, which included him on the cover (though actually, the lower half of his face is obscured in that picture, anyway). The rumour which circulated was that there was a warrant out for Ghost's arrest and hence it wasn't safe for him to appear publicly, but it seems that the mask was adopted not to hide his identity from the authorities but as a conscious performance.

In 1903, sixty years before his own death in Ghana and ninety years before the release of *Enter the Wu-Tang*, W.E.B. Du Bois published his classic work, *The Souls of Black Folk*. A series of essays, both travelogue and autobiography—often remarkably different in tone— plus one short story and some key snippets of sheet music, this hugely influential book is held together by the idea that:

33   It's also possible that the red-faced figure at the very back of the line on the cover of *Enter* is Ghostface in that hockey mask. There's no objective evidence for this supposition, just a lot of squinting.

the Negro is a sort of seventh son, born with a veil, and gifted with second-sight in this American world,—a world which yields him no true self-consciousness, but only lets him see himself through the revelation of the other world. It is a peculiar sensation, this double-consciousness, this sense of always looking at one's self through the eyes of others, of measuring one's soul by the tape of a world that looks on in amused contempt and pity. One ever feels his twoness,—an American, a Negro; two souls, two thoughts, two unreconciled strivings; two warring ideals in one dark body, whose dogged strength alone keeps it from being torn asunder.

The notion of a 'veil' here refers to the caul—the remains of the amniotic membrane which sometimes still covers a baby's eyes at birth—and the belief that this set of circumstances signals the advent of special powers in the newborn child, in particular the ability to see the future. But the metaphoric work that the 'veil' does in the text takes us a bit further than that, too. There's also the sense of it operating as in the phrase 'beyond the veil': 'the unknown state of those who have departed life'. Indeed, there is something of the ghost realm to the situation Du Bois describes, of occupying the same space but being unable to touch or impact upon the existence of those around you: 'shut out from their world as if by a vast veil'. Third, there is the sense of the veil as a kind of mask. White Americans do not 'see' Black Americans, they only see the Veil—the mask they place on them. These metaphors all overlap and intertwine, of course, both in Du Bois' own work and in that of many of the writers who follow him. This can lead to a relatively straightforward expression, such as Paul Laurence Dunbar's 'We Wear the Mask' ('We wear the mask that grins and lies, / It hides our cheeks and shades our eyes'), or to a considerably more complex articulation, as in Ralph Ellison's *Invisible Man*: 'I am invisible, understand, simply because people refuse to see me.' And all these notions are bound up together in Ghostface Killah's choice of name. In 'Can It Be All So Simple' he states his position quite clearly, outlining his plans for the future but saying they are 'just a big dream / Cos I find myself in the place where I'm last-seen'. But the black mask he wears on top of his ghost face, that's something else.

We're back with minstrelsy, the cultural dark star from whose gravitational pull, it seems, America can never escape. Minstrelsy—'the white male mimicry of black song and dance'—revolves around the wearing of the blackface mask (either a literal mask or a layer of soot or boot polish spread across the features). It is 'a quintessential American ritual', says Houston A. Baker Jr. 'That mask is a space of habitation not only for repressed spirits... but also for that deep-seated denial of the indisputable humanity of inhabitants of and descendants from the continent of Africa.' And as we have seen, hip hop stands accused of minstrelsy: 'While hip hop has embodied the continuum of blackface minstrelsy in its trajectory of white appropriation and commercial takeover, the genre embodies the legacy of minstrelsy in another key way: in its specific imagery of black masculinity,' claims Harriet Manning. 'Hip hop unfortunately reaffirms black male tropes of rage, violence, unpredictability and depravity rooted in minstrelsy and projected onto blacks so [as] to inferiorize them.' Or, as Stanley Crouch has put it, 'You like it [rap] and the rest of you white people like it for one very specific reason, and that is whenever you read those lyrics, as they're called, you always know, or assume, that you are superior to the Negro who wrote them' (though Crouch's problem could perhaps be solved by *listening* to the lyrics instead of reading them). For Baker, 'the minstrel mask is a governing object in a ritual of *non-sense*'. And this non-sense is expressed as sound. 'The *sound* emanating from the mask reverberates through a white American discursive universe as the sound of the Negro.'

Let's look closely at Ghostface's 'black mask' verse. As we've already noted, it's from 'Da Mystery of Chessboxin'', and as this is also the name of the film from which he takes his name, it's appropriate to think of this as his solo track, even though he's joined on it by six other members of the Clan (seven if you include RZA, on the beat). He begins, 'Speaking of the devil-psych / No, it's the God, get the shit right.' It's easy to interpret this as a reference to Devil psychology, that bit of mischief that lurks inside even the mind of a god, tempting him to do the wrong thing, and hence it encourages us to read his words as an internal, spiritual dialogue of some sort. After this, though, things become confusing. When Ghost tells us, 'I killed you in a past life', it's not clear if this is the devil or the god in him talking, or if he's addressing some other, outward adversary. He then goes into quite a long description of someone trying to fast-rap badly—suggestive of a standard *wack-rapper* motif—before he *strikes*, in his Timbaland boots 'and a black mask'. I'm going to claim that this is the minstrel devil-psych talking to the god. The latter's failure to master his martial skills (rapping) leaves him open to attack, so the devil pounces, dressed in the minstrel's mask. He asks the god if he remembers this past-life event, when his soul was killed by the mask, but only as a rhetorical exercise, because his opponent remembers nothing (suggesting a reference to slavery). Now we switch to the perspective of the god, who, it transpires, has been playing with the devil: 'you thought I was bugged out and crazy', but actually he's armed and dangerous, 'strapped for nonsense, after me [you] became lazy'. The god sees his opportunity and unleashes a spray of spiritual bullets to vanquish his foe while everyone else flees. He appears to triumph, though there is a note of ambiguity, a sense that he's challenging the devil to a duel and that the conflict is, as yet, unresolved. Then again, you can read the whole verse the other way round, with the god hidden behind the mask, but then the devil is the victor. Or you can see it as a stream-of-consciousness example of Ghost's flyness, barely meant to make sense, a succession of shapes and sounds. Or you can see it as all three at once.

That's probably the nearest we'll come to truth—all three at once—because it hints towards something bigger going on just offstage or behind the words. Ghostface ends by telling the listener to get his 'eight plus one', which in normal circumstances would be translated as a nine-millimetre, a gun. But in the numerology of the Five Percent Nation, eight plus one is BUILD + KNOWLEDGE, a rather different idea. And, once again, perhaps it can mean both at once. This leads us naturally to Ghostface's most famous line on the whole record, one which is immediately followed by the observation (from Raekwon) that 'Ghostface carry a black nine'. Nine stands for BORN or birth in Five Percenter thought, so beneath the obvious meaning—the observation/threat that Mr Coles always comes armed—there's a more spiritual idea: that Ghostface is somehow pregnant with blackness, with divinity and possibility.

The line comes right at the end of 'Can It Be All So Simple', a piece of music that RZA tells us, in his introduction, is about nostalgia, but which turns out to be nothing of the sort. Raekwon's verse is a recollection of times past, of his childhood growing up on Staten Island, but there is no pink tint to his lenses: can it be that it was all so simple, then? Well no, obviously not. Ghostface starts off by saying how much he enjoys making music. He then talks about how he's tired of the violence and wants to focus on this music, but even here, there's some ambivalence. It's now that light as a guiding metaphor makes its first appearance: 'I want to be in the shade / Plus the spotlight.' He then sets out his ambitions (getting an all-night penis massage, owning a yacht, buying land on which to farm cannabis) before stating that none of these are realistic in a country where he's 'last-seen'. From here he goes on to talk about how many of his friends are incarcerated or dead, and the pressure this places him under, before he finds the Lessons of the Nation of Gods and Earths, which enable him to hold it together so he can continue to make music. And then he says it: 'Sunshine plays a major part in the daytime.'

It's a strange line, both blatantly obvious and understated all at once. *Of course* sunshine plays a major part in the daytime. Without sunshine, without light, there is no daytime. But for reasons not immediately apparent it carries a lot of emotional weight, which at first is hard to fathom. Is this another example of Ghost's 'shapes and sounds', a series of words suggesting deep meaning, hitting you at a musical level without actually meaning too much at all? Well no, not exactly.

The first name of the Nation of Gods and Earths was the Suns of Almighty God Allah. 'The Five Percenters teach that those in whom knowledge dawns, rises, and completes itself are "gods," are "Asiatic," are "suns",' Melvin Gibbs points out. 'Clarence 13X Smith taught that the sun as emitter of light is symbolic of knowledge and the black man who is God... As the sun is the dominant body in this solar system, the black male, in Clarence 13X's belief, is the dominant body in day-to-day life.' Sunshine, then, is the fruit of the Black man's labour.

What I want to do here is to suggest that what Ghostface means by 'daytime' is America. It's there in John Winthrop's exhortation, while still aboard the *Arbella* before landing in the New World, to build a city upon a hill—a reference to Jesus's Sermon on the Mount, when he says, 'Ye are the light of the world. A city that is set on an hill cannot be hid.' It surfaces again in George Washington's inaugural address to his newly formed nation, when he says that 'preservation of the sacred fire of liberty' is 'considered as deeply, perhaps as finally staked, on the experiment entrusted to the hands of the American people'. You can see it embodied in the Statue of Liberty in New York Harbor, passed by the ferryboat from Staten Island to Manhattan and back hundreds of times every day. Given to the USA by the people of France to mark the centennial of the Declaration of Independence, the statue's full title is 'Liberty Enlightening the World'. It's an idea that bobs up again in Martin Luther King's famous 'I have a dream' speech, in relation to the Emancipation Proclamation, of which he says that 'this momentous decree came as a great beacon light of hope to millions of Negro slaves who had been seared in the flames of withering injustice. It came as a joyous daybreak to end the long night of captivity.'

America is, to (mis?)use the words of René Magritte, the Empire of Light. But its light is provided by sunshine—the work, the sweat, the blood of African slaves. Not just provided—its light *is* sunshine. The American pursuit of liberty isn't just made possible by slavery. It *is* slavery. The two are one and the same thing. The beacon is the brand (in both senses of the word). Heaven is Hell. Its brightness is attractive but it also burns. Lucifer—morning star, day star—rules the Empire of Death.

On the surface, none of this is so very different from the standard critique of a country whose Declaration of Independence states 'that all men are created equal, that they are endowed by their Creator with certain inalienable Rights, that among these are Life, Liberty and the pursuit of Happiness' and was a document written by slave owners. But there is something else going on here, a realignment of sorts. Earlier, I quoted Huey P. Newton of the Black Panther Party. 'We feel that Black people in America have a moral right to claim nationhood,' he says, 'because we are a colonized people. But history won't allow us to claim nationhood.' The crux of the Panther position is that the African American should be an internationalist because he can never truly be an American—or an African, for that matter. Instead, they are a colonized people without a homeland. But on Ghostface's reading, the offspring of slaves—the suns who shine to make the day—are the most quintessentially American of all Americans. They are the energy powering the Empire of Light. They are ghosts who bring sunshine to the Empire of Death.

It's hard to emphasise sufficiently just how radical this position is. Ghostface is not confronting America—the position of the Black radicals of the sixties. Nor is he

trying to escape America, either through an emphasis
on some halcyon African past or through a shuttling
forward into some future scenario of liberation (the
two directions of Afrofuturism). There is no utopianism
in the Wu's world view, no positing of a perfect world.
Ghostface *inhabits* America, and he inhabits it just as
it is now, in all its contradictions, with all its appetites:
'where I lounge is my stomping grounds'. In the course
of the album he compares himself to an elephant tusk,
Egyptian musk, President Nixon, the burning Waco
compound of the Branch Davidian, to Fort Knox, a car
crash involving a luxury vehicle, a runaway slave, a
spiked bat and a shooting star. In later years, he will
reinvent himself as a series of mythic Americans,
first Tony Stark/Iron Man and later GhostDeini, his
own *now you see me, now you don't* version of Harry
Houdini. (Writing about Houdini, the psychoanalyst
Adam Phillips notes that 'the masked are always great
unmaskers'.)

And maybe Ghostface really doesn't mean to be
understood (or at least didn't mean any of this). Perhaps
he's pushing for a radical transcendence of self through
gibberish, a re-appropriation of non-sense. He collages
words which look and sound good together without
any reference to meaning. Hip hop becomes a machine
not of re-reference but of the destruction of reference.
Its aesthetic function overpowers its communicative
function and the self is dissolved in the ecstasy of
patterning. It's a creative misuse of the technology of
martial arts. After all, hip hop is a battle machine and
surely the ultimate way to win a battle of self-control
is *to have no self*? Anyway, the Western notion of the
self, with its individuated, inalienable rights, relies
on imperialism, colonialism and slavery, not just for

the material conditions necessary to its birth, but at a deeper, conceptual level, too.

Perhaps Ghostface has grown tired of waiting to be understood, of rattling his chains and calling out to people who run from him in terror. Understanding involves an effort from both parties. And, let's face it, the other party to this particular conversation—White America, fingers pushed deep into earholes, humming high-pitched nothings badly remembered from country records—hasn't done too well. As for self-control, which that other party preaches, that puritan ethic they wrap round their appetites like a bib, well, look who they chose for their leader. They have projected everything they want and are scared of onto Ghost and his people and then they've punished them for it. There's no point arguing. Now is the time for occupation.

In the way that he collapses escape routes and chooses instead to occupy America—and in particular the central cultural ground of its own dreams about itself, its deepest subconscious longings and fears— Ghostface is the first of a new generation of rap stars, uninterested in the old battles between 'conscious' and 'gangsta' rap and instead taking a place centrally in the culture as *American*—regardless of what anyone may think or say about that positioning. It's a change in orientation that leads directly to Kanye West, who lives his life as if scripted by F. Scott Fitzgerald, taking the keys to the mansion, enacting the reality show, meeting the Orange Prez, living his life as an embodiment of exactly the aspirational, conspicuously consumptive values which sit at the heart of an American Dream built on slavery.[34] You could say it's a *reductio ad absurdum*

---

[34] And yet, as we noted in the last chamber, West is also capable of creating a

except that it never seems to reduce. 'I feel like I got my whole style from Ghostface,' West has said, 'my whole mentality about hip hop.'

'*My whole mentality about hip hop.*' We've been using the wrong terminology. Neither *inhabiting* or *occupying* are quite right, and this is to do with what happens to hip hop around 1993/1994, widely considered by aficionados—many of them too young to remember, or not even born then—to be hip hop's golden era. This is the point, perhaps during that verse from Ghostface released in November 1993, when hip hop *eats America*. Twenty-one and a half years after the Funkadelic album *America Eats Its Young*, released a couple of weeks after young Dennis Coles' second birthday, hip hop youth returns the favour. As Neil Kulkarni puts it, 'You couldn't simply find a space for Wu-Tang in your schedule, make a lifestyle choice, file them away in a corner of your world. They were too total, their demands on you too huge to negotiate without obsession. They seeped into your body, affected your mind, burrowed into your soul, and coloured your whole experience. Only hip hop can do this. Only Wu can do hip hop like this.'

There's a theory that hip hop grew out of the slashing of music education funding in public schools in American inner cities in the early to mid-seventies. Unable to access instruments or the teaching that went with them, poor young Black kids were forced to make their own organisations of sound using whatever was available. It's a nice story, but perhaps seeing a turntable as a replacement for a bassoon underestimates

---

piece of music as powerful—and beautiful—as 'Ultralight Beam'.

the radical reach of hip hop's praxis. Once you have abandoned (or been forced to abandon) conventional instruments, *everything* becomes an instrument. There is no limit to what you can use. The abstract artist Al Loving said that 'jazz musicians are people who make a radical use of conventional materials'. Hip hop musicians, then, are people who make a radical use of unconventional materials, in fact *all and any* materials. Hip hop is an appropriation engine, an infinite assemblage machine. It sucks up whatever is placed in its path and reconfigures it—re-references it—making it part of its own circuits, its own organism. It looks much like what was there before, but somehow it *means* something different, or sounds new chords. And it spreads rapidly, a kind of musical and conceptual Spanish flu—or, to use the words of Ishmael Reed, the latest, most effective outbreak of the 'anti-plague' he called *Jes Grew*. It's a virus which inhabits and repurposes already-existent technologies, one which, in Kulkarni's vision, seeps into your body, affects your mind, burrows into your soul. And by 1993 or 1994, hip hop eats the world. Whole. When James Baldwin said, 'He who would enter the twenty-first century must come by way of me', he had no idea how true hip hop would make his words. The Wu-Tang Clan obviously did. It's right there in the record's title: *Enter the Wu-Tang...*

America still exists, of course, you can go there, you can walk between its money palaces and buy its cultural products. But it resides now—as do we all—inside the digestive tracts, the vast internal chambers—the conceptual framework, if that's easier to grasp—of hip hop. This is why Gates's claim that hip hop is 'signifying on steroids' is a monumental understatement. This is signifying as virus, as he himself points out, 'a creative process that puts everything up for grabs'. Gilroy claims that 'hybridity… is formally intrinsic to hip hop', but once again, this barely scratches the surface of what's going on. This is not hybridity as strategy but hybridity as the terrain on which any strategy takes place, a kind of paradigmatic shift pulled off without anyone noticing. As we've already noted, hip hop is a technology (a 'systematic treatment' if you break down the Greek), and what it systematically treats is everything else. You can see it as a digitisation of signifying if that makes it easier, a mechanisation of hybridisation—a function of increased processing power, so that we can plot its development on the graph laid out by Moore's Law. (In fact, if you start from the one and a half million people living in the Bronx in 1972 and use Moore's Law to estimate the rate of hip hop's growth, the whole population of the planet was infected sometime around 1995.)

I know that this sounds far-fetched, possibly conceptually confused, definitely self-serving ('how can I appropriate hip hop if hip hop has already appropriated me?'). All I can say in answer is *look at the world*. Not just the world of popular music, where hip hop's predominance is perhaps most obvious, but the world in general. If you want to put a purely positive spin on it, turn to Bakari Kitwana's suggestion that 'Hip-hop is the last hope for this generation and arguably the last hope for America.' He looks to a 'hip hop generation' to reject 'the old racial politics' and organise politically, creating 'a new language for discussing issues once deemed "Black."' He would most likely see current events as symbolic of the final, desperate attempts of an older generation to lash out at these inevitable changes, the painful death throes of White supremacy, the anguished writhing of decrepit bodies being killed by a virus their minds aren't capable of assimilating. On the other hand, for those of a more dystopic mindset, look at the office of the Presidency of the United States and tell me that we aren't trapped inside some recombinatorial process in which disparate, possibly clashing elements are endlessly pushed together and ripped apart with no reference to plausibility, taste or safety. Because that's hip hop, too. Think of it as an extension and intensification of systematic mania. No one said it would never be ugly.

Of course, hip hop paid a price for this move to predominance, for its gargantuan appetite, for swallowing the planet. In becoming the air we breathed it stopped being art. In pulling off this huge reversal, this re-wiring of everything that created it, hip hop itself was re-wired, too. It was the chief sacrifice in its own revolution. It ate itself. Not in one gulp, but gradually, a nibble here and a nibble there, so that we didn't even notice. But was this a sacrifice at all, or a deliberate tactic, a cost or a reward?

Earlier, we drew a comparison between Coltrane's *A Love Supreme* and Ghostface's *Supreme Clientele*, one a spiritual work of high art and the other distinguished by the couplet (on 'Nutmeg'), '[My] dick made the cover / Now count how many veins on it.' As noted at the time, such a comparison only seems likely to play out one way. But while no one could deny the sincerity or the beauty of *A Love Supreme*, it remains a work of art and, arguably, in its spirituality, a work of escape. And this notion of 'art' is itself implicated in the system which it often claims to be critiquing or commenting upon. It is not autonomous, it's a cultural munitions store built with the patronage and approval of rich and powerful men, wrapped in the illusion that it transcends ordinary life. This is our orthodoxy, the warehouse-temple in which we manufacture and maintain cultural value. It's very beautiful and very still, all marble floors, carefully positioned statuary, light and space. Then, *Enter the Wu-Tang*—nine rap assassins crash in through the door, swords drawn. The only aesthetic judgement to be passed on a battle rap is that it's a battle winner. The statues aren't just limbless, they're headless—at least they are now. And the intruders? They're gone. I started out wanting to tell you why *Enter* was a work of art, but I was wrong. It's bigger—or broader, or less limited—than that. As Coltrane himself put it in the poem included on the back of *A Love Supreme*, between the worshipful sentiments, 'It all has to do with it.' *Supreme Clientele* takes the process to its logical conclusion, utterly rejecting any notion of art or artistry—even the values of battle rapping. Instead, it opts for the chaos, the beautiful-ugliness, the wildness and contradiction implicit in being alive, in being not just in the world, but actually *being the world*. We're all breathing hip hop, so art is, finally and forever, dead. Good riddance, rest in peace.

36TH CHAMBER
ENIHCAM EMIT

The only 'WU' logo left on Victory Boulevard is a
Western Union sign outside a cheque-cashing business.
In general, the boulevard itself doesn't really live up
to the grandeur of its name. The area around here is
one of the scruffiest in Staten Island, a whole bunch of
(unfailingly courteous) street drinkers hanging about
the nearby bodegas, the sense of a space caught between
neighbourhoods, not really belonging anywhere and
hence unloved, unlovely. The smartest looking shop by
far is at number 61—a barber's called Against Da' Grain,
which has been in business since 2000, both here and at
another branch in West Brighton. The shop is coloured
bright yellow and black, waspish, either a visual echo of
the killer bees of the Wu or just a punchy way to attract
attention to the premises. They seem to be expanding
into the unit next door.

In 1995, this was the site of the very first Wu-Wear store, a point of pilgrimage for fans from all over the world, a key location only five or ten minutes' walk from where the ferries docked at St George terminal. By 1998, the neighbouring space was occupied by U-God's own shop—apparently called Walking Dogs—while RZA's sister, Sofia Diggs, opened Wu Nails opposite, claiming it to be the first Black-owned nail bar in Staten Island. Wu-Wear, the brainchild of Oliver 'Power' Grant, grew from its foundations in this store on Staten Island to over ten million dollars' worth of sales by 1998 (including around a million in sales from that first Staten Island shop), from a badly printed insert in Raekwon's *Only Built 4 Cuban Linx* CD case to a brand which was 'sold in department stores across the country and appeared in fashion spreads in consumer and trade magazines from *The Source* to *Sportswear International*'.

Power, a close friend of both Raekwon and RZA's brother, Divine, had made his money during the crack boom of the eighties. It was him who paid RZA's bail when he was arrested in Steubenville. Wu-Wear was Power's idea and his moment to shine—and for a while he did. The first really successful artist-owned/branded line of clothing was also 'the first urban brand to get a window display in Macy's flagship Herald Square store, ground zero of mainstream American retail'. And yet, by 1998, new brands like FUBU had begun to overtake it and by the turn of the millennium, that first store had shut.

Twenty-five years since the release of *Enter the Wu-Tang* is also, necessarily, over twenty years since the end of RZA's Five Year Plan. It's twenty-four years since the release of *Tical* by Method Man and *6 Feet Deep* by the

Gravediggaz. Twenty-three have passed since ODB, Raekwon and GZA all released classic albums in one year (*Return to the 36 Chambers: The Dirty Version*, *Only Built 4 Cuban Linx* and *Liquid Swords*, respectively). Twenty-two years have gone since Ghostface's *Ironman* and twenty-one since the double Wu album, *Wu-Tang Forever*, widely criticised at the time as being both rushed and bloated, but now generally considered to be another classic. It's also twenty-two years since Method Man (or 'Cliff', as he's known on set) started his film career, and twenty-one since he was joined by Oli 'Power' Grant and Raekwon as part of James Toback's flawed, ill-fated *Black and White*. Nineteen years have passed since the RZA started working with Jim Jarmusch and fourteen since he hooked up with Quentin Tarantino. It's eighteen years since Ghostface's *Supreme Clientele*, which, as we've seen, is considered (by me at least) to be the only truly great record from the crew since the end of the Five Year Plan. It's also eighteen years since the release of *The W* and seventeen years since the release of *Iron Flag*. Fifteen years ago, Method Man accused RZA's brother, Divine, of taking 'something major from me that he had no intention of giving back'. Fourteen years have gone since U-God left the Wu-Tang Clan, then claimed it was a publicity stunt and rejoined. Perhaps most importantly, it's also fourteen long years since Ol' Dirty Bastard died—curled up, alone, broken, his blood thick with cocaine and Tramadol—in RZA's recording studio in Manhattan. It's thirteen years since Ghostface first sued RZA over royalties and RZA published *The Wu-Tang Manual*. It's eleven years since a new Wu-Tang album, *8 Diagrams*, and Ghostface's new solo record, *The Big Doe Rehab*, came out within a week of one another, something which

GFK could not see as an accident. A decade ago, RZA launched Wuchess.com, 'the world's first online chess and urban social network', and this may be the last time anyone heard of it, as well. Six years past, RZA directed a full-length kung fu movie, *The Man with the Iron Fists*. Four years back, the band released *A Better Tomorrow*. Three years ago, the Wu-Tang Clan (or, at least, RZA and a Dutch-Moroccan producer called Cilvaringz) sold a single-copy edition of the album *Once Upon a Time in Shaolin* to the businessman Martin Shkreli, allegedly for $2 million. Two and a half years ago, Shkreli became notorious for hiking up the price of a drug used to treat AIDS. Two years ago, Shkreli streamed three tracks from the album on the internet to celebrate the election of Donald Trump to the Whitehouse. Just over a year ago, Shkreli ended up in prison for fraud. A year ago the band appeared as guests on what seemed to be their own album, *The Saga Continues*, and even its title expressed a sense of exhaustion, like one of those TV shows which has gone on two or three series too many.

If a trajectory can be perceived in all this, it can't be the one the group or their fans envisaged or hoped for. The great strength of the Wu-Tang plan became its flaw, as solo album followed solo album in a rush of product which eventually began to alienate all but the most committed supporter—as much as anything because if you weren't the most committed supporter you couldn't keep up, couldn't assimilate one record before the next one dropped. Meanwhile, the competition between individual members—for labels, for release spots, for beats from the RZA, for recognition, for attention, for money, for *love*—resulted in jealousy and turmoil within the group, and these feelings weren't helped by a star system which saw the bigger names in the Clan transfer some of their wattage to Hollywood. Plus, let's be honest, it's really hard to keep being original over and over again, to stay ahead of everyone else, to stay ahead of yourself, to second-guess your own habits. Whereas rock bands are allowed to sink into some kind of comfortable middle-aged stupor, hip hop—treated as disposable pop music—has to continue to be genuinely avant-garde, a cutting-edge music made, in ODB's words, 'for the children'. And children are unforgiving, unsentimental consumers of novelty. There is a Wu logo somewhere at the back of the Against Da' Grain shop, with 'ADG' across the middle of it, a blurring of brand boundaries, but this is the only evidence left of the existence of the band's shops in Staten Island. Empires rise and empires fall—and when they're gone, little or nothing remains to mark their passing.

Diagonally across the junction outside Against Da' Grain there's a scrappy green construction fence, drunk-leaning and battered, heading back down the hill. There used to be a Taco Bell on this corner with a parking lot behind it, but that's all gone now. Instead the fence leads round into a small run of scrubby, tenement-style buildings in Bay Street. Opposite is Tompkinsville Square, a bedraggled triangle of public park where the street drinkers like to sit and pass the time between plots of grass and trees enclosed by ornamental fences. On the street side, there's a Spanish diner of some sort, then a phone shop, another bodega, a taxi office, and a wig shop before you reach it: that low plastic box on the ground next to Bay Beauty, stuffed with faded flowers and cuddly toys, the pictures of Eric Garner so sun-bleached you can hardly make them out. This is where he was pulled backward so hard that he and the police officer who had him in a chokehold bounced off Bay Beauty's window. This is where he was pushed to the ground. This is where a group of policemen stood around chatting to one another, some of them still kneeling on his back while he tried to make himself heard. This is where he was choked to death. All of a sudden it feels very quiet, the broad sidewalk extremely empty.

But let's stop. Let's pull the record back. Hip hop, after all, is a time machine and books can be, too. If you want the Daoist take, then 'turning back is how the way moves'. We don't have to end with death, with dissolution, when we can hear the needle ripping the wrong way through the groove. Skip it right back until, once again, we go from the start of the break.

A year ago it was reported that over 100,000 bombs and missiles had been dropped on Iraq, Syria and Libya as part of ongoing operations against ISIS in the region. Less than two years ago, Donald Trump was elected President of the United States of America. Three years ago, gun deaths in the USA surpassed car deaths for the first time on record. Three and a half years ago, China became the world's largest economy. Four years ago, the film of the death of Eric Garner helped launch the Black Lives Matter movement. Six years ago Barack Obama was re-elected. Seven years ago, Occupy Wall Street protesters were evicted from their camp in Zuccotti Park. Seven and a half years ago, Osama bin Laden was shot dead by US special forces at a compound in Pakistan. Nine years ago, the Tea Party movement began to coalesce around issues ranging from mortgage relief to gun control to whether Barack Obama was American. Nine years ago, Michael Jackson died. Ten years ago, Lehman Brothers investment bank collapsed. Ten years ago, Barack Obama became the USA's first Black president. Eleven years ago, the sub-prime mortgage market began to lurch towards crisis. Thirteen years ago, Hurricane Katrina killed almost 2,000 people in Louisiana, Mississippi and Alabama. Fourteen years ago, George W. Bush was re-elected. Fifteen years ago, George W. Bush ordered the invasion of Iraq. Seventeen years ago, the USA invaded Afghanistan. Just over seventeen years ago, two passenger jets were flown into the Twin Towers of the World Trade Center in New York, and another into the Pentagon, killing almost 3,000 people. Eighteen years ago, George W. Bush, like his father before him, became president. Nineteen years ago, two students shot thirteen others at Columbine High School. Twenty years ago, Bill Clinton was accused of having an affair with an intern called Monica Lewinsky. Twenty-one years ago, the Dow Jones Industrial Average fell 7.18% in a single day of trading. Twenty-two years ago Bill Clinton won re-election. Twenty-three years ago, O.J. Simpson was acquitted of killing his wife. Twenty-three and a half years ago, the Oklahoma City bombing killed 168 people. Just under twenty-five years ago, the North America Free Trade Agreement was implemented. Around twenty-five and half years ago, the Branch Davidians burnt in their compound in Texas. A little over twenty-five and a half years ago, a bomb was detonated in a truck in the basement of the North Tower of the World Trade Center, killing six people. Almost twenty-six years ago, Bill Clinton became President.

Around twenty-seven years ago, having paid his friend's bail to get him out of jail in Ohio, Oli 'Power' Grant sorted out Prince Rakeem/RZA with 'a roomful of equipment', using some of the money he had made selling crack. Among that equipment was likely an Ensoniq ASR-10. In retrospect, history has come to fetishise the Akai MPC as the Excalibur or Zulfiqar of hip hop production. You can see why it would. There's something about utilising a drum machine as a sampler which ties in with the culture's rhythmic self-image. RZA, however, has never expressed much interest in or love for the MPC (in fact the classic version, the MPC3000, wasn't released until 1994, the year after *Enter* was released). He had owned the MPC's spiritual forerunner, the Emulator SP-1200, but eventually swapped it with RNS—the producer for Staten Island group The U.M.C.'s—for his Ensoniq EPS. And RZA preferred the Ensoniq because it had a full keyboard rather than drum pads, which allowed him to sample single notes and play with them. In fact, it's claimed that he wrote the main melody part in 'Da Mystery of Chessboxin'' after watching a documentary about Thelonious Monk on TV. When you listen to it knowing that, you can hear Monk in the intervals, while at the same time, the choice of instrumental sound tugs you back towards the Hong Kong movies the Abbot loves so much.

There's actually a time machine built into *Enter the Wu-Tang*. 'Wu-Tang: 7th Chamber' is repeated, remixed, as a 'Part II' at the end of the album. While the CD contains a remix of 'Method Man' as well, this comes after the concluding skit and is obviously meant as a bonus, rather than an essential component of the suite of music. But the remix of '7th Chamber' is integral, the very last track on the vinyl version (although, for some reason, RZA starts it with GZA's chorus from 'Clan In Da Front'). It's hard to imagine that the group couldn't, between them, get together enough material to fill a full hour of music without repeats (in fact, as they were already working on a number of solo albums before *Enter* came out, it wouldn't have been difficult to re-purpose a track from one of these other projects). The decision to include both versions of the tune—and to finish the record with one—must have been deliberate.

Reasons have been offered, of course. There's a rumour that RZA wanted to show that he could compete with the low-end roll of the West Coast, and certainly the remix of the tune is driven along by a killer bassline, a sound which is fathoms deep, warm and harsh all at once. There may be some truth to the story, but it's not the kind of truth which is interesting. Better to think up something which may *not* be true, but which is at least provocative.

So. 'Wu-Tang: 7th Chamber' is the fourth track on *Enter* as well as the twelfth. It's tempting to get numerological and point out that 4+1+2=7. It features seven members of the Wu-Tang—everyone except for U-God and Masta Killa—so there are also seven verses. The original version starts off with a chugging drum loop from Lonnie Smith (cut, chopped and doubled throughout the piece to keep the beat swinging) before RZA drops a piece of tri-tonal pianistics that sounds so much like Thelonious Monk that either the story about his watching the *Straight, No Chaser* documentary refers to this track, or he decided not to credit the sample (the previous two tracks on the record feature the piano player). Over this, he strings out a guitar line from an Otis Redding record, stretched and sharp. The vocalists pile through, one after the other, and in a way, this is an encapsulation of what the Wu-Tang Clan is in miniature. Each of them has at least one great lyric on the tune and each of them sounds exactly like their individual self—distinct, brilliant and unique but all the more powerful for flashing out from the collective for a moment and then being swallowed back into that swampy whole. But it's not perfect and there's a reason you know it.

That reason is '7th Chamber: Part II'. Seven, in Five Percenter numerology, stands for *God*, that is the perfected Black man, and 'Part II' is a perfected Seventh Chamber. Seven plus that two makes nine, meanwhile, which we already know represents *Born*. Hence the album ends with a re-birth, with a beginning. The song has no right to be as perfect as it is. The drum loop is taken from a breaks record[35] and there's no clever doubling up or chopping, just a few drop-outs, sounding like they've been done by the RZA using a fader during mixdown. So solid is this break, though, so driving, that these drop-outs feel like chasms and you keep falling and falling until the beat hits again. This is made only too apparent on Raekwon's opening verse, which sounds off, fighting against the pulse of the music until—snap!— the drums come back and everything locks. Above it, a ghostly chorus, a moaned '*Wuuu-uuu-uuu*' and stabs of icy noise. Last, a saxophone note played up and down a scale, presumably on the keyboard.[36]

Then there's the bassline, which is, in effect, the tune, the world, the universe. Four notes circling round themselves so that without the snap of the snare you'd never know what was the start and what the finish, they

---

35   This isn't any old breaks record, though, but the classic *Funky Drummer Vol. 1*, played and put together by Ralph Vargas and the man engineering most of these sessions, the one and only Carlos Bess, who would go on to play drums as well as engineer on *Wu-Tang Forever* and produce 'Cherchez LaGhost' for GFK's *Supreme Clientele*, among many other credits.

36   The original misused technology of African American musical genius, here misused.

walk over the bars like the bootprints of a god, utterly magnificent, utterly heartless, a fact. It's been suggested that this is the fascination of electronically generated bass—that it conjures up the sound of natural disasters, of the sublime. Until its advent, the only simulacrum for the rumble of an earthquake was the sound of an organ in church. Now we hear it in nightclubs, even at home, that buzz in your sternum a kind of religious awakening, your soul trying to clamber its way out.

We've already talked a little about the sound generated. RZA made it on the ASR-10 by playing a bass sound through two of the fifty pre-set filters the machine contained. The first was a guitar amp filter, which gives it its fuzzy, overdriven edge. The other was called a Van der Pol filter. The Van der Pol oscillator plays a fêted role in chaos theory. Originally a vacuum tube built by Balthasar van der Pol in the 1920s, on experimenting with it, the Dutch electrical engineer discovered the occasional irregular frequency sneaking into his results as he increased the current. At the time he dismissed these irregularities, but later they would be crucial to the development of a mathematical model of chaos. Van der Pol 'was one of many scientists who got a glimpse of chaos but had no language to understand it'. RZA on the other hand 'was trusting chaos and confusion—not judging it, not fearing it, not reaching for an immediate solution'. The remix is a demonstration of his skill because with it he makes the lyrics sound new, too. But in doing so, he demonstrates their intrinsic power, the talent involved, the sheer drive of their delivery—human life, desperate, funny, violent, sad, wild and beautiful. The Wu-Tang hold it all—'the paradoxes of the American psyche'—in a delicate, perfect balance, apparently pulling and pushing in at least two contrary directions at once and finding some kind of equilibrium. They are breathing, both individually and as a collective organism, the fast patter of their separate panting a hi-hat line above the thump and snap of their monstrous group-lung.

There is no orthodoxy. Anyone who tells you otherwise is lying. There's no correct sampler to use, no particular source which should be sampled, not even any way you should put the pieces together beyond the simple (and complex) stipulation that the result should be *dope*. RZA has reminisced about sitting in a studio with the producer True Master, who thought a particular channel of the music RZA was making was 'off'—that is, that it sat out of time with everything around it. RZA ignored his protests and continued mixing. 'When I finished,' he says, 'he realized that it was only off until it was balanced.' RZA goes on to spell out the very basis of his philosophy. 'That's the whole secret of it: It's off, but it isn't off. It's off and on at the same time.' This is a sense not just of balance as we would normally understand it, but of something more profound, something closer to Hegelian synthesis or even quantum superposition. Although, really, call it what you like, show off. All that matters is that it's on and off at the same time. It's on and off at the same time. It's twenty-five years ago and it's yesterday. It's angry and it's beautiful. It's testosterone-soaked and delicate. It's old-fashioned and brand new. It's constructed and it's real. It's individual and collective. It's flawed and it's perfect. It's sad and it's funny. It's high-tech and nostalgic. It's the future and the past, it's wrong and it's right. It's the man held, stretched and squashed across the sidewalk and the man putting a brick through a police car's windshield. It's the one drinking wheatgrass and the one passing the bone. It's shouting and it's music. It's anguish and it's joy. It's drunk and it's sober. It's the dandy and the ascetic. It's funky and it's jagged. It's weed and PCP. It's laughter and tears. It's literal and figurative. It's Black and White. It's devil and god. It's the in breath and the out.

Breath—the final switch. To continue breathing is a victory if you live in an environment seemingly designed to make you stop. A study estimates that Black American males living in urban locales and aged 16 in the year 2000 will, individually, have only a 50–62% chance of making it to the age of 65. The Wu-Tang Clan are older so their odds are even worse. That means we could expect over half of them—five—to be dead by the fortieth anniversary of *Enter the Wu-Tang*. At the moment, eight are still breathing, in and out, in and out. There is no orthodoxy, there's only surviving. Perhaps that's RZA's personal heresy, a misuse of the technology of Chan Buddhism, which he folds back into hip hop as the most basic and essential of survival tools—the flow of chi as air moving in and out of your chest. Beneath the riddles, the battling, the guns and swords, the jokes, the bravado, the pain, *Enter* reveals the most fundamental rule of hip hop—perhaps the only rule of hip hop.

Keep breathing.

SAMPLES

FRONT QUOTES

vii   'What if history…': Ralph Ellison, *Invisible Man* (Random House, 1953), p. 424 (Penguin Classics, 2016).

vii   'The only thing I rely on…': quoted in Gene Ching, 'Hip Hop Fist: Wu Tang Clan's RZA and his Sifu Shaolin Monk Shi Yan Ming' in *Kung Fu Magazine*, 1 September 1999. http://www.kungfumagazine.com/magazine/article. php?article=100

2ND CHAMBER–DON'T CRY

p. 7   'me and God…': quoted in Michael Segell, *The Devil's Horn: The Story of the Saxophone, from Noisy Novelty to King of Cool* (Picador, 2005), p. 139.

p. 8   'After that…': *The Devil's Horn*, p. 140.

p. 9   'The musician was not…': Arnold Shaw, *Honkers and Shouters: The Golden Years of Rhythm and Blues* (Macmillan, 1978), p. 172.

p. 9   'frustration, hostility and alienation…': Dean Tudor & Nancy Tudor, *Black Music* (Libraries Unlimited, 1979), p. 120.

p. 9   'The point, it seemed…': LeRoi Jones, *Blues People* (Payback, 1995), p. 172.

p. 9   'By resorting to such tactics…': quoted in *Honkers and Shouters*, p. 170.

p. 10   'sheer vocal power': Kip Lornell, *'Happy in the Service of the Lord': African-American Sacred Vocal Harmony Quartets in Memphis* (University of Illinois, 1988), p. 27.

p. 10   'Archie could demolish…': Bobby Womack with Robert Ashton, *Midnight Mover* (John Blake, 2006), pp. 27–28.

p. 11   'I seen him… jump…': quoted in Robert Darden, *People Get Ready: A New History of Black Gospel Music* (Continuum, 2005), p. 235.

p. 12   'He'd scream and scream and scream…': Nik Cohn, *Awopbopaloobop Alopbambamboom: Pop from the Beginning* (Vintage, 2004), p. 25.

p. 12   'to imitate them talking…': Charles White, *The Life and Times of Little Richard*, (Pan, 1984), p. 29.

p. 12   'The sisters didn't like me screaming…': *Life and Times of Little Richard*, p. 28.

p. 13   'he lets out a series of screams…': *Awopbopaloobop Alopbamboom*, p. 107.

p. 13   'The scream was a transfer…': RJ Smith, *The One: The Life and Music of James Brown* (Gotham, 2012), p. 113.

p. 15   'when I met him…': James Brown with Bruce Tucker, *James Brown: The Godfather of Soul* (Sidgwick & Jackson, 1987), p. 218.

p. 16   'The "cry" was the trademark…': Ben Sidran, *Black Talk* (Payback, 1995), p. 36.

p. 16   'The introduction of the saxophone…': *Black Talk*, p. 74.

p. 19   'That weird screechy sound…': quoted in Henry Louis Gates Jr, *The Signifying Monkey: A Theory of African-American Literary Criticism*, 25th Anniversary Edition (Oxford University Press, 2014) p. xxx.

p. 19   'that sample had to be taken off…': quoted in John Tatlock, 'The Noise and How to Bring It: Hank Shocklee Interviewed,' *The Quietus,* February 4th 2015. http://thequietus.com/articles/17101-hank-shocklee-interview

p. 20   'C'mon! C'mon Robert!': James Brown, 'Super Bad', from 4 minutes in. https://www.youtube.com/watch?v=LJ9CLOEOB5U

p. 20   'i didn't cry…': Don L. Lee, *Don't Cry, Scream* (Broadside Press, 1969) p. 29.

p. 21   'the kettle noise': quoted in Kembrew McLeod & Peter DiCola, *Creative License: The Law and Culture of Digital Sampling* (Duke University Press, 2011), p. 23.

p. 22   'There was no compromise…': LeRoi Jones, *Tales* (MacGibbon & Kee, 1969), p. 76.

4TH CHAMBER–HERE AND THERE

p. 29   'a triumph of…' and 'a structure of…': both quoted in Carol V. Wright, *Staten Island: A Blue Guide Travel Monograph* (Somerset, 2013), p. 154.

p. 30   '"White flight,"…': Daniel C. Kramer & Richard M. Flanagan, *Staten Island: Conservative Bastion in a Liberal City* (University Press of America, 2012), p. 5.

p. 30   'larger homes…': Aarian Marshall, 'It's Far Too Simple To Dismiss Staten Island for "Being Staten Island",' *CityLab*, 8 December 2014. https://www.citylab.com/equity/2014/12/its-too-simple-to-dismiss-staten-island-for-being-staten-island/383458/

p. 32   'struggle as a form…': Kevin Young, *The Grey Album: On the Blackness of Blackness* (Graywolf, 2012), p. 361.

p. 33   'How art thou fallen…': Isaiah 14:12, Holy Bible, King James Version (CollinsBible, 1957), p. 657.

5TH CHAMBER–CREATIVE REORGANISATION

p. 36   'the only times when…': LeRoi Jones (Amiri Baraka), *Blues People*
(Payback Press, 1963/1995), p. 41.

p. 36   'outwardly abiding by…': Robert Farris Thompson, *Flash of the Spirit:
African and Afro-American Art & Philosophy* (Vintage, 1984), p. 18.

p. 37   'human sampler': quoted in '100 Greatest Hip Hop Songs of All
Time,' *Rolling Stone*, no. 49, 2 June 2017. http://www.rollingstone.
com/music/lists/100-greatest-hip-hop-songs-of-all-time-w435246/
grandmaster-flash-and-the-furious-five-the-adventures-of-grandmaster-
flash-on-the-wheels-of-steel-w441006

p. 38   'Even if I didn't know the words…': quoted in Insanul Ahmed,
'Method Man Breaks Down His 25 Most Essential Songs,'
Complex, 9 October 2011. http://uk.complex.com/music/2011/10/
method-man-25-essential-songs/wu-tang-clan-method-man-1993

p. 39   'I'm black as…': Brian Hiatt, 'The Rolling Stones' New Blues:
Inside their Roots Revival, Bright Future,' *Rolling Stone*, 16
November 2016. http://www.rollingstone.com/music/features/
inside-the-rolling-stones-new-album-blue-lonesome-w450645

p. 39   'I was sampling it…': quoted in 'Method Man Breaks Down His 25 Most
Essential Songs.'

7TH CHAMBER–IMPURE THOUGHTS

p. 46   When an Indian…': quoted in Gaynell Stone (ed.), *The Shinnecock
Indians: A Culture History* (Suffold County Archeological Association,
1990), p. 54.

p. 46   'a diffuse community…': John A. Strong, *The Montaukett Indians of
Eastern Long Island* (Syracuse University Press, 2001), p. 130.

p. 46   'prevailing racial…': *The Montaukett Indians*, p. 131.

p. 46   'disintegrated and been absorbed…': quoted in *The Montaukett Indians*,
p. 139.

p. 47   'last of the…': *The Shinnecock Indians*, pp. 7–8.

p. 47   'When I first came here…': quoted in Russ Buettner, 'For
Shinnecocks, Forecasts of Doom Finally Give Way to One of
Prosperity,' *New York Times*, 29 December 2009, p. A22 of
New York edition. http://www.nytimes.com/2009/12/29/
nyregion/29shinnecock.html?action=click&contentCollection=N.Y.%20
%2F%20Region&module=RelatedCoverage&region=
EndOfArticle&pgtype=article

p. 47   'one of the largest…': Jean-Paul Salamanca, 'Annual Shinnecock
Powwow Puts Heritage on Display,' *Newsday*, 3 September
2016. http://www.newsday.com/ long-island/suffolk/
annual-shinnecock-powwow-puts-heritage-on-display-1.12263884

pp. 47-8   'required the dispossession…' and 'in addition to rendering…': Patrick Wolfe, *Traces of History: Elementary Structures of Race* (Verso, 2016) p. 80.

p. 48   'Kill the Indian…': quoted in Hayes Peter Mauro, *The Art of Americanization at the Carlisle Indian School* (University of New Mexico Press, 2011), p. 88.

p. 48   'Cut off from their families…': Donald R. Wharton & Brett Lee Shelton, quoted in Jacqueline Fear-Segal & Susan D. Rose (eds), *Carlisle Indian Industrial School: Indigenous Histories, Memories, and Reclamations* (University of Nebraska Press, 2016), p. 11.

p. 49   'I was an outcast…': quoted in *Carlisle Indian Industrial School*, p. 3.

p. 49   'Sand Creek, Camp Grant, Wounded Knee': see N. Scott Momaday, 'The Stones at Carlisle,' in *Carlisle Indian Industrial School*, p. 45.

p. 49   'Too much negro': the card can be viewed online at http://carlisleindian. dickinson.edu/student_files/fred-cuffee-student-file

8TH CHAMBER–THROWING AWAY THE KEY

p. 50   'Seven of the nine…': RZA quoted in Jaime Lowe, 'RZA on Eric Garner and "The Non-value of a Black Life",' *The Gawker*, 23 December 2014 (http://gawker.com/rza-on-eric-garner-and-the-non-value-of-a-black-life-1674239684). RZA may well be counting Cappadonna among the seven, but as that would be in place of ODB it doesn't change the statistic.

p. 51   'Security from domestic violence…': 'Goldwater's 1964 Acceptance Speech,' *Washington Post*, http://www.washingtonpost.com/wp-srv/ politics/daily/may98/goldwaterspeech.htm

p. 51   'his embrace of…': Michael W. Flamm, 'The Original Long, Hot Summer: The Legacy of the 1964 Harlem Riot,' *New York Times*, 15 July 2014. https://www.nytimes.com/2014/07/16/opinion/16Flamm.html?mcubz=3

p. 51   'a war against crime…': quoted in 'The Original Long, Hot Summer'.

p. 51   'the use of crime…': Ian Haney López, *Dog Whistle Politics: How Coded Racial Appeals Have Reinvented Racism and Wrecked the Middle Class* (Oxford University Press, 2014), p. 51.

p. 51   'the New Right's…': Katherine Beckett, *Making Crime Pay: Law and Order in Contemporary American Politics* (Oxford University Press, 1997), p. 42.

p. 52   'The mood toward drugs…': 'Radio Address to the Nation on Federal Drug Policy,' 2 October 1982. http://www.presidency.ucsb.edu/ws/index. php?pid=43085&st=war&st1=drugs

p. 52   'a system of social control…': Michelle Alexander, *The New Jim Crow: Mass Incarceration in the Age of Colorblindness* (New Press, 2010/2012), p. 8.

p. 52   'Between 1965 and 1993…': *Making Crime Pay*, p. 3.

p. 52   'no other country…': *The New Jim Crow*, p. 6.

p. 52   'The current system of control…': *The New Jim Crow*, p. 13.

p. 53   'more than half of the young black men…': *The New Jim Crow*, p. 16.

p. 54   'it is questionable…': *The New Jim Crow*, p. 73.

p. 55   'this Court has become…': quoted in *The New Jim Crow*, p. 62.

p. 55   'this drug forfeiture regime…': *The New Jim Crow*, p. 79.

p. 55   'extraordinarily punitive…': *The New Jim Crow*, p. 53.

p. 55   'with charges that carry…': *The New Jim Crow*, p. 88.

p. 55   'In the drug war…': *The New Jim Crow*, p. 98.

p. 56   'slavery just meant…': RZA quoted in Jaime Lowe, 'RZA on Eric Garner and "The Non-value of a Black Life",' *The Gawker*, 23 December 2014, http://gawker.com/rza-on-eric-garner-and-the-non-value-of-a-black-life-1674239684

p. 56   'a closed circuit…': Loïc Wacquant, quoted in *The New Jim Crow*, p. 95.

p. 56   'a criminal record…': NAACP, 'Criminal Justice Fact Sheet.' http://www.naacp.org/criminal-justice-fact-sheet/

p. 57   'Whites have their government…': Ishmael Reed, *Another Day at the Front: Dispatches from the Race War* (Basic Books, 2003) p. 64.

p. 59   'the State is not a…': Emma Goldman at the International Anarchist Congress, Plancius Hall, Amsterdam, Tuesday 27 August 1907. https://theanarchistlibrary.org/library/freedom-ed-the-international-anarchist-congress

9TH CHAMBER–CRACK IN THE SYSTEM

p. 60   'a measure of how addictive…': Dan Charnas, *The Big Payback: The History of the Business of Hip-Hop* (New American Library, 2010), p. 483.

p. 61   'We made money…': The RZA with Chris Norris, *The Tao of Wu* (Riverhead, 2009), p. 90.

p. 62   'The drive to achieve…': Stuart Walton, *Out of It: A Cultural History of Intoxication* (Hamish Hamilton, 2001), p. xxv.

p. 62   'I inhaled…': Ruben Castaneda, *S Street Rising: Crack, Murder and Redemption in D.C.* (Bloomsbury, 2014), p. 11.

p. 62   'He feels the high…': Bill Clegg, *Portrait of an Addict as a Young Man* (Jonathan Cape, 2010) pp. 114–15.

p. 62   'You feel this…': quoted in *Out of It*, pp. 126–7.

p. 62   'whole body…': quoted in Craig Reinarman & Harry G Levine (eds), *Crack in America* (University of California Press, 1998), p. 45.

p. 62   '… and then…': *Portrait of an Addict*, p. 115.

p. 63   'first criminalized when the…': Craig Reinarman, 'The Social Construction of Drug Scares', in P.A. Adler & P. Adler (eds), *Constructions of Deviance: Social Power, Context and Interactions* (Wadsworth, 1994), p. 94.

p. 63   'There is no doubt…': quoted in Edward Marshall, 'Uncle Sam is the Worst Drug Fiend in the World,' *New York Times*, 12 March 1911. http://druglibrary.net/schaffer/History/history.htm

p. 63   'cocaine is often…': quoted in Alexander Cockburn & Jeffrey St. Clair, *Whiteout* (Verso, 1998), p. 71.

p. 63   'its aura…': *Out of It*, p. 109.

p. 64   'the sensations…': *Out of It*, p. 104.

p. 64   'it is a perfect…': *Out of It*, p. 110.

p. 65   'Powder cocaine…' and 'We cooked…': Rick Ross with Cathy Scott, *Freeway Ricky Ross: The Untold Autobiography* (Freeway Studios, 2014), p. xxi.

p. 65   'crack was a marketing…': *Crack in America*, p. 2.

p. 65   'the key to a good product…': *Freeway Ricky Ross*, p. 186.

p. 66   'All the way through…': *Whiteout*, p. 14.

p. 66   'Ross recalls…': *Freeway Ricky Ross*, p. 207.

p. 66   'miniature video…': *Whiteout*, p. 7.

p. 67   'none of us knew…': *Freeway Ricky Ross*, p. xiii.

p. 67   'Crack literally changed…': Albert Samaha, 'Cheaper, More Addictive, and Highly Profitable: How Crack Took Over NYC in the '80s,' *The Village Voice*, 12 August 2014. http://www.villagevoice.com/news/cheaper-more-addictive-and-highly-profitable-how-crack-took-over-nyc-in-the-80s-6664480

p. 67   'In October 1985…': Michelle Alexander, *The New Jim Crow: Mass Incarceration in the Age of Colorblindness* (New Press, 2010/2012), p. 52.

p. 67   'crack was a godsend…': *Crack in America*, p. 38.

p. 68   'an epidemic…': Richard M. Smith, quoted in *Crack in America*, p. 35.

p. 68   'a plague…': quoted in *Crack in America*, p. 21.

p. 68   'crack is the most addictive…': quoted in *Crack in America*, p. 3.

p. 68   'faulty testimony…': *Whiteout*, p. 75.

p. 68   'There is no evidence…': John P. Morgan & Lynn Zimmer, 'Social Pharmacology of Smokeable Cocaine: Not All It's Cracked Up To Be' in *Crack in America*, p. 147.

p. 69   'Like food consumption…': 'Social Pharmacology of Smokeable Cocaine,' p. 135.

p. 69   'The drug problem…': Clarence Lusane, *Pipe Dream Blues* (South End Press, 1991), p. 19.

p. 69   'Black people's need…': *Pipe Dream Blues*, p. 13.

p. 70   'Just about all…': *Freeway Ricky Ross*, p. 132.

p. 70   'The primary means…': Eloise Dunlap & Bruce D. Johnson, 'The Setting for the Crack Era: Macro Forces, Micro Consequences (1960-1992)' in *Journal of Psychoactive Drugs*, 24(4), October–December 1992, p. 317.

p. 71   'out of control…': quoted in *Crack in America*, p. 39.

p. 71   'drug-taking disrupts…': *Out of It*, p. 15

p. 71   'If all you have…': Jefferson Morely, quoted in *Crack in America*, p. 92.

p. 71   'Self-control…': 'The Social Construction of Drug Scares,' p. 99.

p. 72   'the constant cultivation…': 'The Social Construction of Drug Scares,'
         p. 100.

10TH CHAMBER–DEALING

p. 73   'unite eight…': The RZA with Chris Norris, *The Tao of Wu* (Riverhead,
         2009), p. 105.
p. 75   'Every label…': Dan Charnas, *The Big Payback: The History of the Business
         of Hip-Hop* (New American Library, 2010), p. 450.
p. 75-6 'You bargain…', 'The contract…' and 'I wanted…': The RZA with Chris
         Norris, *The Wu-Tang Manual* (Riverhead, 2005), p. 76.

11TH CHAMBER–YOUNG GODS

p. 80   'spooky mindedness…': quoted in Herbert Berg, *Makers of the Muslim
         World: Elijah Muhammad* (Oneworld, 2013), p. 55.
p. 80   'to make slaves…': answer to Question 12 of 'Lost-Found Muslim
         Lesson #2'. https://thefivepercentnation.wordpress.com/2011/05/01/
         lost-found-muslim-lesson-no-2-1-40/
p. 81   'The original man…': answer to Question 1 of 'Student Enrollment'.
         https://thefivepercentnation.wordpress.com/2011/03/15/
         student-enrollment-1-10/
p. 81   'the Holy Koran or Bible…': answer to Question 1 of 'Lost-Found Muslim
         Lesson #2'. https://thefivepercentnation.wordpress.com/2011/05/01/
         lost-found-muslim-lesson-no-2-1-40/
p. 82   'We teach that the Blackman…': no. 7 in 'What We Teach'. https://genius.
         com/Nation-of-gods-and-earths-what-we-teach-what-we-will-achieve-
         annotated
p. 83   'she was tawny…': quoted in Janet Malcolm, *Forty-One False Starts*
         (Granta, 2013), p. 74.
p. 84   'Like cubist chemists…': Chris Kraus, *I Love Dick* (Tuskar Rock, 2015),
         p. 209.
p. 86   'With scorching flames and boulders…': Virgil, *The Aeneid*, trans. Robert
         Fitzgerald (Vintage Classics, 1990), lines 740–745, p. 179.
p. 87   'You know you are Allah…': quoted in Michael Muhammad Knight, *The
         Five Percenters: Islam, Hip Hop and the Gods of New York* (Oneworld,
         2007), p. 90.

12TH CHAMBER–A PROBLEM IN MATHEMATICS

p. 88   Statistics taken from:
         Eloise Dunlap & Bruce D. Johnson, 'The Setting for the Crack Era: Macro
             Forces, Micro Consequences (1960–1992)' in *Journal of Psychoactive
             Drugs*, 24(4), October–December 1992, pp. 307–319.

'Social and Economic Issues of the 1980s and 1990s,' *Amistad Digital Resource*, http://www.amistadresource.org/the_future_in_the_present/social_and_economic_issues.html

Tony L. Whitehead, 'The Formation of the US Racialized Urban Ghetto,' *CuSAG Special Problems Working Paper Series in Urban Anthropology*, 15 September 2000.

Susan Aud, 'Status and Trends in the Education of Racial and Ethnic Groups,' *National Center for Educational Statistics*, US Department for Education, July 2010. https://nces.ed.gov/pubs2010/2010015.pdf

David Weisburd & Rosann Greenspan, 'Police Attitudes Toward Abuse of Authority: Findings from a National Study,' *National Institute of Justice*, May 2000. https://www.ncjrs.gov/pdffiles1/nij/181312.pdf

Ryan Gabrielson, Ryann Gorchowski Jones & Eric Sagara, 'Deadly Force, in Black and White,' *ProPublica*, 10 October 2014. https://www.propublica.org/article/deadly-force-in-black-and-white

13TH CHAMBER–CROSSING THE BORDER

p. 93   'Across the clear blue…': 'Wu-Tang Clan Ain't Nuthing Ta F' Wit'.

p. 93   'For the Bambara…': W. Jeffrey Bolster, *Black Jacks: African American Seamen in the Age of Sail* (Harvard University Press, 1997), pp. 62–63.

p. 94   'marine maroon colony': quoted in Kevin Young, *The Grey Album: On the Blackness of Blackness* (Graywolf, 2012), p. 81.

p. 94   'undo the transformative…': *Black Jacks*, p. 64.

p. 94   'the sea brought us…': quoted in *Black Jacks*, p. 65.

p. 96   'It's an area that's…': quoted in John Leland, 'On the Edge of Staten Island,' *New York Times*, 12 February 2016. https://lens.blogs.nytimes.com/2016/02/12/christine-osinski-staten-island-summer-days-photos/?_r=0

14TH CHAMBER–COLLECTIVE INSULATION

p. 99   'had this blues…': quoted in Philip Mlynar, 'Clan in Da Back: The Behind-the-Scenes Oral History of "Enter the Wu-Tang (36 Chambers)",' *Spin*, 5 November 2013. http://www.spin.com/2013/11/wu-tang-clan-enter-the-wu-tang-36-chambers-oral-history/

15TH CHAMBER–SECRETS AND LIES

p. 103   '*Another aspect discussed…*': https://vault.fbi.gov/russell-tyrone-jones/russell-tyrone-jones/view p. 65.

p. 104   'there's something addicting…': Curt Gentry, *J. Edgar Hoover: The Man and the Secrets* (W.W. Norton, 1991), p. 13.

p. 104   'that blacks would…': Theodore Kornweibel, Jr (ed.), *Federal Surveillance of Afro-Americans (1917–1925)* (University Publications of America, 1986), p. x.

p. 104   'Black radicalism…': quoted in *Federal Surveillance*, p. xii.

p. 105   'Hoover was a racist': Kenneth O'Reilly, *'Racial Matters': The FBI's Secret Files on Black America, 1960–1972* (Free Press, 1989), p. 46.

p. 105   'Edgar kept…': Anthony Summers, *Official and Confidential: The Secret Life of J. Edgar Hoover* (Victor Gollancz, 1993), p. 57.

p. 105   'the foremost radical…': quoted in *'Racial Matters'*, p. 15.

p. 105   'neutralizing [him]…': quoted in *Official and Confidential*, p. 353.

p. 105   'a massive surveillance…': *Official and Confidential*, p. 352.

p. 105   'the most notorious liar…': quoted in *'Racial Matters'*, p. 142.

p. 106   'created the climate…': quoted in *'Racial Matters'*, p. 364.

p. 106   'the very lies…' and 'the fact…': Brian Glick, 'Preface', in Ward Churchill & Jim Vander Wall (eds), *The COINTELPRO Papers: Documents from the FBI's Secret Wars Against Domestic Dissent* (South End, 1990), p. xvi.

p. 106   'we set up…': quoted in *Official and Confidential*, p. 384.

p. 106   'twenty-seven guns…': *'Racial Matters'*, p. 311.

p. 107   'to be a black revolutionary…': quoted in Ekwueme Michael Thelwell, 'H. Rap Brown/Jamil Al-Amin: A Profoundly American Story,' *The Nation*, 18 March 2002, 4(10).

p. 107   'there were two things…': quoted in *Official and Confidential*, pp.350–51.

p. 108   'by 1990…': numbers from *Official and Confidential*, p. 60.

p. 108   'Tyrone Powers': Tyrone Powers, *Eyes To My Soul: The Rise or Decline of a Black FBI Agent* (Majority Press, 1986), particularly pp. 290, 320, 375-7.

p. 108   'the bureau agreed…': Philip Shenon, 'Black FBI Agent Looks Back on Years of Harassment,' *New York Times*, 12 August 1990. http://www.nytimes.com/1990/08/12/us/black-fbi-agent-looks-back-on-years-of-harassment.html

p. 108   'It did not…': Glick, 'Preface', in *The COINTELPRO Papers*, p. xii.

p. 109   'religious fanatics…': S. Culbertson, 'Memorandum for Mr Ladd,' 24 July 1942. https://vault.fbi.gov/Moorish%20Science%20Temple%20of%20America/Moorish%20Science%20Temple%20of%20America%20Part%202%20of%2031/view, p. 8.

p. 109   'a fanatic Negro organization…': Central Research Section, 'The Muslim Cult of Islam – Captioned Monograph,' 26 June 1955. https://vault.fbi.gov/Nation%20of%20Islam/Nation%20of%20Islam%20Part%201%20of%203/view, p. 8.

p. 110   'a loosely knit group…': Federal Bureau of Investigation, 'Disturbance By Group Called "Five Percenters", Harlem, New York City, July 29 1965', 26 August 1965. https://vault.fbi.gov/5percent/five-percenters-part-01-of-01/view, p. 14.

p. 110   'does not feel that…': Special Agent in Charge, NYC, 'Disturbance by Group Called "Five Percenters", Harlem, NYC, 5/31/65', 2 June 1965. https://vault.fbi.gov/5percent/five-percenters-part-01-of-01/view, p. 23.

p. 110   'the WTC is heavily…': https://vault.fbi.gov/russell-tyrone-jones/russell-tyrone-jones/view, p. 63.

p. 111   'radical freedom of information activist': all quotes in this passage taken from email correspondence.

p. 113   'Federal prosecutors…': William L. Anderson & Candice E. Jackson, 'Law as a Weapon: How RICO Subverts Liberty and the True Purpose of Law,' in *The Independent Review*, IX(1), Summer 2004, p. 86.

p. 113   'an open invitation…': quoted in 'Law as a Weapon,' p. 95.

p. 113   'overturn the…': 'Law as a Weapon,' pp. 86–7.

p. 113   'once individuals have proved themselves…': https://vault.fbi.gov/russell-tyrone-jones/russell-tyrone-jones/view, p. 64.

16TH CHAMBER–WALKIN'

p. 116   'I walked every day…': The RZA with Chris Norris, *The Tao of Wu* (Riverhead, 2009), p. 101.

p. 116   'By walking, you escape…': Frédéric Gros, *A Philosophy of Walking* (Verso, 2015), p. 6.

p. 116   'the logic of identity…': David Graeber, *Debt: The First 5,000 Years* (Melville House, 2011), p. 111.

p. 118   'while walking, you hold yourself…': *A Philosophy of Walking*, p. 196.

p. 119   'funkier…' and 'I felt there was…': *Tao of Wu*, p. 110.

p. 120   'Like most meditation…': *Tao of Wu*, p. 102.

17TH CHAMBER–FAKING FOR REAL

p. 125   'Linda Hamlin…': Dan Charnas, *The Big Payback: The History of the Business of Hip-Hop* (New American Library, 2010), p. 434.

p. 125   'Some of the best…': 'Martin Scorsese on *Goodfellas*,' American Film Institute. https://www.youtube.com/watch?v=qV7btRCs3Wc

p. 125   'a hallucinatory…': Richard Brody, 'Scorsese's Achievement with "Goodfellas",' *The New Yorker*, 19 June 2015 http://www.newyorker.com/culture/richard-brody/scorseses-achievement-with-goodfellas

p. 126   'If you read the script…': quoted in Ryan Vlastelica, 'Goodfellas Turned Wiseguy's Simple Prose into Cinematic Gold,' A.V. Club, 18 September 2015. http://www.avclub.com/article/goodfellas-turned-wiseguys-simple-prose-cinematic-224013

p. 126   'any changes from the book…': 'Goodfellas Turned Wiseguy's Simple Prose into Cinematic Gold'.

p. 126   'Any narrative account…': David Shields, *Reality Hunger: A Manifesto* (Penguin, 2010), #192, p. 65.

p. 127   'We are all in flight…': *Reality Hunger*, #215, p. 72.

p. 127   'What I love to read…': John D'Agata, 'We Might As Well Call It The Lyric Essay,' *Seneca Review*, Fall 2015, p. 8. https://www.hws.edu/senecareview/dagata_le.pdf

p. 127   'the conviction that art…': Wolfgang Funk, Florian Groß & Irmtraud Huber (eds), *The Aesthetics of Authenticity: Medial Constructions of the Real* (Transcript, 2012), p. 42.

p. 128   'Heaven knows…': quoted in Miles Orvell, *The Real Thing: Imitation and Authenticity in American Culture 1880–1940* (University of North Carolina Press, 1989), p. xvi.

p. 128   'both expressed…': Travis Elborough, *The Long-Player Goodbye* (Sceptre, 2008), p. 175.

p. 129   note 16: 'At the time we developed…': quoted in *The Long-Player Goodbye*, p. 377.

p. 129   'the concept of authenticity…': *The Real Thing*, p. xvii.

p. 129   'misuse language': Ludwig Wittgenstein, *The Blue and Brown Books* (Basil Blackwell, 1958), p. 45.

p. 129   'the problem of authenticity…': *The Real Thing*, p. xvii.

p. 130   'partly a response…': *The Real Thing*, p. xvi.

p. 130   'It was as if…': *The Real Thing*, p. 145.

p. 130   'Minstrelsy swept…': Robert C. Toll, *Blacking Up: The Minstrel Show in 19th Century America* (Oxford University Press, 1974), pp. 31, 33.

p. 130   'Some Northerners…': *Blacking Up*, p. 38.

p. 131   'Minstrelsy provided…': *Blacking Up*, p. 272.

p. 131   'There is little evidence of culture…': quoted in Katie J. Graber, '"A Strange, Weird Effect": The Fisk Jubilee Singers in the United States and England,' *American Music Research Center Journal*, 14 (University of Colorado, 2004), p. 34.

p. 131   'The perceived purity…': Ronald Radano, quoted in Patrick Burke, *Come In And Hear The Truth: Jazz and Race on 52nd Street* (University of Chicago Press, 2008), p. 6.

p. 132   'the story of African…': Hugh Barker & Yuval Taylor, *Faking It: The Quest for Authenticity in Popular Music* (Faber & Faber, 2007), p. 39.

p. 132   'Jewish Jazz–Moron Music': *The Dearborn Independent*, 6 August 1921. http://chroniclingamerica.loc.gov/lccn/2013218776/1921-08-06/ed-1/seq-1/

p. 132   'the most authentic…': *Faking It*, p. 61.

p. 132   'the most racially pure…': *Faking It*, p. 70.

p. 133   'They saw the jazz…': Ted Gioia, *The Imperfect Art* (Oxford University Press, 1988), p. 29.

p. 133   'Both the front-porch…': *Faking It*, pp. 89–90.

p. 134   'In his semi-memoir': The RZA with Chris Norris, *The Tao of Wu* (Riverhead. 2009), pp. 1–2.

p. 134   'for me, my pictures…': quoted in *The Aesthetics of Authenticity*, p. 29.

18TH CHAMBER–PRIMARY COLOURS

p. 136   'something that I felt…': Karizza Sanchez, '#TBT: Raekwon
Talks Making the Polo "Snow Beach" Jacket Famous,'
Complex, 25 June 2015. http://uk.complex.com/style/2015/06/
raekwon-talks-ralph-lauren-polo-snow-beach-jacket

p. 136   'The first thing I thought…': '#TBT'.

p. 137   'a lot of us came…': quoted in Elliot Aronow, 'Meet the Crew that Brought
Ralph Lauren and Hip Hop Together,' *GQ*, 8 July 2016. http://www.
gq.com/story/ralph-lauren-hip-hop-thirstin-howl-lo-lifes-book

p. 137   'Watch polo matches…': Stephen Koepp, 'Selling a Dream of Elegance
and the Good Life,' *Time Magazine*, 1 September 1986. http://content.
time.com/time/subscriber/article/0,33009,962179,00.html

p. 138   'Aryan youth…': Margaret Carlson, 'Where Calvin Crossed The Line,' *Time
Magazine*, 11 September 1995. http://content.time.com/time/subscriber/
article/0,33009,983406,00.html

p. 138   'Polo purchasers…': 'Selling a Dream'.

p. 138   'The youth market came after us…': Jason Russell, quoted in
Michel Marriott, 'Out of the Woods,' *New York Times*, 7 November
1993. http://www.nytimes.com/1993/11/07/style/out-of-the-woods.
html?pagewanted=all

p. 139   'an orthodox Jewish immigrant…': 'Selling a Dream'.

p. 139   'We made our own custom garments…': quoted in 'Meet the Crew'.

p. 140   'For those without…': quoted in Alice Gregory, 'A Brief History of the Zoot
Suit,' *Smithsonian Magazine*, April 2016. http://www.smithsonianmag.
com/arts-culture/brief-history-zoot-suit-180958507/

p. 140   'We all lived hip hop…': quoted in 'Meet the Crew'.

p. 140   'With its ceaseless boom…': Mark Fisher, *Capitalist Realism: Is There No
Alternative?* (O Books, 2009), p. 35.

19TH CHAMBER–RESPECTING VIOLENCE

p. 143   'You seem to be…': quoted in George P. Fletcher, *A Crime of Self-Defense:
Bernhard Goetz and the Law on Trial* (Free Press, 1988), p. 1.

p. 143   'I don't know why I did it…': quoted in Lillian B. Rubin, *Quiet Rage: Bernie
Goetz in a Time of Madness* (Faber & Faber, 1987), p. 4.

p. 143   'My intention…': quoted in *Quiet Rage*, p. 38.

p. 144   'indict a ham sandwich…': quoted in Marcia Kramer & Frank Lombardi,
'New Top State Judge: Abolish Grand Juries and Let Us Decide,' *New York
Daily News*, 31 January 1985, p. 3. http://www.nydailynews.com/news/
politics/chief-judge-wanted-abolish-grand-juries-article-1.2025208

p. 144 'the fault in failing to convict…': Mark Lesly with Charles Shuttleworth, *Subway Gunman: A Juror's Account of the Bernhard Goetz Trial* (British American, 1988) p. 315.

p. 145 'I don't think I've paid…' and 'was just what the doctor…': Larry King Live, CNN, 17 December 2004. Transcript: http://transcripts.cnn.com/TRANSCRIPTS/0412/17/lkl.01.html

p. 145 'This type of hysterical…': quoted in Shayna Jacobs & Bill Hutchinson, '"Subway Vigilante" Bernie Goetz Refuses Plea Bargain for Selling Marijuana,' *New York Daily News*, 18 December 2013. http://www.nydailynews.com/new-york/nyc-crime/subway-vigilante-refuses-plea-bargain-selling-pot-article-1.1551829

p. 146 'Don't touch me…': quoted in Al Baker, J. David Goodman & Benjamin Mueller, 'Beyond the Chokehold: The Path to Eric Garner's Death,' *New York Times*, 13 June 2015. https://www.nytimes.com/2015/06/14/nyregion/eric-garner-police-chokehold-staten-island.html

p. 146 'seven disciplinary complaints…': Jack Jenkins & Carimah Townes, 'EXCLUSIVE DOCUMENTS: The disturbing secret history of the NYPD officer who killed Eric Garner,' *ThinkProgress*, 21 March 2017. https://thinkprogress.org/daniel-pantaleo-records-75833e6168f3/

p. 146 'What happened on…': quoted in 'EXCLUSIVE DOCUMENTS'.

p. 147 'the precinct was ranked 11th…': Barry Paddock, Rocco Parascandola, Sarah Ryley & Dareh Gregorian, 'Staten Island, Borough where Eric Garner Died, Has Highest Number of Most-Sued NYPD Officers,' *New York Daily News*, 28 July 2014. http://www.nydailynews.com/new-york/staten-island-highest-number-most-sued-nypd-officers-article-1.1882160

p. 147 'There's a culture…': quoted in 'Staten Island'.

p. 148 'a coroner's report…': Richard Bernstein, 'One Neighborhood, Two Lives. A Special Report. A Death on Staten Island: 2 Paths Cross on Familiar Ground,' *New York Times*, 15 May 1994. The report also mentions the shooting of U-God's two-year-old son in a separate incident. http://www.nytimes.com/1994/05/15/nyregion/one-neighborhood-two-lives-special-report-death-staten-island-2-paths-cross.html?pagewanted=all

p. 148 'Not just the one…' and 'racism is played…': quoted in Jaime Lowe, 'RZA on Eric Garner and "The Non-Value of a Black Life",' *The Gawker*, 23 December 2014. http://gawker.com/rza-on-eric-garner-and-the-non-value-of-a-black-life-1674239684

pp. 148-9 'It's like, enough is enough…' and 'If you ask me…': quoted in Zach Schwartz, 'Ghostface Killah Is Sick and Tired of Police Brutality in America,' *Vice*, 6 December 2014. https://www.vice.com/en_uk/article/9bzjk8/ghostface-killah-isnt-down-with-the-peaceful-protesting-456

20TH CHAMBER–A SHAW THING

p. 153   'razzle-dazzle…': Chuck Stephens, 'The Shaw Brothers' Elephant,' in *Film Comment*, 40(5), September/October 2004 (Film Society of the Lincoln Center), p. 52.

p. 154   'Run Run Shaw…': Chang Cheh, *A Memoir* (Hong Kong Film Archive, 2004), p. 59.

p. 154   'Sometimes it borders on…': quoted in Stephanie Chung Po-yin (ed.), *The Shaw Screen: A Preliminary Study* (Hong Kong Film Archive, 2003), p. 9.

p. 155   'colour *wuxia* century': quoted in Law Kar, 'The Origin and Development of Shaws' Colour Wuxia Century,' in *The Shaw Screen*, p. 132.

p. 155   'Hong Kong cinema's…': *A Memoir*, Introduction, p. 11.

p. 156   'employing a repertoire…': Stephen Teo, 'Shaws' *Wuxia* Films: The Macho Self-Fashioning of Zhang Che / Change Cheh,' in *The Shaw Screen*, p. 144.

p. 156   'two things symbolise…': 'Shaws' *Wuxia* Films', p. 153.

p. 156   'martial arts mavens…': 'The Shaw Brothers' Elephant,' p. 55.

p. 156   'vertical death': 'Shaws' *Wuxia* Films,' p. 151.

p. 156   'the deepest impression…': Sek Kei, in *A Memoir*, Introduction, p. 16.

p. 156   'I use dance…': quoted in 'The Origin and Development of Shaws' Colour Wuxia Century,' p. 139.

p. 157   'The colony's Communist…': Maynard Parker, 'Reports: Hong Kong,' *The Atlantic*, November 1967. https://www.theatlantic.com/past/docs/issues/67nov/hk1167.htm

p. 157   'a fragile, unstable…' and 'Chang depicts…': Lui Tai-lok & Yiu Wai-hung, in *The Shaw Screen*, pp. 163, 171.

p. 157   'find the hero's…': David Bordwell, *Planet Hong Kong: Popular Cinema and the Art of Entertainment* (Harvard University Press, 2000), p. 249.

p. 157   'in Zhang's…': 'Shaws' *Wuxia* Films,' p. 150.

p. 157   'became more violent…': 'The Origin and Development of Shaws' Colour Wuxia Century,' p. 139.

p. 158   'Zhang's male bias…': 'Shaws' *Wuxia* Films,' p. 154.

p. 158   'idiosyncratic personality…': 'Shaws' *Wuxia* Films,' p. 146.

p. 158   'martial arts experts…': *Planet Hong Kong*, p. 252-3.

p. 159   'stressing the training…': *The Shaw Screen*, p. 322.

22ND CHAMBER–THE SUN RISES IN THE EAST

p. 171   'the appeal of the genre…': David Desser, 'The Kung Fu Craze: Hong Kong Cinema's First American Reception,' in Poshek Fu & David Desser (eds), *The Cinema of Hong Kong: History, Arts, Identity* (Cambridge University Press, 2000), p. 38.

p. 172   'The original man…': from the 120, quoted in The RZA with Chris Norris, *The Wu-Tang Manual* (Riverhead, 2005), p. 43.

p. 172   'The people of Islam…': quoted in Herbert Berg, *Elijah Muhammad (Makers of the Muslim World Series)* (Oneworld, 2013), p. 58.

p. 172   'saw Africa as a mere extension…': *Elijah Muhammad*, p. 99.

p. 172   'the nationality of the Moors…': Drew Ali, 'Koran,' v. 47 17, quoted in Melvin Gibbs, 'Thuggods: Spiritual Darkness and Hip-Hop,' in Greg Tate (ed.), *Everything But The Burden* (Harlem Moon, 2003), p. 88.

p. 173   'The key of civilization…': 'Koran,' v. 47 17, in *Everything But The Burden*, p. 89.

p. 173   'The problem of the twentieth century…': W.E.B. Du Bois, *The Souls of Black Folks* (A.C. McCLurg, 1903), pp. 17–18 (Simon & Schuster, 2009).

p. 173   'bestowed an obligation…': Huey P. Newton, quoted in Sundiata Keita Cha-Jua, 'Black Audiences, Blaxploitation and Kung Fu Films, and Challenges to White Celluloid Masculinity,' in Poshek Fu (ed.), *China Forever: The Shaw Brothers and Diasporic Cinema* (University of Illinois Press, 2008), p. 204.

p. 173   'the main intellectual issue…': Edward W. Said, *Orientalism* (Routledge & Kegan Paul, 1978), p. 53.

p. 174   '"Asiatic" is a state of…': 'Thuggods,' in *Everything But The Burden*, p. 89.

p. 174   'share nonsecular interest…': Fanon Che Wilkins, 'Shaw Brothers Cinema and the Hip-Hop Imagination,' in *China Forever*, p. 238.

p. 174   'I think all barriers…': quoted in 'Shaw Brothers Cinema,' p. 240.

p. 175   'One of the characteristics…': 'Thuggods,' in *Everything But The Burden*, p. 91.

p. 176   'Before we were an hour…' and 'because that movie…': The RZA with Chris Norris, *The Tao of Wu* (Riverhead, 2009), pp. 57–8.

p. 176   'lost China…': Geoffrey O'Brien, 'Made in Hong Kong,' in *Artforum International*, 1 September 2004, 43(1), p. 253.

p. 176   'bunch of dudes…': *Tao of Wu*, p. 58.

pp. 177-8 'in the manner' to 'these were movies': all 'Made in Hong Kong,' p. 253.

p. 178   'reflexively repeats…': quoted in James Goodwin, *Eisenstein, Cinema, and History* (University of Illinois Press), p. 30.

p. 178   'By impelling us…' and 'The very cogency…': David Bordwell, *Planet Hong Kong: Popular Cinema and the Art of Entertainment* (Harvard University Press, 2000), p. 244.

pp. 178-9 'post-slave populations' and 'It is nothing new': Paul Gilroy, *The Black Atlantic: Modernity and Double Consciousness* (Verso, 1993), p. 75.

p. 179   'Kung fu movies resonate…': quoted in Gene Ching, 'Hip Hop Fist: Wu-Tang Clan's RZA and his Shifu, Shaolin Monk Shi Yan Ming,' *Kung Fu Magazine*, September 1999. http://www.kungfumagazine.com/magazine/article.php?article=100. Da'Mo, more commonly known as Damo or the Bodhidharma, brought Chan Buddhism from India to China.

p. 179   'rhythmic theatre…': 'Hip Hop Fist,' p. 224.

p. 179   'move like sound…': 'Hip Hop Fist,' p. 222.

p. 180   'Directors rhythmicize…': 'Hip Hop Fist,' p. 229.

p. 180   'drum tap micro-rhythm…': 'Hip Hop Fist,' p. 222.

p. 181   'a mental survival tool…': KRS-One, *The Science of Rap: Second Edition* (L. Parker, 1996), p. 5.

p. 182   'Battling is foundational…': Joseph G. Schloss, *Foundation: B-boys, B-girls, and Hip-Hop Culture in New York* (Oxford University Press, 2009), p. 10.

p. 182   'breaking was a form…': ibid, p. 118.

p. 182   'are commonly carried on…': Thomas A. Green, 'Surviving the Middle Passage: Traditional African Martial Arts in the Americas,' in Thomas A. Green and Joseph R. Svinth (eds), *Martial Arts in the Modern World* (Praeger, 2003), p. 130.

p. 183   'battling is the best venue…': *Foundation*, p. 107.

p. 183   'regardless [of] where…': *Foundation*, p. 120.

p. 184   'Each borough…': David Toop, *Rap Attack* (Pluto Press, 1984), p. 141.

p. 185   'People compare rap…': quoted in Adam Bradley, *Book of Rhymes: The Poetics of Hip Hop* (Basic Civitas, 2009), p. 177.

p. 185   'vicarious violence': Burton Peretti, quoted in Mark Katz, *Capturing Sound: How Technology Has Changed Music* (University of California Press, 2010, revised edition), p. 142.

p. 185   'If you don't like…': quoted in *Capturing Sound*, p. 143.

p. 187   'And I cried for like…': quoted in Jeff Chang, *Can't Stop Won't Stop: A History of the Hip-Hop Generation* (Ebury, 2005), p. 113.

p. 187   note 24: 'running the recordings backwards…': Peter Manning, *Electronic and Computer Music* (Oxford, 1985), pp. 11–12.

p. 187   'peace, unity, love, and having fun': quoted in Mark Katz, *Groove Music: The Art and Culture of the Hip-Hop DJ* (Oxford University Press, 2012), p. 88.

p. 188   'chess is also…': *Tao of Wu*, p. 46.

23RD CHAMBER–SOUND TECHNIQUE

p. 190   'Born…': The RZA with Chris Norris, *The Wu-Tang Manual* (Riverhead, 2005), p. 45.

p. 192   'social phenomenon': Jonathan Sterne, 'Bourdieu, Technique & Technology,' *Cultural Studies*, 17(3/4), 2003, p. 384. http://sterneworks. org/BourdieuTechandTech.pdf

p. 192   'At what point': 'Bourdieu, Technique & Technology,' pp. 373–4.

p. 193   'The word is now a virus…': William Burroughs, 'Operation Rewrite,' in James Grauerholz & Ira Silverberg (eds), *Word Virus: The William S. Burroughs Reader* (Grove, 1998), p. 744.

p. 194   'Man's first and most natural…': Marcel Mauss, quoted in 'Bourdieu, Technique & Technology,' p. 380.

24TH CHAMBER–THE DEUCE

p. 195 'the world's most notorious…': Mary C. Henderson & Alexis Greene, *The Story of 42nd Street: The Theaters, Shows, Characters, and Scandals of the World's Most Notorious Street* (Back Stage, 2008).

p. 195 'a hub of sensational thrills…': Austin Fisher & Johnny Walker (eds), 'Introduction,' in *Grindhouse: Cultural Exchange on 42nd Street, and Beyond* (Bloomsbury Academic, 2016), p. 1.

p. 196 'cesspool…': *The Story of 42nd Street*, p. 27.

p. 196 'By the last decade…': Marc Eliot, *Down 42nd Street: Money, Culture and Politics at the Crossroads of the World* (Rebel Round, 2001), pp. 71–2.

p. 196 'helped transform…': *Down 42nd Street*, p. 24.

p. 197 'The business of sex…': *Down 42nd Street*, p. 25.

p. 198 'the rare business…': Anthony Bianco, *Ghosts of 42nd Street: A History of America's Most Infamous Block* (William Morrow, 2004), p. 101.

p. 198 'these became…': *Down 42nd Street*, p. 96.

p. 199 'Bill Gates…': *Ghosts of 42nd Street*, p. 157.

p. 199 'We looked around…': Mr. X, a member of the Gambino organisation, interviewed by and quoted in *Down 42nd Street*, p. 112.

p. 200 'His immediate goal…': *Down 42nd Street*, p. 226.

p. 200 'by 1987…': quoted in *Down 42nd Street*, pp. 228–9.

p. 200 'the city's only…': *Down 42nd Street*, p. 189.

p. 200 'moral leper…': *Down 42nd Street*, p. 39.

p. 200 'pretty much every…': quoted in Shawn Setaro, 'Kung Fu Kenny Is Just the Latest Example of Hip-Hop's Fascination With Martial Arts,' *Complex*, 19 April 2017. http://www.complex.com/music/2017/04/kendrick-lamar-kung-fu-kenny-hip-hops-obsession-with-martial-arts

p. 201 'in 1979…': quoted in Jason Gross, 'RZA's Edge,' *Film Comment*, May/June 2008. https://www.filmcomment.com/article/rzas-edge-the-rzas-guide-to-kung-fu-films/

p. 201 'anus…': quoted in *Down 42nd Street*, p. 143.

p. 201 'We wound up at…': The RZA with Chris Norris, *The Tao of Wu* (Riverhead, 2009), pp. 55–6.

p. 202 'discipline and struggle…': *Tao of Wu*, p. 58.

p. 202 'it was through these films…': quoted in 'Kung Fu Kenny'.

p. 202 'living where shit…': *Tao of Wu*, p. 3.

p. 202 'hard seats, sticky floors…': Bill Landis & Michelle Clifford, *Sleazoid Express: A Mind-twisting Tour through the Grindhouse Cinema of Times Square* (Fireside, 2002), p. 6.

p. 202 'a turgid waft of human sweat…': *Down 42nd Street*, p. 7

p. 202 'young boys, young girls…': *Down 42nd Street*, p. 7.

25TH CHAMBER–CASH RULES

p. 205   'the Four-Bar Killer…': The RZA with Chris Norris, *The Wu-Tang Manual* (Riverhead, 2005), p. 32.

p. 206   'a musical composition…': quoted in Damon Krukowski, *The New Analog: Listening and Reconnecting in the Digital World* (New Press, 2017), excerpted at https://www.theparisreview.org/blog/2017/04/21/surface-noise/

p. 207   'Mechanical reproduction': *The New Analog.*

p. 209   'an artist once demanded…': Helienne Lindvall, 'Behind the Music: Why Topline Melody Writing Creates Disputes between Artists and Songwriters,' *Guardian*, 26 August 2011. https://www.theguardian.com/music/musicblog/2011/aug/26/topline-melody-disputes-artists-songwriters

p. 209   'By assuring that…': Alan Page, *Enter the Wu-Tang: How Nine Men Changed Hip-Hop Forever* (Lone Gunman, 2014), p. 78.

p. 209   'When it comes to the beats…': quoted in Sean Michaels, 'Wu-Tang Clan's RZA to Appeal Royalties Lawsuit,' *Guardian*, 30 September 2009. https://www.theguardian.com/music/2009/sep/30/wu-tang-clan-rza

26TH CHAMBER–IN AND OUT

p. 211   'it's all about…': quoted in Paul Edwards, *How To Rap: The Art & Science of the Hip-Hop MC* (Virgin, 2012), p. 128.

p. 212   'Breath control…': Adam Bradley, *Book of Rhymes: The Poetics of Hip Hop* (Basic Civitas, 2009), p. 39.

p. 214   'techniques of the body': Marcell Mauss, quoted in Jonathan Sterne, 'Bourdieu, Technique & Technology,' *Cultural Studies*, 17(3/4), 2003, p. 384. http://sterneworks.org/BourdieuTechandTech.pdf

p. 214   'music is harmonious…': quoted in Gene Ching, 'Hip Hop Fist,' *Kung Fu Magazine*, 1999. http://www.kungfumagazine.com/magazine/article.php?article=100

p. 214   'Tai chi translates…': The RZA with Chris Norris, *The Tao of Wu* (Riverhead, 2009), p. 60.

p. 215   'Life is a mere…': Zhuangzi, *The Complete Works of Zhuangzi*, trans. Burton Watson (Columbia University Press, 2013), p. 181.

27TH CHAMBER–WARRIORS COME OUT TO PLAY

p. 216   'the invincible…': The RZA with Chris Norris, *The Wu-Tang Manual* (Riverhead, 2005), p. 8.

p. 217   'GZA's the only one…': *The Wu-Tang Manual*, p. 9.

p. 217   'I felt good…': quoted in Brian Coleman, *Check the Technique: Liner Notes for Hip Hop Junkies* (Villard, 2007), p. 452.

p. 217　'commissioned a single…': Dan Charnas, *The Big Payback: The History of the Business of Hip-Hop* (New American Library, 2010), p. 431.

p. 218　'The ideal, it seems…': Joseph G. Schloss, *Foundation: B-boys, B-girls, and Hip-Hop Culture in New York* (Oxford University Press, 2009), p. 113.

p. 219　'Self-control is really the essence…': *Foundation*, p. 114.

p. 219　'the Dozens can be tricky…': Elijah Wald, *Talking 'Bout Your Mama: The Dozens, Snaps, and the Deep Roots of Rap* (Oxford University Press, 2012), p. 3.

p. 220　'we played the Dozens…': H. Rap Brown, *Die Nigger Die!* (Dial Press, 1969), p. 26.

p. 220　'Signifying allowed you…': *Die Nigger Die!*, p. 29.

p. 220　'while the dozens is part of…': *Talking 'Bout Your Mama*, p. 11.

p. 221　'the most prevalent manifestation of signifying…': Henry Louis Gates Jr, *The Signifying Monkey: A Theory of African-American Literary Criticism*, 25th Anniversary Edition (Oxford University Press, 2014), p. xxix.

p. 221　'until the rap era there was no…': *Talking 'Bout Your Mama*, p. 185.

p. 221　'Tapes of this confrontation…': *Talking 'Bout Your Mama*, pp. 195–6.

p. 221　'Such combat was nothing new…': *Talking 'Bout Your Mama*, p. 194.

28TH CHAMBER–TORTURE

p. 226　'schooled me…': quoted in Ming Tzu, 'RZA Talks About His Image at Tommy Boy, Prince Paul and Being Forsaken,' 14 April 2008. http://grandgood.com/2008/04/14/rza-talks-about-his-image-at-tommy-boy-prince-paul-and-being-forsaken/

p. 226　'I realized…': quoted in Jeff Weiss, 'A History of the Hip Hop Skit,' *Red Bull Music Academy Daily*, 7 July 2015. http://daily.redbullmusicacademy.com/2015/07/hip-hop-skits-history

p. 226　'skits don't just…': Gabriel Alvarez, 'The 50 Greatest Hip-Hop Skits,' *Complex*, 6 December 2011. http://uk.complex.com/music/2011/12/the-50-greatest-hip-hop-skits/

p. 227　'like you're eavesdropping…': 'The 50 Greatest Hip-Hop Skits'.

p. 227　'instead of having…': Serengeti, quoted in 'A History of the Hip Hop Skit'.

p. 228　'Signifyin(g) is…': *The Signifying Monkey*, pp. 56–7.

p. 228　'aggressive…' and 'is synonymous…': *The Signifying Monkey*, p. 87.

p. 228　'do not forget that a poem…': Ludwig Wittgenstein, *Zettel*, trans. G.E.M. Anscombe (Blackwell, 1967), p. 28e.

p. 228　'the relationship between…': *The Signifying Monkey*, p. 61.

p. 229　'In hip-hop and in…': The RZA with Chris Norris, *The Tao of Wu* (Riverhead, 2009), p. 76.

p. 230　'lamentably sexist…' and 'Taking their lyrics…': *The Signifying Monkey*, p. xxix.

p. 230　'leaving the question of…': Paul Gilroy, *The Black Atlantic: Modernity and Double Consciousness* (Verso, 1993), p. 84.

p. 231　'a form of rhetorical…': *The Signifying Monkey*, p. 76.

29TH CHAMBER–PASS THE BONE

p. 233　'I don't advocate…': The RZA with Chris Norris, *The Wu-Tang Manual* (Riverhead, 2005), p. 118.

p. 233　'I don't mean to advocate…': *The Wu-Tang Manual*, p. 120.

p. 234　'It is difficult to generalize…': Martin A. Lee, *Smoke Signals: A Cultural History of Marijuana–Medical, Recreational and Scientific* (Scribner, 2012), p. 6.

p. 234　'the herb's capriciousness…': *Smoke Signals*, p. 7.

p. 234　'the drug defies…': quoted in *Smoke Signals*, p. 59.

p. 235　'fat bags of skunk…': from 'Method Man'.

p. 235　'open like…': from 'Wu-Tang: 7th Chamber'.

p. 235　'mythillogical': Kodow Eshun, *More Brilliant Than The Sun: Adventures in Sonic Fiction* (Quartet, 1998), p. 46.

p. 235　'deregulates the means…': *More Brilliant Than The Sun*, p. 47.

p. 236　'"Keeping it real"…': *More Brilliant Than The Sun*, p. 46.

p. 236　'to escape from…': quoted in *Smoke Signals*, p. 36.

p. 236　'we always looked at…': quoted in *Smoke Signals*, p. 12.

p. 237　'marijuana causes…': quoted in *Smoke Signals*, p. 52.

p. 237　'Marijuana leads to pacifism…': quoted in *Smoke Signals*, p. 62.

p. 237　'several musicians…': *Smoke Signals*, p. 11.

p. 237　'on auditory perception…': Michael E. Veal, *Dub: Soundscapes & Shattered Songs in Jamaican Reggae* (Wesleyan University Press, 2007), p. 81.

p. 237　'the first time…': quoted in *Dub*, p. 82.

p. 238　'Under the spell…': Ralph Ellison, *Invisible Man* (Penguin Classics, 2001 edition), p. 8.

p. 238　'you could hear space…': quoted in David Toop, *Ocean of Sound: Aether, Talk, Ambient Sound and Imaginary Worlds* (Serpents Tale, 1995), p. 114.

p. 238　'I was getting help…': *Ocean of Sound*, p. 115.

p. 239　'I haven't smoked…': *Invisible Man*, p. 12.

p. 239　'They might play…': *Dub*, p. 82.

p. 240　'gin and reefer': Robin D.G. Kelley, *Thelonious Monk: The Life and Times of an American Original* (Simon & Schuster, 2009), p. 74.

p. 241　'there has been no…': Paul Gilroy, *The Black Atlantic: Modernity and Double Consciousness* (Verso, 1993), p. 100.

p. 241　'Five Percenter praxis…': Melvin Gibbs, 'Thuggods: Spiritual Darkness and Hip-Hop,' in Greg Tate (ed.), *Everything But The Burden* (Harlem Moon, 2003), p. 91.

p. 241　'the moment it drugs…': *More Brilliant Than The Sun*, p. 46.

30TH CHAMBER–THANATASIA

p. 243 'hitting cats…': from 'Da Mystery of Chessboxin''.

p. 243 'chrome TECs…': from 'Da Mystery of Chessboxin''.

p. 243 'The year 1993 itself was a highpoint…': gun stats taken from http://www.npr.org/sections/thetwo-way/2013/05/07/181998015/rate-of-u-s-gun-violence-has-fallen-since-1993-study-says and http://www.pewsocialtrends.org/2013/05/07/gun-homicide-rate-down-49-since-1993-peak-public-unaware/. Toddler stat: https://www.washingtonpost.com/news/wonk/wp/2015/10/14/people-are-getting-shot-by-toddlers-on-a-weekly-basis-this-year/?utm_term=.aeb0e1a0e9c1. More guns than Americans: https://www.washingtonpost.com/news/wonk/wp/2015/10/05/guns-in-the-united-states-one-for-every-man-woman-and-child-and-then-some/?utm_term=.da64e12573f3

p. 244 note 29: 'Wu-Tang… means…': quoted in Mike Diver, 'Wu-Tang Clan: The 10 Laws of Shaolin, Part 1,' *Clash*, 5 September 2013. http://www.clashmusic.com/features/wu-tang-clan-the-10-laws-of-shaolin-part-1

p. 246 'to be a Black revolutionary…': quoted in Ekwueme Michael Thelwell, 'H. Rap Brown/Jamil Al-Amin: A Profoundly American Story,' *The Nation*, 18 March 2002, 4(10).

p. 246 'a fearsome cult…': Mike Dash, *Thug: The True Story of India's Murderous Cult* (Granta, 2005), p. x.

p. 246 'the One Primordial…': Melvin Gibbs, 'Thuggods: Spiritual Darkness and Hip-Hop,' in Greg Tate (ed.), *Everything But The Burden* (Harlem Moon, 2003), p. 86.

p. 246 'a dark goddess…': 'Thuggods,' p. 93.

p. 247 'overcome their caste…': 'Thuggods,' p. 92.

p. 247 'For some people in…': Dan Charnas, *The Big Payback: The History of the Business of Hip-Hop* (New American Library, 2010), p. 467.

p. 250 'Thirty-six chambers of death…': on 'Clan In Da Front'.

p. 250 'horrorcore': at 2.42 minutes on https://www.youtube.com/watch?v=ApTn9n19XoY

p. 250 'I was like…': at 3:00 minutes on https://www.youtube.com/watch?v=ApTn9n19XoY

31ST CHAMBER–JUMPING FREE

p. 252 'Wu-Tang is for the children': 0:29 seconds on https://www.youtube.com/watch?v=ENQ9qbUVdg4

p. 253 'I rap but I…': 0:28 seconds on https://www.youtube.com/watch?v=bB6EkeWoG2I

p. 253 'He scares some people…': The RZA with Chris Norris, *The Wu-Tang Manual* (Riverhead, 2005), p. 13.

p. 254 note 30: 'the calabash rattle…': Milo Rigaud, *Secrets of Voodoo*, trans. Robert B. Cross (City Lights, 1969), pp. 35–36.

p. 256 'straight alcohol…': Buddha Monk, quoted in Jaime Lowe, *Digging For Dirt: The Life and Death of ODB* (Faber & Faber, 2008), p. 67.

p. 256 'suggestive and…': quoted in Colin Larkin, *The Virgin Encyclopaedia of the Blues* (Virgin, 1998), p. 152.

p. 256 'the most outrageous…': Ron Wynn, in Michael Erlewine, Vladimir Bogdanov, Chris Woodstra, Cub Koda (eds), *All Music Guide to the Blues* (Miller Freeman, 1996), p. 106.

p. 256 'he was different…': in *Screamin' Jay Hawkins – I Put A Spell On Me*, directed by Nicholas Triandafyllidis. 2 minutes 45 seconds. https://www. youtube.com/watch?v=qecYcFZR6Mk

p. 257 'One, I can't sing…': *Screamin' Jay Hawkins*, 26 minutes 10 seconds.

p. 257 'I don't like…': *Screamin' Jay Hawkins*, 6 minutes 13 seconds.

p. 258 'Do you feel like your life…': Jaime Lowe, *Digging for Dirt: The Life and Death of ODB* (Faber & Faber, 2008), p. 55.

p. 258 'wilder use…': Vladimir Simosko, *Eric Dolphy: A Musical Biography and Discography* (Da Capo, 1979), p. 65.

p. 259 'the musical nonsense' and 'Coltrane…': both John Tynan, 'Take Five,' *Down Beat*, 23 November 1961, p. 40.

p. 259 'That's got to be…': from *Down Beat*, 1964, quoted in Macy Halford, 'A New Yorker Blindfold Test,' *New Yorker*, 21 June 2011. https://www. newyorker.com/books/page-turner/a-new-yorker-blindfold-test

p. 259 'It is mainly…': quoted in 'Take Five,' p. 40.

p. 260 'a logic was operating…': Geoff Dyer, *But Beautiful: A Book About Jazz* (Vintage, 1991), p. 34.

p. 260 'Big leaps…': Alan Lomax, *The Land Where The Blues Began* (Minerva, 1993), p. 354.

p. 261 'My impression was…': quoted in *Digging for Dirt*, p. 78.

p. 262 'Dirty was a mastermind…': quoted in *Digging for Dirt*, p. 227.

32ND CHAMBER–THE LAST BATTLE

p. 264 'the visible god-head' and 'the transformation…': Karl Marx, 'On Money,' in David McLellan (ed.), *Selected Writings* (Oxford University Press, 1977), p. 110.

p. 265 'My whole thing…': in an interview on *Halftime Online*, 10 November 2004. http://halftimeonline.net/portfolio/inspectah-deck-wu-tang/

p. 267 'We got n***s who think they're gangsta': interview on *Halftime Online*.

p. 267 'it's time to go back to…': interview on *Halftime Online*.

p. 268 'I bake the cake…': from 'Wu-Tang Clan Ain't Nuthing Ta F' Wit'.

p. 268 'like he's battling himself…' and 'Who is the illest…': both from interview on *Halftime Online*.

p. 269 'that kung fu was…': The RZA with Chris Norris, *The Tao of Wu* (Riverhead, 2009), p. 60.

p. 270 'brothers from the same…': *Enter The Wu-Tang Documentary 1994*, 5 minutes 43 seconds. https://www.youtube.com/watch?v=xXWGEH74w20

p. 270 'All we did…': *Enter The Wu-Tang Documentary 1994*, 11 minutes 20 seconds.

p. 270 'It's the same thing Ghostface says…': 'Ghostface Killah Came Up with Wu-Tang's Name, Talks Rich Chigga and Bruce Lee!' *88Rising*, 5 minutes 53 seconds. https://www.youtube.com/watch?v=PkvRo0jcClw

33RD CHAMBER—WHOSE PROBLEM?

p. 272 'According to…': Karen Fields & Barbara J. Fields, *Racecraft* (Verso, 2012), p. 3.

p. 273 'Americans believe in…': Ta-Nehisi Coates, *Between the World and Me* (Text, 2015), p. 7.

p. 273 'racial classification does not…': Michael Yudell, Dorothy Roberts, Rob DeSalle & Sarah Tishkoff, 'Taking Race Out of Human Genetics,' *Science*, 351(6273), 5 February 2016, p. 565.

p. 273 'who sought to demonstrate…': Adam Sutherland, 'He May Have Unravelled DNA, but James Watson Deserves to be Shunned,' *Guardian*, 1 December 2014. https://www.theguardian.com/commentisfree/2014/dec/01/dna-james-watson-scientist-selling-nobel-prize-medal

p. 273 'race is the child…': *Between the World and Me*, p. 7.

p. 274 'have been brought up…': *Between the World and Me*, p. 7.

p. 274 'racism, to separate…': Edward S. Morgan, quoted in Theodore W. Allen, *The Invention of the White Race, Volume Two: The Origin of Racial Oppression in Anglo-America* (Verso, 1997/2012), p. 249.

p. 274 'is the insistence…': *The Invention of the White Race*, p. 243.

p. 275 'the subordination of class…': *The Invention of the White Race*, p. 240.

p. 275 'the founding fathers' emancipatory…': Patrick Wolfe, *Traces of History: Elementary Structures of Race* (Verso, 2016), p. 67.

p. 275 'though born of slavery…': *Traces of History*, p. 74.

p. 276 'Black blood took on…': *Traces of History*, p. 82.

p. 277 'race is inextricably…': Scott DeVeaux, *The Birth of Bebop: A Social and Musical History* (University of California Press, 1997), p. 231.

p. 277 'colonisers…': *Traces of History*, pp. 65–6.

p. 277 'there is every reason…': David Graeber, *Debt: The First 5,000 Years* (Melville House, 2011), p. 165.

p. 277 'some of the most genuinely archaic…': *Debt*, p. 171.

p. 278 '"symbolic capital"': *Debt*, p. 445, n.76.

p. 278 'social technology': Felix Martin, *Money: The Unauthorised Biography* (Vintage, 2014), p. 29.

p. 278   'there is a paradox…': *Money*, p. 157.

p. 279   'the saxophone is not…': Jaap Kool, *Das Saxophon: The Saxophone*, trans. Lawrence Gwozdz (Egon, 1987), pp. 243–4.

p. 279   'a kind of amplification…': Ross Russell, *Jazz Style in Kansas City and the Southwest* (University of California Press, 1971), p. 232.

p. 280   'less a fighting style and more about the cultivation of spirit': The RZA with Chris Norris, *The Tao of Wu* (Riverhead, 2009), p. 60.

p. 281   'We generally believe that…': Master Sheng-yen with Dan Stevenson, *Hoofprint of the Ox: Principles of the Chan Buddhist Path as Taught by a Modern Chinese Master* (Oxford University Press, 2001), p. 85.

p. 281   'As property…': *Traces of History*, p. 68.

p. 281   'that the slave…': *Debt*, p. 168.

34TH CHAMBER–LEVELS OF DEVILS

p. 283   'came to believe…': quoted in Loren Glass, 'The Mighty Mezz, Marijuana, and the Beat Generation,' *Los Angeles Review of Books*, 7 May 2015. https://lareviewofbooks.org/article/the-mighty-mezz-marijuana-and-the-beat-generation/

p. 284   'real golden-leaf': quoted in 'The Mighty Mezz'.

p. 284   'Dreamed about a reefer…': quoted in Martin A. Lee, *Smoke Signals: A Social History of Marijuana–Medical, Recreational and Scientific* (Scribner, 2012), p. 46.

p. 284   'There I could hardly…': Milton 'Mezz' Mezzrow & Bernard Wolfe, *Really The Blues* (Random House, 1946), p. 306.

p. 285   'the backward…': Sven Lindqvist, 'Exterminate All the Brutes', trans. Joan Tate, collected in *Saharan Journey* (Granta, 2012), p. 201.

p. 285   'Our most important…': 'Exterminate All the Brutes', p. 200.

p. 285   'The "gunboat"…': 'Exterminate All the Brutes', p. 202.

p. 286   'a new epoch…': 'Exterminate All the Brutes', p. 201.

p. 286   'first they came…': quoted in 'Exterminate All the Brutes', p. 222.

p. 287   'the first really good…': 'Exterminate All the Brutes', p. 203.

p. 287   'only three…': John Laband, *Kingdom in Crisis: The Zulu Response to the British Invasion of 1879* (Pen & Sword, 2007), p. 108.

p. 287   'was the scene of an atrocity…': Rory Carroll, 'Rorke's Drift Battle was War Crime Scene,' *Guardian*, 29 April 2003. https://www.theguardian.com/world/2003/apr/29/schools.southafrica

p. 288   'monstrous…': Will Heaven, 'Zulu: Is This the Greatest Ever British War Film?' *Telegraph*, 23 December 2014. http://www.telegraph.co.uk/culture/film/10589719/Zulu-is-this-the-greatest-ever-British-war-film.html

p. 288   'there are hundreds…': Jeff Chang, *Can't Stop Won't Stop: A History of the Hip-Hop Generation* (Ebury, 2005), pp. 93–94.

p. 288   'I see this movie…': quoted in *Can't Stop Won't Stop*, p. 94.

p. 289   'although rap…' 'rap's hour…' and 'The ways in which…': David Samuels, 'The Rap on Rap: The Black Music That Isn't Either,' *New Republic*, 11 November 1991. https://newrepublic.com/article/120894/david-samuels-rap-rap-1991

p. 289   'data pool…': Bakari Kitwana, *Why White Kids Love Hip Hop: Wankstas, Wiggers, Wannabes and the New Reality of Race in America* (Basic Civitas, 2005), p. 83.

p. 290   'White youth…': quoted in *Why White Kids Love Hip Hop*, p. 103.

p. 290   'that to be oppressed…' and 'In place of the old disgust…': Zadie Smith, 'Getting In and Out: Who owns Black Pain?' *Harper's*, July 2017. https://harpers.org/archive/2017/07/getting-in-and-out/

p. 291   'Of course there are many…': William Upski Wimsatt, *Bomb the Suburbs* (Subway & Elevated, 1994), p. 22.

p. 291   'I wouldn't categorically…': The RZA with Chris Norris, *The Tao of Wu* (Riverhead, 2009), p. 191.

p. 291   'the white race…': quoted in Michael Muhammad Knight, *The Five Percenters: Islam, Hip Hop and the Gods of New York* (Oneworld, 2007), p. 226.

p. 291   'neither pro-black…': *The Five Percenters*, p. 227.

p. 292   '"But big enough…' and 'the great-grandmother': Sven Lindqvist, *Terra Nullius: A Journey through No One's Land*, trans. Sarah Death (Granta, 2007), pp. 11, 12.

p. 292   'taking–from a culture…': Resolution of the Writers' Union of Canada, quoted in Bruce Ziff & Pratima V. Rao, 'Introduction to Cultural Appropriation: A Framework for Analysis,' in Bruce Ziff & Pratima V. Rao (eds), *Borrowed Power: Essays on Cultural Appropriation* (Rutgers University Press, 1997), p. 1.

p. 293   'I am hopeful…': Lionel Shriver, 'Fiction and Identity Politics,' Brisbane Writers Festival, in the *Guardian*, 13 September 2016. https://www.theguardian.com/commentisfree/2016/sep/13/lionel-shrivers-full-speech-i-hope-the-concept-of-cultural-appropriation-is-a-passing-fad

p. 293   'it is as if…': Timothy Morton, *Human Kind* (Verso, 2017), p. 12.

p. 293   'Membership of a larger group…' and 'both as writers…': 'Fiction and Identity Politics'.

p. 294   'a virtual "strip mining"…': Perry A. Hall, 'African-American Music: Dynamics of Appropriation and Innovation,' in *Borrowed Power*, p. 33

p. 294   'a people from whom so much…': 'Getting In and Out'.

p. 296   'a nearly isotopic sizzle…': Eric Lott, *Love & Theft: Blackface Minstrelsy & the American Working Class* (Oxford University Press, 1993/2013), p. 249.

p. 296   'Every time you hear…': *Love & Theft*, p. 5.

p. 296   'what white people have to do…': James Baldwin, in *I Am Not Your Negro*, directed by Raoul Peck (2016).

p. 297   'the real fantasy…' and 'no getting out…': 'Getting In and Out'.

pp. 297-8 'the power, beauty and alienation…', 'verifications of what…', 'Over the last few years…' and 'I've promised myself…': all quoted in Antwaun Sargent, 'Arthur Jafa and the future of Black Cinema,' *Interview* magazine, 11 January 2017. https://www.interviewmagazine.com/art/arthur-jafa

p. 298 'the music is a riotous solemnity…': Fred Moten, *Black and Blur* (Duke University, 2017), p. xiii.

p. 298 'God and the Devil…': quoted in *The Five Percenters*, p. 236.

35TH CHAMBER–MASKED AVENGER

p. 301 'he the smartest motherfucker': from the 'Intermission' skit on *Enter the Wu-Tang (36 Chambers)*.

p. 303 'it was definitely spoken on…': 'Raekwon Opens Up About Wu-Tang Drama,' VladTV, 1 minute 44 seconds. https://www.youtube.com/watch?v=tCw4pxnii5c

p. 304 'the chief of the kung fu…': quoted in 'Ghostface Killah Came Up with Wu-Tang's Name, Talks Rich Chigga and Bruce Lee!' 4 minutes 42 seconds. https://www.youtube.com/watch?v=PkvRo0jcClw

p. 304 'I played it to RZA…': 'Ghostface Killah Came Up with Wu-Tang's Name,' 4 minutess 47 seconds.

p. 304 'the closest hip hop ever…': Jeff Weiss, 'Ghostface Killah – *Supreme Clientele*,' *Pitchfork*. http://pitchfork.com/reviews/albums/23207-supreme-clientele/. I honestly think this one review renders most of this book pointless, but there we are. Respect to Mr Weiss.

p. 305 'Ghost was Moses…': The RZA with Chris Norris, *The Tao of Wu* (Riverhead, 2009), p. 93.

p. 305 'one of the most famous…': The RZA with Chris Norris, *The Wu-Tang Manual* (Riverhead, 2005), p. 144.

p. 305 'that's really true…': *The Wu-Tang Manual*, p. 141.

p. 306 'some official beats…': 'Ghostface Killah – *Supreme Clientele*'.

p. 306 'capable of being in uncertainty': quoted in Walter Jackson Bate, *John Keats* (Harvard University Press, 1963), p. 249.

p. 306 'when I struck': from 'Da Mystery of Chessboxin''

p. 307 'he was the best, best…': *The Wu-Tang Manual*, p. 24.

p. 308 'the Negro is a sort of…': W.E.B. Du Bois, *The Souls of Black Folks* (Simon & Schuster, 2005), p. 7.

p. 308 'the unknown state of…': Ivor H. Evans, *Brewer's Dictionary of Phrase & Fable* (Cassell, 1981), p. 1160.

p. 308 'shut out from their…': *The Souls of Black Folks*, p. 6.

p. 308 'We wear the mask…': quoted in Houston A. Baker Jr, *Modernism and the Harlem Renaissance* (University of Chicago Press, 1987), p. 39.

p. 308 'I am invisible…': Ralph Ellison, *Invisible Man* (Random House, 1953), p. 3.

p. 309 'the white male…': Harriet J. Manning, *Michael Jackson and the Blackface Mask* (Ashgate, 2013), p. 1.

p. 309   'a quintessential American ritual…': *Modernism and the Harlem Renaissance*, p. 17.

p. 309   'While hip hop…': *Michael Jackson and the Blackface Mask*, p. 64.

p. 309   'You like it…': quoted in Bakari Kitwana, *Why White Kids Love Hip Hop: Wankstas, Wiggas, Wannabes and the New Reality of Race in America* (Basic Civitas, 2005), p. 108.

p. 310   'the minstrel mask…': *Modernism and the Harlem Renaissance*, p. 21.

p. 310   'The *sound*…': *Modernism and the Harlem Renaissance*, p. 22.

p. 313   'The Five Percenters…': Melvin Gibbs, 'Thuggods: Spiritual Darkness and Hip-Hop,' in Greg Tate (ed.), *Everything But The Burden* (Harlem Moon, 2003), pp. 89–90.

p. 313   'Ye are the light of the world': Matthew 5:14, New Testament, Holy Bible, King James Version (CollinsBible, 1957), p. 6.

p. 313   'preservation of the sacred fire of liberty': George Washington, First Inaugural Address, April 30 1789. http://avalon.law.yale.edu/18th_century/wash1.asp

p. 313   'this momentous decree…': Martin Luther King, 28 August 1963, Lincoln Memorial, Washington, DC. http://www.americanrhetoric.com/speeches/mlkihaveadream.htm

p. 314   'We feel that Black people…': quoted in Poshek Fu (ed.), *China Forever: The Shaw Brothers and Diasporic Cinema* (University of Illinois Press, 2008), p. 204.

p. 315   'the masked are…': Adam Phillips, *Houdini's Box: On the Arts of Escape* (Faber & Faber, 2001), p. 124.

p. 317   'I feel like I got my whole style…': quoted in 'Ghostface Killah – *Supreme Clientele*'.

p. 317   'You couldn't simply find a space…': Neil Kulkarni, *The Periodic Table of HIP HOP* (Ebury, 2015), p. 116.

p. 318   'jazz musicians are…': quoted in Mark Godfrey, 'Notes on Black Abstraction,' in Mark Godfrey & Zoe Whitley (eds), *Soul of a Nation: Art in the Age of Black Power* (Tate, 2017), p. 149.

p. 318   'anti-plague': Ishmael Reed, *Mumbo Jumbo* (Penguin Classics, 2017), p. 6. 'Jes Grew is as electric as life and is characterized by ebullience and ecstasy.'

p. 318   'He who would enter…': quoted in *Modernism and the Harlem Renaissance*, p. 61.

p. 318   'signifying on steroids…': Henry Louis Gates, *The Signifying Monkey: A Theory of African American Literary Criticism*, 25th Anniversary Edition (Oxford University Press, 2014), p. xxix.

p. 318   'a creative process…': *The Signifying Monkey*, p. xxxi.

p. 319   'hybridity…': Paul Gilroy, *The Black Atlantic: Modernity and Double Consciousness* (Verso, 1993), p. 107.

p. 319   'Hip-hop is the last hope…': Bakari Kitwana, *Why White Kids Love Hip Hop: Wankstas, Wiggers, Wannabes and the New Reality of Race in America* (Basic Civitas, 2005), p. 209.

p. 319   'a new language…': *Why White Kids Love Hip Hop*, p. 192.

p. 321   'It all has to do with it': John Coltrane, *A Love Supreme* (EMI, 1965), although I actually came across the phrase quoted in Jarrett Earnest's interview of Fred Moten for Brooklyn Rail, 2 November 2017 (https://brooklynrail.org/2017/11/art/FRED-MOTEN-with-Jarrett-Earnest). Coltrane used the poem as his 'notation' for the fourth part of *A Love Supreme*, 'Psalm', and you can see the words and music combined here: https://vimeo.com/38345026

36TH CHAMBER–ENIHCAM EMIT

p. 323   'U-God's own shop…': the only reference I can find to Walking Dogs is in the following old piece in the *New York Times*, which makes me wonder if someone was winding up the writer: Amy Waldman, 'The Revolution Will Be Merchandised,' New Yorkers & Co, *New York Times*, 11 January 1998. http://www.nytimes.com/1998/01/11/nyregion/new-yorkers-co-the-revolution-will-be-merchandised.html

p. 323   'sold in department…': Dan Charnas, *The Big Payback: The History of the Business of Hip-Hop* (New American Library, 2010), p. 506.

p. 323   'the first urban brand…': *The Big Payback*, p. 480.

p. 325   'the world's first online…': Sean Michaels, 'Wu Tang Clan Promote Unity through Chess,' *Guardian*, 4 June 2008. https://www.theguardian.com/music/2008/jun/04/urban

p. 327   'turning back is how the way moves': Laozi, *Tao Te Ching*, trans. D.C. Lau (Chinese University, 1982), p. xxii.

p. 328   'a roomful…': *The Big Payback*, p. 484.

p. 332   'was one of many…': James Gleick, *Chaos: Making a New Science* (Cardinal, 1987), p. 49.

p. 332   'was trusting…': The RZA with Chris Norris, *The Tao of Wu* (Riverhead, 2009), pp. 116–17.

p. 332   'the paradoxes of the American psyche': Robert Pogue Harrison, 'The True American,' *New York Review of Books*, 17 August 2017. http://www.nybooks.com/articles/2017/08/17/henry-david-thoreau-true-american/

p. 333   'When I finished…': *Tao of Wu*, p. 115.

p. 333   'That's the whole secret…': *Tao of Wu*, p. 116.

p. 334   'A study estimates…': Arline T. Geronimus, John Bound & Cynthia G. Colen, 'Excess Black Mortality in the United States and in Selected Black and White High-Poverty Areas, 1980–2000,' *American Journal of Public Health*, 101(4), April 2011, pp. 720–9. https://www.ncbi.nlm.nih.gov/pmc/articles/PMC3052342/

ACKNOWLEDGEMENTS

As is always the case, many more people have contributed to this book than you'd guess from looking at the cover. As ever, I'm very grateful for all the help.

Matthew Shapland, Nick Midgley and Alastair Siddons. Phil Mlynar, Mike Lewis, Theresa Adebiyi, Amaechi Uzoigwe and Raj Gandesha. Skiz Fernando, Angus Batey, Rich Jones and Joshua Astrachan. Nick White, Jon Baker, Rob Shanks, Peter Quicke and Mark Hart. Matt Thorne and Ben Thompson. My agent, Patrick Walsh, John Ash and William Clark. Prune, JR, Lucca, Marc and everyone at the Family, NYC. All the staff of the Rare Books & Music reading room at the British Library. Kenny A La Fu, Mike Ladd and Juice Aleem.

My editor, Max Porter (without whom this book wouldn't exist), Alex Bowler, Christine Lo, Sarah Wasley, Lindsay Nash, Jon Gray, Mandy Woods, Pru Rowlandson, Nat Shaw, Katie Hayward and everyone at Granta.

This book couldn't exist without the work of the writers and thinkers quoted. If you've found it interesting, please go crate-digging in the Samples section and follow up with the original heavyweight grooves.

I owe a huge debt to all the artists I worked with at Big Dada, plus those I was lucky enough to chat with or to interview in the years before. These are the people who pointed out a path to me—along with my dad, whose Miles

Davis, Fats Waller and Jelly Roll Morton LPs set me on that path in the first place. This book is dedicated to the many, many people who have taught me about hip hop and the music of the African slave diaspora more generally—thank you, it was a privilege.

Last, to Leila, Miriam and Saul, because it's both boring and trying living with a writer—and you very rarely get the house to yourself.

The cover image of *Enter The Wu-Tang (36 Chambers)* appears with the kind permission of Sony Music Entertainment.

INDEX